1991

Shelleyan Eros

Shelleyan Eros

THE RHETORIC OF ROMANTIC LOVE

William A. Ulmer

PRINCETON UNIVERSITY PRESS

PRINCETON, NEW JERSEY

Library of Congress Cataloging-in-Publication Data

Ulmer, William Andrew.
Shelleyan eros : the rhetoric of romantic love / William A. Ulmer.
Includes bibliographical references.
1. Shelley, Percy Bysshe, 1792–1822—Criticism and interpretation.
2. Love poetry, English—History and criticism. 3. Love in
literature. I. Title.
PR5442.L6U46 1990 821′.7—dc20 90-8189

ISBN 0-691-06829-1 (alk. paper)

This book has been composed in Linotron Baskerville

Princeton University Press books are printed on acid-free paper
and meet the guidelines for permanence and durability of the
Committee on Production Guidelines for Book Longevity of the
Council on Library Resources

Printed in the United States of America by Princeton University Press,
Princeton, New Jersey

10 9 8 7 6 5 4 3 2 1

For Kelly

*What is all this sweet work worth
If thou kiss not me?*

CONTENTS

PREFACE

THIS BOOK investigates the interrelation of language, politics, and sexuality in Shelley's poetry. I approach that constellation of interests by way of *Alastor, The Revolt of Islam, Prometheus Unbound, The Cenci,* and *Epipsychidion* (chapters 2–6). These poems' representations of erotic experience—ranging from nocturnal emission, to the sexual consummation of Titanic marriage, to incestuous rape—make them an important poetic sequence. To this sequence I add *The Triumph of Life* (chapter 7) as a revaluation of *Alastor* and as the almost inevitable terminus for reflection on Shelley's poetic development. Chapter 1 sketches my approach to Shelley by reconstructing his poetics, which I take to be predominately idealist—neither specifically Platonic nor Berkeleyan (as in the notion of a metaphysically absolute "One Mind"), but idealist in its logocentric symbiosis of contraries. For me, the logic governing the interaction of idealism and skepticism in Shelley is itself idealizing. It is a dialectical form of metaphor. As such, it divides presence into manifest and latent phases so that antitheses can cyclically displace and recuperate one another. As a temporalizing or differential model, it remains an occluded tautology, however, so that Shelley's idealism sustains itself only by eliding time and difference.

I hope this argument will encourage Shelleyans to rethink the relationship of Shelley's skeptical allegiances—which I fully grant—to the actual aspirations and claims of his poetry. In demoting the role of skepticism in Shelley's poetry, I also hope to encourage modifications in the use of critical theory for reading Shelley. Some recent theoretical accounts of Shelley's career happily wed skepticism and deconstruction. They portray a poet who assents philosophically and politically to the deferral of truth continually effected by his writing, a poet who makes indeterminacy the measure of psychic and social freedom. The Shelley my book portrays was morally and artistically committed to the idea of truth. His doubts about both the possibility and the wisdom of discovering or representing the truth were quite real, but they dominated only one part of a mind that thought and imagined antithetically. Consequently, my greatest debts to critics working in poststructuralism are to individuals who have represented the disruptions and deferrals of Shelley's work as its problem rather than its solution. Here I am thinking especially of J. Hillis Miller, Tilottama Rajan, and Paul de Man, and above all of de Man's seminal "Rhetoric of Temporality" essay.

I concur with some, not all, of these thinkers in finding the humanistic project of Shelley's poetry to be ultimately unsuccessful. As his poems increasingly fail to displace their inherent contradictions, his faith in redemptive community grows increasingly tentative. Shelley finally fails to reconcile imagination and world, to transform idealist ideologies into an effective revolutionary program. I return to the work of Ross Woodman and Earl R. Wasserman, then, in arguing that Shelley's poetry rejects earthly mediations in favor of death conceived as an apocalypse of consciousness. Beyond my obligations to these Shelleyans, I owe particular debts to the work of Harold Bloom, Daniel J. Hughes, William Keach, Stuart M. Sperry, and Jerrold E. Hogle—debts repaid in disagreement as well as in admiration. I trust that my footnotes will acknowledge how much I have learned from other scholars working in Shelley and English Romanticism.

I am also indebted to Robert E. Brown, literature editor at Princeton University Press, for his unfailing helpfulness, to my copyeditor, Jane Lincoln Taylor, to my anonymous readers at Princeton, and to two journals for permission to reprint material: part of chapter 2 borrows from my "Some Hidden Want: Aspiration in 'To a Sky-Lark,' " *Studies in Romanticism* 23 (1984): 245–58; and chapter 6 is a revised version of "The Politics of Metaphor," *Journal of English and Germanic Philology* 87 (1988): 535–57. The jacket illustration, Burne-Jones's *The Mirror of Venus*, is reproduced courtesy of The Calouste Gulbenkian Museum, Lisbon, Portugal. I must thank Lisa Rashley, Charlotte Pass, and Ellen Ryan, my three research assistants, for their diligence and energy, and the University of Alabama for sabbatical leave in the spring of 1987. Special thanks to Cecil Y. Lang, who introduced me to Shelley's poetry, and whose influence imbues the best of this book. Within my department, my gratitude goes to my chairperson, Claudia D. Johnson, for release time and friendship, and to Matt Marino, for help with computer problems. Edward Haworth Hoeppner and Richard Rand thoughtfully criticized sections of the manuscript. John P. Hermann and Joseph Hornsby took time off from weightier endeavors to read the entire manuscript at a crucial stage. My greatest intellectual debt, however, is to David Lee Miller, who virtually taught me to write, and then had to deal with the consequences by reading what I'd written; his talent for turning phrases and shaping arguments improved literally every page of this book.

Nearer to home, I must also mention Tommy and Percy, whose insistence on rising early often got me to my computer earlier than I had either intended or wished. The muse who enabled me to complete this study of Shelleyan love—she could have inspired a Shelley book on no other topic—usually doesn't rise so early. She is my wife, Kelly Brennan, the only person as pleased as I am that this book is completed. Both my gratitude and my priorities are indicated in the dedication.

EDITIONS AND ABBREVIATIONS

I USE the following editions: *Lord Byron: The Complete Poetical Works*, ed. Jerome J. McGann, 8 vols. (Oxford: Clarendon Press, 1980–); *Dante: The Divine Comedy of Dante Alighieri*, trans. and intro. Allen Mandelbaum (Berkeley and Los Angeles: University of California Press, 1980–1984); *Homer: The Odyssey*, trans. Robert Fitzgerald (Garden City: Doubleday and Company, 1961); *John Keats: Complete Poems*, ed. Jack Stillinger (Cambridge: Harvard University Press, 1982); *John Milton: Complete Poems and Major Prose*, ed. Merritt Y. Hughes (Indianapolis: Odyssey Press, 1957); *Plato: The Collected Dialogues*, ed. Edith Hamilton and Huntington Cairns, Bollingen Series 71 (Princeton: Princeton University Press, 1961); *William Shakespeare: The Complete Works*, ed. Alfred Harbage (Baltimore: Penguin Books, 1969); *William Wordsworth: Poetical Works*, ed. Thomas Hutchinson, rev. Ernest de Selincourt (London: Oxford University Press, 1936). The following journals and editors are referred to by abbreviation:

CW   *The Complete Works of Percy Bysshe Shelley*, ed. Roger Ingpen and Walter E. Peck, 10 vols. (London: Ernest Benn, 1926–1930)

CWC   *The Collected Works of Samuel Taylor Coleridge*, ed. Kathleen Coburn, Bollingen Series 75, 16 vols. (Princeton: Princeton University Press, 1969–)

ELH   *ELH: A Journal of English Literary History*

ELN   *English Language Notes*

JEGP   *Journal of English and Germanic Philology*

KSJ   *Keats-Shelley Journal*

KSMB   *Keats-Shelley Memorial Bulletin*

Letters *The Letters of Percy Bysshe Shelley*, ed. Frederick L. Jones, 2 vols. (Oxford: Clarendon Press, 1964)

LMWS   *The Letters of Mary Wollstonecraft Shelley*, ed. Betty T. Bennett, 3 vols. (Baltimore: Johns Hopkins University Press, 1980–1988)

MLQ   *Modern Language Quarterly*

PMLA   *Publications of the Modern Language Association*

PQ   *Philological Quarterly*

PW   *Shelley: Poetical Works*, ed. Thomas Hutchinson, 2d ed., corrected and rev. G. M. Matthews (New York: Oxford University Press, 1971)

RES   *Review of English Studies*
SEF   *The Standard Edition of the Complete Psychological Works of Sigmund Freud*, gen. ed. and trans. James Strachey, 24 vols. (London, Hogarth Press, 1953–1974)
SEL   *Studies in English Literature, 1500–1900*
SHC   *Shelley and His Circle*, ed. Kenneth Neill Cameron and Donald H. Reiman, 8 vols. (Cambridge: Harvard University Press, 1973–1986)
SIR   *Studies in Romanticism*
SPP   *Shelley's Poetry and Prose*, ed. Donald H. Reiman and Sharon B. Powers (New York: Norton, 1977). Unless otherwise noted, Shelley's texts are cited from this edition.

Shelleyan Eros

Chapter 1

SHELLEY'S POETICS OF LOVE

This spiritual Love acts not nor can exist
Without Imagination.
—Wordsworth, *The Prelude*

IF ANGELS have reason to blush, as did Milton's "rosy red" Raphael
(*Paradise Lost* 8.619), angelic poets surely must as well. And if carica-
tures of Shelley as an "ineffectual angel"[1] have been thoroughly dis-
credited, it should prove that much easier to appreciate the materi-
alist investments of his idealism—its strong grasp of the physical
sciences, its political conversancies, and its commitment to bodily pas-
sion. Shelleyan love can hardly be reduced to eros. Yet the poet him-
self declared sexual intercourse "the link and type of the highest
emotions of our nature," and commonly represented the range of
human relationships "by categories which are patently derived from
erotic attraction and sexual union."[2] For Shelley the psychology of
desire cannot be dissociated from even the most sublime adoration,
nor can it be dissociated from imaginative issues. Shelley's poetics cor-
relates love and imagination as variant forms of each other: the "great
secret of morals is Love; or a going out of our own nature. . . . A man,
to be greatly good, must imagine intensely and comprehensively."[3] If
Yeats himself deemed Shelley's poetry "the poetry of desire," he did
so not just because the poems are *about* desire but because, in their
distinctly Shelleyan imaginativeness, they appear to be linguistic con-

[1] Matthew Arnold's notorious "ineffectual angel" phrase appears in his essay "By-
ron," in *The Complete Prose Works of Matthew Arnold*, ed. R. H. Super, vol. 9, *English
Literature and Irish Politics* (Ann Arbor: University of Michigan Press, 1973), 237.

[2] The quotations come respectively from Shelley's *A Discourse on the Manners of the
Antient Greeks Relative to the Subject of Love*, in James A. Notopoulos, *The Platonism of
Shelley: A Study of Platonism and the Poetic Mind* (Durham: Duke University Press, 1949),
410, and M. H. Abrams, *Natural Supernaturalism: Tradition and Revolution in Romantic
Literature* (New York: Norton, 1971), 298. Shelley's views on love and sexuality are
compiled and discussed in Nathaniel Brown, *Sexuality and Feminism in Shelley* (Cam-
bridge: Harvard University Press, 1979). Among interpretive studies touching or cen-
tering on Shelleyan love, Stuart M. Sperry's recent *Shelley's Major Verse: The Narrative
and Dramatic Poetry* (Cambridge: Harvard University Press, 1988) has proven most use-
ful to me, in part for its concurrent emphasis on Shelley's idealism.

[3] *A Defence of Poetry*, *SPP*, 487–88. All of Shelley's works are cited from *SPP* unless
otherwise noted.

figurations *of* desire.[4] Yeats's respect for Shelley is verbal, a respect compelled by continual rediscovery in sacred books such as *Prometheus Unbound* of "words that have gathered up the heart's desire of the world."[5]

These words make up a rhetoric of Romantic love. They subject eros, as Shelley's virtuosity grows, to figurations of extraordinary complexity and beauty. Nowhere more clearly than in Shelley does one find warrant for Paul de Man's equation of "the rhetorical, figural potentiality of language with literature itself."[6] Of course, Shelley thoroughly appreciated the conceptual problems raised by poetic tropes. He inherited a philosophical tradition stressing the referential arbitrariness of the sign, studied contemporary linguistic theorists such as Monboddo and Horne Tooke, had Asia proclaim the priority of speech to thought (*Prometheus Unbound* 2.4.72), and acknowledged verbal inadequacies in poem after poem.[7] Instructively, one of the most frank of such acknowledgments, "These words are inefficient and metaphorical—Most words so—No help," appears in a note to his fragment "On Love" (474). In this essay Shelley's association of love and language ends by implicating philosophy in rhetoric and by demanding that a poem's moral or political analysis of love be gauged against the performance of its language as a mode of love. "On Love" locates desire in the self's thirst for an antitypical complement, a beautiful other pursued for its promise of wholeness. By adding this erotic model to its confession of metaphorical inefficiency, "On Love" grounds Shelley's poetics in contradiction. Shelley's career was largely an exploration of the artistic possibilities of this contradiction.

THE EROTIC SUPPLEMENT

The importance of the problem of language for Shelley's treatment of desire can be inferred from the relationship of "On Love" to its

[4] W. B. Yeats, *"Prometheus Unbound,"* in *Essays and Introductions* (New York: Macmillan, 1961), 419. I am also indebted to Harold Bloom's reconstruction of Shelley's career as an "internalized quest to reach the limits of desire," in *Shelley's Mythmaking* (1959; reprint, Ithaca: Cornell University Press, 1969), vii.

[5] W. B. Yeats, "The Philosophy of Shelley's Poetry," in *Essays and Introductions*, 65.

[6] Paul de Man, *Allegories of Reading: Figural Language in Rousseau, Nietzsche, Rilke, and Proust* (New Haven: Yale University Press, 1979), 10.

[7] For late eighteenth- and early nineteenth-century linguistic theory, see Hans Aarsleff, *From Locke to Saussure: Essays on the Study of Language and Intellectual History* (Minneapolis: University of Minnesota Press, 1982), which shows that certain principles of structuralist linguistics are clearly anticipated in the ideas about language formulated by Locke and other thinkers in the skeptical tradition (375–76, for example). Shelley's ideas about language are discussed in the first chapters of William Keach, *Shelley's Style* (London: Methuen, 1984), and in Richard Cronin, *Shelley's Poetic Thoughts* (New York: St. Martin's Press, 1981).

Platonic model. Shelley wrote "On Love" in late July 1818, shortly after finishing his elegant translation of *The Symposium* and shortly before beginning his *Discourse on the Manners of the Antient Greeks Relative to the Subject of Love*, an essay seemingly intended as an introduction to the translation. Clearly, "On Love" emerged from a period of sustained immersion in Platonic philosophy and "should be read as Shelley's response to Plato's *Symposium*."[8] The human race, Aristophanes claims in one of the best-known passages of *The Symposium*, consisted originally of anatomically doubled androgynous beings whom Jupiter prudently cut in half. "Immediately after this division," says Aristophanes,

> as each desired to possess the other half of himself, these divided people threw their arms around and embraced each other, seeking to grow together. . . . From this period, mutual Love has naturally existed in human beings; that reconciler and bond of union of their original nature, which seeks to make two, one, and to heal the divided nature of man. . . . Whenever, therefore, any such as I have described are impetuously struck, through the sentiment of their former union, with love and desire and the want of community, they are ever unwilling to be divided even for a moment. These are they who devote their whole lives to each other, with a vain and inexpressible longing to obtain from each other something they know not what; for it is not merely the sensual delights of their intercourse for the sake of which they dedicate themselves to each other with such serious affection; but the soul of each manifestly thirsts for, from the other, something which there are no words to describe, and divines that which it seeks, and traces obscurely the footsteps of its obscure desire. . . . The desire and pursuit of integrity and union is that which we all love.[9]

Here in turn are the analogous passages from "On Love":

> [Love] is that powerful attraction towards all that we conceive or fear or hope beyond ourselves when we find within our own thoughts the chasm of an insufficient void and seek to awaken in all things that are, a community with what we experience within ourselves. . . . We are born into the world and there is something within us which from the instant that

[8] As Donald H. Reiman urges, in *SHC* 6:639. Reiman also argues that Shelley's concept of love changes from 1818 to 1821, at which point Shelley denies that "the external world [must] respond or conform to the ideal within the self; rather the self seeks the beautiful without" (*SHC* 6:645). I agree with Jerrold E. Hogle that the egocentrism of "On Love" and the "total 'going out of ourselves' in the *Defence*" are essentially continuous, as Hogle argues in "Shelley's Poetics: The Power as Metaphor," *KSJ* 31 (1982): 188 n. 32. The differing emphases Reiman notes are merely complementary aspects of a single self/other model.

[9] *The Banquet Translated from Plato*, in Notopoulos, *Platonism*, 430–32.

we live and move thirsts after its likeness. . . . We dimly see within our intellectual nature a miniature as it were of our entire self, yet deprived of all that we condemn or despise, the ideal prototype of every thing excellent or lovely that we are capable of conceiving as belonging to the nature of man. Not only the portrait of our external being, but an assemblage of the minutest particulars of which our nature is composed: a mirror whose surface reflects only the forms of purity and brightness: a soul within our soul that describes a circle around its proper Paradise which pain and sorrow and evil dare not overleap. To this we eagerly refer all sensations, thirsting that they should resemble or correspond with it. (473–74)

"On Love" and the androgynous myth of *The Symposium* concur in viewing desire as an impulse to reunify sundered psychic complements. Yet the Aristophanic and Shelleyan accounts of love (themselves each other's antitype) also differ significantly. Their differences can be summed up by observing that the words "likeness," "portrait," "mirror," "resemble," and "correspond"—so crucial to Shelley's sense of the relationship of self and antitype—are entirely missing from the relevant passages of *The Symposium* as he translated it. The role accorded similitude in "On Love" is hardly original in Shelley, needless to say. But his repeated insistence on the likeness of lovers, especially in so short an essay, testifies to his deeply felt commitment to the idea. Shelley's poetry affords similar testimony. As the "veiled maid" of *Alastor* has a voice "like the voice of [the Poet's] own soul / . . . Herself a poet" (ll. 153, 161), so Laon declares of Cythna, "As mine own shadow was this child to me, / A second self" (*The Revolt of Islam*, *PW*, ll. 874–75); as Asia and Prometheus describe themselves as the shadows of each other's souls, so the speaker of *Epipsychidion* addresses Emily as a "soul out of my soul" (l. 238). Arising as a pursuit of integral likeness, Shelleyan eros is metaphorically constituted and structured. For Shelley, Jerrold E. Hogle remarks, "love is the action of metaphor inhabiting our deepest emotional drives."[10]

---

[10] Hogle, "Shelley's Poetics," 188. Paul Fry notes that for Shelley "love is the perception of similitude in dissimilitude of which the emblem and vehicle is metaphor," in *The Reach of Criticism* (New Haven: Yale University Press, 1983), 162. John W. Wright similarly contends that Shelley considered "metaphoric apprehension . . . to be the fundamental power of the human mind and a mental counterpart of the primal capacity for self-transcendence he found in love," in *Shelley's Myth of Metaphor* (Athens, Ga.: University of Georgia Press, 1970), 22. In his 1800 Preface to *Lyrical Ballads*, Wordsworth similarly attributes "the direction of the sexual appetite, and all the passions connected with it" to "the pleasure which the mind derives from the perception of similitude in dissimilitude," in *The Prose Works of William Wordsworth*, ed. W.J.B. Owen and Jane Worthington Smyser, 3 vols. (Oxford: Clarendon Press, 1974), 1:148.

Shelley's idealization of love requires an idealization of metaphor as the vehicle for emotional closure and union. When the speaker of *Epipsychidion* declares "I am not thine: I am a part of *thee*" (l. 52), he affirms metaphor's power to organize difference into identity. Because such identity reharmonizes separated counterparts, Shelley's sense of metaphor invests it with synecdochical and symbolic powers. Since imagination signifies "the principle of synthesis" and poetic language must be "vitally metaphorical," tropes of similitude assume the obligations of unity (*Defence of Poetry*, 480, 482). Metaphor reconciles tenor and vehicle "As a lover or a chameleon / Grows like what it looks upon" (*Prometheus Unbound* 4.483–84), acting as the trope of a symbolism that (as Coleridge wrote) "always partakes of the Reality which it renders intelligible; and while it enunciates the whole, abides itself as a living part in that Unity, of which it is the representative."[11] In the *Defence of Poetry*, similarly, imagination employs an incarnating poetics that "reproduces all that it represents" so as to "unveil the permanent analogy of things by images which participate in the life of truth" (487, 485). Returned to their contexts in Shelley's essay, these phrases assume positions in an eclectic argument more complex and empirical than I indicate here. Yet that empiricism neither nullifies nor fully controls the residual idealism of Shelley's faith in the reconciliatory power of poetry. By no means does the skepticism of the *Defence of Poetry* absolve Shelleyan figuration of the "inseparability of the nature of metaphor from the metaphysical chain."[12]

What results, ironically, is a unitive poetics divided against itself. The divisions and contradictions are legacies of a metaphorical idealism. By nominating metaphor as the imagination's harmonizing mechanism, Shelley inscribes metaphor with the larger contradictions of his antithetical vision. He slights metaphor's presupposition of ab-

[11] Coleridge's well-known definition of the symbol is from *The Statesman's Manual*, reprinted in *Lay Sermons*, ed. R. J. White, *CWC* 6:30. Wright associates Shelleyan metaphor and the Coleridgean symbol on the basis of their integrative function (*Shelley's Myth of Metaphor*, 27). Metaphor has been frequently identified with fusion and identity, as shown by the entry in *The Princeton Encyclopedia of Poetry and Poetics*, ed. Alex Preminger, enlarged ed. (Princeton: Princeton University Press, 1974), 490. Coleridge's poetics were by no means simplistically unitive, as Emerson R. Marks reminds us in *Coleridge on the Language of Verse* (Princeton: Princeton University Press, 1981), 60, 99–102, where he points to the interaction of likeness and difference in Coleridgean mimesis and the dynamic, tensive reconciliations of Coleridgean metaphor. Yet Coleridge finally stresses the coalescent power of imagination and locates language on "a hierarchical continuum [that] joins ordinary speech with the divine Logos" (Marks, *Coleridge*, 10). See Abrams, *Natural Supernaturalism* (141–95, for example) for the prevalence of "unity" and "fragmentation" in the conceptual and mythopoeic vocabulary of Romanticism.

[12] Jacques Derrida, "White Mythology," *New Literary History* 6 (1974): 37.

sence and difference; he tries to make metaphor do too much. The
problem refers ultimately to the discrepant roles accorded antitypes
in Shelley's appropriation of *The Symposium*. Indebted to Plato yet
dedicated to resemblance, "On Love" pursues an impossible nego-
tiation of completion and similitude. In Shelley, antitypes "must be
inadequate because they are not what they should duplicate *and*
because what they should match is itself dependent on them for self-
completion."[13] The antitype's inadequacy betrays the reliance of Shel-
leyan eros on what Derrida calls the "logic of the supplement":

> The concept of the supplement . . . harbors within itself two significa-
> tions whose cohabitation is as strange as it is necessary. The supplement
> adds itself, it is a surplus, a plenitude enriching another plenitude, the
> *fullest measure* of presence. . . . But the supplement supplements. It adds
> only to replace. It intervenes or insinuates itself *in-the-place-of*; if it fills,
> it is as if one fills a void. If it represents and makes an image, it is by the
> anterior default of a presence.[14]

The Shelleyan antitype supplements the self by filling an interior in-
sufficiency, functioning as an interlocking opposite completing the
self. Yet the antitype also corresponds to the self, acting as its essential
"likeness." So the antitype resembles and completes the self, but *can*
complete the self only by differing from it, by possessing what the
self lacks.

   This impasse illustrates the paradoxes of mirroring, since the erotic
supplement is the self's specular avatar. Shelley employs specular
models to figure the relation of self and other in "On Love"—where
the antitype acts as "a mirror whose surface reflects only the forms of
purity and brightness" (474)—but returns to them throughout his
love poetry as well. In all of these poems, specularity prevents desire
from transcending the otherness of the antitype because mirroring
transposes the symmetrical axes of representation. Shelleyan eros
arises through a specular encounter reversing the self into its mirror
image. In this mirror stage the role of the (at first) necessarily un-
recognizable other ensures the ineluctable otherness of desire. Desire
alienates the subject by inscribing it with the difference and insuffi-
ciency that produces it: the reflected other "is that which introduces
'lack' and 'gap' into the operations of the subject and which, in doing
so, incapacitates the subject for selfhood, or inwardness, or appercep-
tion, or plenitude; it guarantees the indestructibility of desire by

[13] Hogle, "Shelley's Poetics," 188.
[14] Jacques Derrida, *Of Grammatology*, trans. Gayatri Chakravorty Spivak (Baltimore:
Johns Hopkins University Press, 1976), 144–45.

keeping the goals of desire in perpetual flight."[15] It makes love go on until it is stopped, and prevents it from stopping.[16] From this perspective, all images of closure and fusion, including the unity of Shelleyan lovers, are backward configurations of an inaugural harmony that cannot be reattained because it never existed.

As a result, Shelley's affirmations of correspondence and concord do violence to the truth, or expose the violence *of* truth. His amatory ideal memorializes a metaphorical imperialism founded on the repression of difference. Shelleyan desire doubles itself through attempted appropriations of otherness. Although envisioned as the male self's feminine complement, the Shelleyan antitype—supplement and specular image—is a variant of the double as well. For Shelley, "writing is a kind of doubling in which the author's self is reconstituted within the realm of language as the Other, a narcissistic mirroring of the self."[17] Doubles are always the progeny of repression, projections outside the self of inadmissible impulses and secret guilt. Obligated to the dynamics of doubling, Shelleyan eros corroborates Otto Rank's claim that "the double is the rival of his prototype in anything and everything, but primarily in the love for woman,"[18] and shows that even supernal love arises in the wake of power, created by economies of force and resistance, banishment and return. Desire modeled on doubling disseminates violence, remaking the double as an "uncanny harbinger of death."[19] Erotic realization in Shelley frequently occurs as an apotheosis of violence in death. The association of eros and death is of course traditional in Western culture,[20] but Shelley's representations of desire insistently ask readers,

[15] Malcolm Bowie, "Jacques Lacan," in *Structuralism and Since: From Lévi-Strauss to Derrida*, ed. John Sturrock (Oxford: Oxford University Press, 1979), 134. Bowie succinctly summarizes one of the main ideas of Lacan's "The Mirror Stage as Formative of the Function of the I as Revealed in Psychoanalytic Experience," in *Écrits: A Selection*, trans. Alan Sheridan (New York: Norton, 1977), 1–7. For an analysis of Shelleyan mirroring from the vantage point of a traditional phenomenology, see Beverly Taylor, "Shelley's Mirrors of Consciousness," in *The Cast of Consciousness: Concepts of the Mind in British and American Romanticism*, ed. Beverly Taylor and Robert Bain (New York: Greenwood Press, 1987), 86–103.

[16] Shelley told Trelawny, "I always go on until I am stopped, and I never am stopped," according to *Trelawny's Recollections of the Last Days of Shelley and Byron*, ed. Edward Dowden (London: Henry Frowde, 1906), 45.

[17] John Irwin makes this claim about Faulkner in *Doubling and Incest/Repetition and Revenge: A Speculative Reading of Faulkner* (Baltimore: Johns Hopkins University Press, 1975), 159.

[18] Otto Rank, *The Double: A Psychoanalytic Study*, trans. and ed. Harry Tucker, Jr. (New York: New American Library, 1979), 76.

[19] Freud's comment, from "The Uncanny," *SEF* 17:235.

[20] See, for instance, Denis De Rougement, *Love in the Western World*, trans. Montgom-

Heardst thou not, that those who die
Awake in a world of extacy?
That love, when limbs are interwoven,
And sleep, when the night of life is cloven,
And thought, to the world's dim boundaries clinging,
And music, when one beloved is singing,
Is death?

                    (*Rosalind and Helen*, *CW*, ll. 1123–29)

This violence invests song as well as sexuality. It is partly rhetorical, latent in metaphor as the trope of doubling. In Shelley's poetry the repetition crucial to metaphor, which replicates tenor in vehicle and figure in referent, often activates the compulsive repetitions of Thanatos.[21] In its nostalgia for identities prior to differentiation, Shelley's metaphorical idealism will finally accept death as the negative form (specular image) of erotic transcendence.

But this climactic gesture remains a last resort. It is an option selected when visionary maidens prove irrecoverable and revolutions doomed. Shelleyan eros begins by embracing earthly mediations. This embrace includes difference, freely granting that comparison takes its rationale from dissimilarity. Following that admission, Shelley's rhetoric can present itself as a "dialectics of likeness and difference within which it is crucially necessary to register dissimilitude."[22] Yet within this dialectic difference remains an epiphenomenon, marking a necessary but surpassed stage in metaphor's progress toward unity and identity. Shelley accords unlikeness a place in love's metaphorical circuitry in an effort to co-opt the enemy and circumscribe its disruptive force. Shelleyan dialectic operates as a temporalized mode of metaphor—as metaphor-become-story, resemblance given a beginning, middle, and end. This progression presupposes the identity of origin and end, thereby confessing its enmity to time and difference. Confronted by the problems of metaphorical idealism, Shelley recreates that idealism in an occluded form that resituates its contradictions without resolving them. This dialectical vari-

---

ery Belgion, rev. and augmented ed. (1940; reprint, Princeton: Princeton University Press, 1983), 18–21, 42–46.

[21] Freud connects Thanatos and the repetition compulsion in explaining instinctual regression to a stabilized sameness prior to life, in *Beyond the Pleasure Principle*, *SEF* 18:7–64. Shelley attributed the idea of postmortal existence to attraction to sameness in "On a Future State": "This desire to be for ever as we are; the reluctance to a violent and unexperienced change, which is common to all the animated and inanimate combinations of the universe, is, indeed, the secret persuasion which has given birth to the opinions of a future state" (*CW* 6:209).

[22] Fry, *Reach of Criticism*, 163.

ation of metaphor organizes his poetry's rhetorical energies and philosophical themes.

METAPHORICAL IDEALISM

No position in Shelley studies enjoys greater esteem than the claim that a skeptical outlook prevails in his poetry. Underlying this claim are reconstructions of Shelley's thinking that merit considerable respect. There can be little doubt about the poet's debts to Hume's skepticism and Drummond's "intellectual philosophy." Yet also underlying the case for Shelleyan skepticism, unavoidably, are certain assumptions about the relationship of antitheses in Shelley: since no one denies Shelley's profound debts to the idealist tradition, defenders of his skepticism must insist that the interaction of ideal and skeptical elements in Shelley is *itself* ultimately skeptical. And so most of them do, deriving Shelley's idealism from his skepticism. C. E. Pulos argues that skepticism gave Shelley a principle by which he "reconciled ideas generally associated with antagonistic traditions" so that he could write as "a consistent Platonist in the sceptical tradition."[23] But is a skepticism that "reconciles" not deeply implicated in idealism when reconciliation, mediation, and unity are idealizing prerogatives? Have our criteria for gauging the bankruptcy of idealisms been too uncritical? When the aestheticizing of historical conflict leaves *Prometheus Unbound* as vulnerable as Hegel to the materialist critique of Marx's *German Ideology*,[24] how conclusive was Shelley's rejection of idealism? When critics deem that rejection complete, and grant Shelley a secular outlook, the poet's moral passion can too readily be reduced, following Eliot on Arnold's religious humanism, to "counsel to get all the emotional kick out of [idealism] one can without the bother of believing it."[25]

For me, Earl R. Wasserman's approach to Shelley is especially compelling not merely for its sensitivity to dialectical tensions but for its

[23] C. E. Pulos, *The Deep Truth: A Study of Shelley's Scepticism* (Lincoln: University of Nebraska Press, 1954), preface, 109. There is an overview of the skeptical tradition in the first chapter of Donald H. Reiman's *Intervals of Inspiration: The Skeptical Tradition and the Psychology of Romanticism* (Greenwood, Fl.: Penkevill Publishing Company, 1988). By repeatedly noting the positive side of skepticism, Pulos acknowledges the involvement of skepticism with philosophies basically opposed to it, such as Platonism. Unfortunately the critical tradition he initiated has occasionally led, contra Pulos, to radically secularizing interpretations in which Shelley's poems affirm an earthbound humanism or gladly embrace indeterminacy.

[24] As William Keach claims, in "Radical Shelley?" *Raritan* 5 (1985–1986): 120.

[25] T. S. Eliot, "Arnold and Pater," in *Selected Essays*, new ed. (New York: Harcourt, Brace & World, 1964), 385.

tendency to view skepticism "as intermediate rather than terminal: a way of strengthening the idealism which is Shelley's final position."[26] In the aftermath of New Critical polemics, Shelley scholarship sought to establish a consistent philosophic outlook for the poet. By constructing the meaning of individual poems in terms of that outlook, this criticism conceded the special rhetorical purposes of Shelley's poetry without fully accepting the implications of that concession. If the poet's thinking was neither sloppy nor contradictory, and if his thought was committed to skepticism, his poems *must* be skeptical. Rather than nullifying skeptical tenets, the poems' idealist affirmations confirmed those tenets in the mode of irony—invoking them as a standard from which Shelley was consciously departing, either in the interest of moral affect or simply as a hypothetical projection of hope. But if Shelley's poems suspend his disbelief, why doesn't that suspension, to the degree that the poems imaginatively realize it, render the disbelief suspended? Are we to read by retrieving what the text discards? Why should we understand a poem's idealizing gestures by referring them to the ideas they formally and intellectually displace? If Shelley's "beautiful idealisms of moral excellence" originate as conjectural renderings of those possibilities "which exalt and ennoble humanity" (Preface to *Prometheus Unbound*, 135; "Shelley's Notes on Hellas," *CW* 3:56 n. 2), they quickly acquire a dramatic authenticity and emotional power neither conditional nor tentative. The problem lies not merely with the fact, for instance, that Demogorgon's reference to an unknowable deep truth is followed by the truth-claim that love is eternal and not subject to "Fate, Time, Occasion, Chance and Change" (*Prometheus Unbound* 2.4.119); it lies also with the fact that *Prometheus Unbound* dramatizes love's triumph as an actually occurring event and not simply as a possibility that skepticism cannot disavow. As obvious as this may be, its importance for reading

---

[26] Tilottama Rajan's comment on Earl R. Wasserman is from *Dark Interpreter: The Discourse of Romanticism* (Ithaca: Cornell University Press, 1980), 58 n. 2. Rajan herself claims that Shelley's "encounter with skepticism leads him to postpone or relocate rather than revise his idealism, to respond to skepticism sentimentally rather than ironically or tragically" (59), though she exempts *The Triumph of Life* from this generalization. I do not accept the doctrinal understructure Wasserman constructs for Shelleyan idealism. He argues for a development from Lockean dualism to a quasi-Berkeleyan "One Mind," regarded as the inevitable ontological implication of the epistemological inseparability of perception and existence, in *Shelley: A Critical Reading* (Baltimore: Johns Hopkins University Press, 1971), 131–53. For criticism of Wasserman's position, see Charles E. Robinson's appendix on the "One Mind," in *Shelley and Byron: The Snake and Eagle Wreathed in Fight* (Baltimore: Johns Hopkins University Press, 1976), 245–48; and Kenneth Neill Cameron's review of *Shelley: A Critical Reading*, in *MLQ* 33 (1972): 463–66.

Shelley's poetry has not been duly allowed. Too often Shelley criticism marginalizes the poet's representations of transcendence by explaining them according to skeptical principles that remain marginally represented (at best) in the poems themselves.[27]

The issue here is obviously one of degree—the comparative weighting of idealism and skepticism. Shelley's idealism undeniably receives its due in many readings, and has been unduly emphasized in some.[28] Still, few Shelleyans would dispute the claim that at present skepticism retains its privileged interpretive position. Critics ordinarily cite the fideistic options of a positive skepticism, stress Shelley's faith in the moral efficacy of hopeful representations, and treat his poetry's manifest idealisms as heuristic fictions—accommodating an idealistic superstructure to a skeptical base, rather than the other way around. I would argue conversely that Shelley's poetry subsumes its antitheses in an idealist logic, the transition from Platonism to skepticism occurring only within an encompassing logocentrism. Skepticism and idealism are equally oriented toward truth-as-presence. If the former doubts while the latter affirms, they merely assume reversed orbits around the same center. As interrelated antitheses, skepticism and idealism operate in Shelley as antitypical counterparts. That hardly leaves them equal partners, however, for the very idea of the antitype is weighted toward idealism. So is the notion of the reciprocity of tenor and vehicle in metaphorical exchanges.

Shelley's idealism rests with his rhetoric, and above all with his conception of metaphor as the subsumption of difference in unity. Admittedly, his rhetoric articulates what appears to be a dialectical irony akin to skepticism. The dialectic emerges in the antithetical conflicts

[27] The congruence of Shelleyan skepticism and idealism can be overstated. Skepticism allowed theocentric beliefs (as in the case of Drummond) and an ethics based on emotional conviction. But even if Shelley derived his poetry's beautiful idealisms from his awareness of uncertainty with anything like the closely reasoned connections of "On Life," that by itself would hardly prevent idealist fictions from ramifying beyond their motivating assumptions in the poems themselves. The skeptical tradition was (for the most part) politically conservative, emotionally cautious, and dedicated to the suspension of judgment. By no means does it automatically sanction visionary projections of any order or emotional intensity. C. E. Pulos describes Drummond as a "sceptic who tends toward a *provisional* idealism," and declares that Shelley "expresses *tentative* feelings about things recognized as unknowable" (*Deep Truth*, 41, 77; emphasis added). I would again suggest that in many cases—with Laon and Cythna's transcendence, and the apotheosis of love in *Prometheus Unbound* 4, for example—Shelley's poems suspend their disbelief to lend ideals far more than an emotionally tentative, provisional reality.

[28] In the Platonizing notes in *The Complete Poetical Works of Percy Bysshe Shelley*, ed. Neville Rogers, vol. 1 (Oxford: Clarendon Press, 1972). See the comments on Rogers' notes in the reviews by E. B. Murray, *KSJ* 25 (1976): 152; Donald H. Reiman, *JEGP* 73 (1974): 258; and Kenneth Neill Cameron, *SIR* 12 (1973): 698–99.

of his figures. Their ostensibly ironic character appears when they motivate a simultaneously creative and de-creative dynamic inimical to closure.[29] In its self-perpetuating drive, this dynamic links Shelleyan contraries in a mutually recuperative complicity, allotting them the successive phases of a cycle in which, as Daniel J. Hughes puts it, moments of "coherence and collapse" continually banish and reinstate each other:

> Shelley was more interested in reconstituting the initial state out of which the poem came and less interested in the total structure extrapolated from inconstant and unremembered beginnings. This is why his poetry constantly returns to its own sources and attempts to mirror the potential from which it sprang. The pattern of his imagery is a pattern of insufficient wholes, the image breaking as it is made; the larger pattern of his total poem is a constant seeking after a stability once glimpsed but now expressible only in fragments and a slowly-unfolding and self-discovering revelation. His poetry bears ceaseless witness to its own destruction, organized, as it is, as a series of fading coals leading to an overall structure which, like the phoenix, rises from its ashes.[30]

This structure remains unaltered by variations in its constituent antitheses—idealism and skepticism, desire and death, similarity and difference—which (as antitheses) prove functionally interchangeable. Potentiality has proven an influential concept in Shelley studies because to all appearances it too validates the poet's skepticism. When coherence relapses on a reenergizing matrix, truths are temporally and rhetorically deferred by a self-perpetuating succession of displacements. As commonly viewed, potentiality disdains final truths, rejects all possibilities of closure, and validates the text's assent to indeterminacy.

My own view (and the readings that follow will test and expand on it) is that the recycling of opposites in Shelley remains idealist. When opposites must reconstitute each other, by their very inclusion in a recuperative economy, they serve as the successively manifest and la-

[29] In *English Romantic Irony* (Cambridge: Harvard University Press, 1980), 5, Anne K. Mellor offers this account of the Romantic ironist: "Having ironically acknowledged the fictiveness of his own patternings of human experience, he romantically engages in the creative process of life by eagerly constructing new forms, new myths. And these new fictions and self-concepts bear with them the seeds of their own destruction. They too die to give way to new patterns, in a never-ending process that becomes an analogue for life itself. The resultant artistic mode that alone can properly be called romantic irony must therefore be a form or structure that simultaneously creates and de-creates itself."

[30] Daniel J. Hughes, "Coherence and Collapse in Shelley, with Particular Reference to *Epipsychidion*," *ELH* 28 (1961): 261–62.

tent complements of a holistic design. When the collapse of coherence can only engender a new moment of coherence, such collapses are merely alienated coherence in the process of returning to itself—like Hegelian Spirit assuming the body of history in a temporary lapse from autonomy. Shelleyan contraries are linked in a dynamic symbiosis that takes place within the closed circle of metaphorical form. This form makes the identity of self and antitype a narrative tautology in which the Same oscillates between obverse, interconvertible instances of itself. Skeptical or ironic approaches to Shelley often overlook the complicities of this oscillation. They place Shelleyan idealism at one of the poles circumscribing an alternation of opposites and ignore ways in which alternation is itself idealizing because it is interrelating. Romantic irony need not yield a synthesis to empower a subliminal idealism. Claims that "the romantic-ironic work . . . sustains two modes of figural discourse without privileging one over the other"[31] ignore the way in which such sustaining *is* a privileging, for it promotes notions of inclusion and mediation given to a reconciliatory imperative, and to the elevation of symbolic copresence over allegorical absence. When irony of this sort is revealed as a mystified idealism, it clarifies the idealist logic of Shelleyan dialectic.

This is not to claim that Shelley's poetry incarnates presence, but to advocate a certain perspective on its inability to do so. Hogle has convincingly shown that Shelleyan metaphor produces meanings "from a process of transfer and substitution rather than from a first Unity or grounding Presence."[32] The transferential energies of Shelley's poems disperse Meaning into a succession of differential meanings, a sequence of vanishings in which terms quickly exhaust and displace themselves. Granted, Shelleyan texts arise in the wake of truth's passage, but how do such texts view their belatedness? For some recent critics, deferral of presence in Shelley's poetry reveals metaphor fortunately actualizing its iconoclastic and disruptive potential. These disruptions unbind the allegorical errancies of metaphor, freeing it from the tyranny of symbolic closure and making it a "rhetoric of temporality."[33] So understood, Shelley's rhetoric celebrates multivalence and becoming as the hallmarks of emotional fulfillment. As Ronald Tetreault writes, such poetry locates "literary meaning . . . in the mutual implication of reader and author in the

---

[31] Mellor, *English Romantic Irony*, 23.

[32] Hogle, "Shelley's Poetics," 159.

[33] Paul de Man associates allegory and irony on the basis of their authentically temporal structure in "The Rhetoric of Temporality," in *Blindness and Insight: Essays in the Rhetoric of Contemporary Criticism*, 2d ed., rev. (1971; reprint, Minneapolis: University of Minnesota Press, 1983).

experience of the text, not in some transcendental signified outside
it."[34] Shelley's verbal anarchism is thus seen to dissolve high truth in
a play of possibilities, a figural *jouissance* freeing the reader for self-
discovery. Such accounts of Shelley's poetic project stress its ironic
"avoidance . . . of determinate meanings" in celebrating readerly
freedom.[35]

There are two problems with these arguments. First, they get the
indeterminacy right but the affirmation wrong. Shelley sometimes as-
sociated stability of meaning with ideological fixation, the ossifying
power of "Large codes of fraud and woe" ("Mont Blanc," l. 81). As in
the last act of *Prometheus Unbound*, his poems can celebrate an un-
bounded vitality that achieves expression by assuming verbal forms it
must break in the act of assuming. But one should not construe Shel-
leyan figuration as a pseudodialectic of chaos and cosmos in which
every instance of dislocation liberates life's essential energies and ev-
ery instance (or appearance) of nodal closure thwarts those energies.
That would be morally and intellectually simplistic. Shelley's artistic
commitment to "ideas which exalt and ennoble humanity" rests on
their possibility as truth, not on their beauty as lies. Claims that Shel-
ley embraces an indeterminacy that "does not strive for truth"[36] ex-
aggerate his assent to unknowability and slight his poetry's moral and
philosophic aspirations. "That there is a true solution of the riddle
[of human existence]," he wrote, "and that in our present state the
solution is unattainable by us, are propositions which may be re-
garded as *equally* certain" ("Shelley's Notes on Hellas," *CW* 3:56 n. 2,
emphasis added). Shelley retained his appreciation of the difficulty,
and the dangers, of determinate and universal meanings. Yet he
never wholeheartedly accepted the antic disposition of irony, or sur-
rendered the dream of fathoming and expressing life's deepest
truths.

The second problem lies with the inability of deconstruction to es-
cape logocentrism, or with the fact that the self-deconstructing fig-
ures of Shelley's poetry are reflexes rather than negations of its ide-
alism. Critics occasionally suggest that centered motifs are
unrecognizably dismantled by the decentering energies inhabiting
them. What results, ironically, is a marginalizing of tension and dif-

[34] Ronald Tetreault, *The Poetry of Life: Shelley and Literary Form* (Toronto: University
of Toronto Press, 1987), 7.

[35] David Simpson, *Irony and Authority in Romantic Poetry* (Totowa, N.J.: Rowman and
Littlefield, 1979), 190. Simpson argues that Romantic texts frequently cultivate unsta-
ble meanings, leaving interpretation open to readers' creative responses, as part of a
campaign against authority.

[36] Tetreault, *Poetry of Life*, 241.

ference in Shelley's work, an evasion of the conflict between what a
writer "commands and what he does not command of the patterns of
the language that he uses."[37] While transference can relapse into hi-
erarchical abjection, there can be no clash of equally energized antith-
eses in Shelley's poems, as Jerrold E. Hogle reads them, for example,
because their idealist energies are always already transferentially
structured. For Hogle, the Shelleyan One is not merely transferen-
tially complicated by its contextualization in particular Shelley texts
but so radically refashioned that it *signifies* transference; it is so di-
vested of its traditional unitive associations that no truly evenhanded
clash of centrifugal and centripetal energies can result. In Shelley's
late work, as Hogle reads it, there is no conflict between attraction
toward the One-as-such and commitment to dispersal, but rather a
co-opting of the One by transferential deep structures that predomi-
nate at every moment: "Instead of the One drawing [Shelley] away
from transference," Hogle argues, "the poet draws the One *toward*
transference and reinstalls that notion at the heart of the One's vari-
ous forms."[38] I argue conversely that transference is meaningless ex-
cept in relation to an otherness ("various forms" of closure, including
the idea of a "heart," or core identity) as endemic to Shelley as trans-
ference itself. When we fail to construe transferential processes in
relation to such unassimilable otherness, even the most systematic ex-
positions of Shelleyan decenteredness can only evoke texts that, ev-
erywhere refusing to be one with themselves, are by the ubiquity of
that refusal rendered massively one with themselves. We must "rec-
ognize that the text cannot simply be replaced by a subtext, and that

---

[37] Derrida, *Of Grammatology*, 158. This quotation comes from a section of *Grammatol-
ogy* in which Derrida addresses the "question of method," the same section to which
Jerrold E. Hogle refers in *Shelley's Process: Radical Transference and the Development of
His Major Works* (New York: Oxford University Press, 1988), 345 n. 22, when he writes,
"I do not claim that my study always performs the 'deconstructive' process of reading
defined by Derrida." Most deconstructive readings of Shelley—and Hogle also disso-
ciates his critical practice from them (*Shelley's Process*, 18–24)—characterize the relation
between the text's authorially commanded and uncommanded aspects as one of trans-
gression, rupture, and aporia—as a "*tension* between text and subtext," a "*lacuna* be-
tween rhetoric and content" (Rajan, *Dark Interpreter*, 60, 72; emphasis added). When
Hogle defines "Shelley's process" as (among other things) the transferential activity of
"arche-writing" *and* "the task of revising Western thought that [Shelley] undertook"
(*Shelley's Process*, 26), he makes language, as a system prior and inimical to authorial
command, continuous with the revisionary objectives of Shelley's poetic project. This
continuity is highly dubious, in my view, and Hogle's transferential readings (the pur-
ported revelations of a distinctly Shelleyan process) critical exercises that could be per-
formed for any text or figure, including those he allows to be "ultimately centered"
(*Shelley's Process*, 326).

[38] Hogle, *Shelley's Process*, 266.

the official content of a work does not cease to exist because it is undermined from within."[39] Just as the erotic imagination projects its antitype through an act of repression, Shelley's rhetoric begins in a negative gesture, banishing the truth of the origin's textualization. His poetry envisions an ideal and originary ground of being, and in its quest for this ontologically higher ground resists recognizing it as an effect of language, a kind of textual mirage. This resistance is as clearly thematized, and enjoys as much dramatic immediacy, as the figural errancies that subvert it. The result is a poetry riven by a clash of antagonists, neither of which could disappear without its counterpart instantly disappearing with it.

The mutual dependence of antitheses in Shelley leaves the ideal at once intact and inaccessible. Shelley's idealism serves as the vehicle of his prophetic optimism, but also sanctions pessimism by wedding the aspirations of his poems to the ultimate. When metaphorical exchanges of self and antitype, idealism and skepticism, continually withhold completion, transferential allegory emerges in Shelleyan metaphor as the dark double of its symbolic orientation. As the mode of metaphor in its inadequacy to presence, allegory both disclaims and recuperates Shelley's figures of likeness. Yet the recuperations finally prove exhaustible. The allegorical subplot of Shelley's poetry gradually exposes the contradictions of his metaphorical idealism, its willed fictions and covert violence. With that exposure, Shelley's poems accept death as the telos of desire and gravitate increasingly toward a visionary despair.

REFORMING THE READER

Shelley adopted a poetics of love in part because it could accommodate his political commitments. Since "the release of Love, as everyone knows, is the basis of social revolution for Shelley,"[40] the self/antitype model lent itself easily to his efforts to have love "celebrated every where as the sole law which should govern the moral world" (Preface to *The Revolt of Islam*, CW 1:247). We must therefore read Shelley's politics as an aspect of his rhetoric of Romantic love. That means allowing "for the elaboration of a politics of form" and avoiding "crude expressive theories of politics in literature that fail to deal with textual strategies."[41] It also means recognizing the politics of Shelley's poetry as a politics of the ideal. As a radical activist and pam-

[39] Rajan, *Dark Interpreter*, 21.
[40] Hogle, "Shelley's Poetics," 181.
[41] Dana Polan, "The Ruin of a Poetics: The Political Practice of *Prometheus Unbound*," *Enclitic* 7 (1983): 38.

phleteer, Shelley accepted the necessary expediencies of practical pol-
itics. He remained "one of those whom nothing will fully satisfy, but
who [is] ready to be partially satisfied by all that is practicable" (*Letters*
2:153). His poems, however, attempt to affirm regenerative love as
an ever-present possibility. They try to lay the psychological ground-
work for revolution in the belief "that until the mind can love, and
admire, and trust, and hope, and endure, reasoned principles of
moral conduct are as seeds cast upon the highway of life," trampled
into uselessness (Preface to *Prometheus Unbound*, 135). Shelley's poetry
strives to promulgate millennial ideals, to empower them causally in
representations enacting their realization. Shelley wished to join the
line of prophetic poets who "perceive the future, but [who] also cre-
ate what they foresee, if only by rendering that future more proxi-
mate and accessible."[42]

He consequently internalizes politics in the reading experiences his
poems encourage. The politics of Shelley's poetry centers on its affec-
tive dynamics and develops imaginatively as a correlative of his self/
antitype paradigm. The specular interplay organizing the relation of
lover and antitype, poet and text, also governs the phenomenology
of poet and reader in Shelley—which he expressly conceives as psy-
chic coincidence. He regards poems as "sacred links of that chain . . .
which descending through the minds of many men is attached to
those great minds [the poets], whence as from a magnet the invisible
effluence is sent forth, which at once connects, animates and sustains
the life of all" (*Defence of Poetry*, 493). The "more essential attribute
of Poetry," he comments, remains "the power of awakening in others
sensations like those which animate my own bosom" (Preface to *The
Revolt of Islam*, *CW* 1:244). Shelley intended his texts to transmit re-
semblances by which the reader's consciousness would be linguisti-
cally reshaped to accord with the poet's consciousness, to reflect the
poet's emotions and values as mirrored in turn by the words of his
poem.[43] Poets and readers are lovers in Shelley, and the text, like
Byron's Plato, "no better than a go-between." Shelley dramatizes this
mediation in the reading scenes of *Prometheus Unbound*, for instance,
and when Cythna acquires her selfhood through an empathic con-

[42] Sperry, *Shelley's Major Verse*, 68.

[43] Tetreault describes Shelley's poetry as a "transaction between author and audience
through the medium of the text, which, if form follows function, will manifest a struc-
tural design that will facilitate that relation" (*Poetry of Life*, 18). While Shelley may have
meant metonymy or metalepsis in referring to "that figure of speech which considers
the effect as a synonime of the cause" (*Defence of Poetry*, 483), his phrase accurately
describes the causal power his poetics consistently attribute to metaphor, as John W.
Wright notes (*Shelley's Myth of Metaphor*, 38).

centration on Laon: her face, Laon reports, "was turned on mine with speechless grace, / Watching the hopes which there her heart had learned to trace" (*The Revolt of Islam, PW*, ll. 944–45). She is thereby transformed just as the chameleonic lover of *Prometheus Unbound* "Grows like what it looks upon" (4.484).

Obviously Shelley's prophetic politics will be implicated in the ambiguities of his idealized mirrorings. The most important political contradiction in his poetry follows from the metaleptic indeterminacy of self and antitype. When a lover's soul becomes a site of desire through the reflexive force of a specular image, but those images remain derivations of a supposedly antecedent entity, then self and antitype are mutually constitutive, which is to say that they toss the origin back and forth between them, leaving the locus of causal power highly unstable. Such circular reciprocity allows for mutual influence of writer and reader, calling the poet's prophetic authority into question. Shelley tries to shore up that authority by assuming certain moral and psychological universals. He takes "the mind of the creator [as] . . . itself the image of all other minds" (*Defence of Poetry*, 485), positing a reader imaginatively redirected only by a liberation of potentials native to every mind. Poetry of this kind aspires to the condition of drama as Shelley described it in commenting on classical tragedy:

> The tragedies of the Athenian poets are as mirrors in which the spectator beholds himself, under a thin disguise of circumstance, stript of all but that ideal perfection and energy which *every one* feels to be the internal type of all that he loves, admires, and would become. . . . The drama, so long as it continues to express poetry, is as a prismatic and many-sided mirror, which . . . multiplies all that it reflects, and endows it with the power of propagating its like wherever it may fall. (*Defence of Poetry*, 490–91; emphasis added)

Such mirrors promote moral improvement through an accurate psychic mimesis: the "ideal perfection and energy" captured by the text reflect realities ordinarily hidden but ultimately true.

Yet the notion of an idealizing mimesis finally embroils Shelley in considerable difficulties. In accepting a communicative process valorizing resemblance as a catalyst for change, he envisions a reader who changes by becoming like the poet, yet who can do so only to the extent that he is *already* like the poet. In this paradox we see the supplemental logic of the text's specular relation to its audience. A revolutionary poetry can alter readers to the extent that it differs from them, but can engage them only insofar as they discover themselves in the mirror of art. This ideal of readerly empathy and moral catharsis accepts difference but again relegates it to the status of an epiphenomenon. The result is a hierarchy. Signification arises as an effect of power, as Shelleyan poems produce meaning through an alternate domination by poet or reader of what, for a poetics of love, should be a marriage of true minds in the text.

The poet can usurp the reading process in numerous ways. Shelley dominates his poetry through an elitism that makes excessive demands on readers and, in his earlier poems, through dogmatic preaching. His favorite strategy for controlling the social effect of his poems was to will a highly select readership for them—an "elect," an "esoteric few" (*Letters*, 2:200, 263). This readership is a narcissistic projection, of course, a social group hypothesized in the poet's own image. Readers so enlightened allowed Shelley to eschew dogmatism. He could administer "to the effect by acting upon the cause" (*Defence of Poetry*, 488), promoting social betterment simply by awakening the dormant imaginations of his naturally benevolent audience. He rarely rested easy with so narrowly defined a readership, however, or sustained so purely optimistic a view of humankind at large.[44] Shelley's ambivalence toward readers informs even *Prometheus Unbound*, addressed though it was to "the more select classes of poetical readers" (Preface to *Prometheus Unbound*, 135). Employing the Preface to *Prometheus Unbound* "in order to reassure himself that he has ultimate control over the reactions of his audience," P.M.S. Dawson observes, Shelley tacitly confesses that "he has not quite reconciled himself to trusting the autonomous imagination of his readers, though such trust is demanded by the moral scheme of philosophical anarchism."[45] Granting his readers an equal role in the construction of intersubjective meanings, Shelley realized, meant granting them the capability to disfigure the most beautiful idealisms in the very process of assimilating them—as the public reception of his work amply demonstrated. Shelley feared conceding an audience so much power, and continued to privilege authorial consciousness as the locus of truth. When the learning, complexity, and heterodoxy of his work left him few readers, he embraced his isolation as a sign of uncompromised principles and prophetic election.[46]

Authorial determinations of meaning in Shelley presume and em-

---

[44] For example, from the "Speculations on Morals," *CW* 7:73: "The immediate emotions of [man's] nature, especially in its most inartificial state, prompt him to inflict pain, and to arrogate dominion. He desires to heap superfluities to his own store, although others perish with famine. He is propelled to guard against the smallest invasion of his own liberty, though he reduces others to a condition of the most pitiless servitude. He is revengeful, proud and selfish."

[45] P.M.S. Dawson, *The Unacknowledged Legislator: Shelley and Politics* (Oxford: Clarendon Press, 1980), 215.

[46] Of course, Shelley for the most part lamented his inability to reach a wide, appreciative audience. See *Letters* 2:331, 374, 436.

power a negative counterpart: the possibility of audience control. With Shelley's poetry the audience usurps the reading process by personifying social intransigence. Audiences allow "society" access to the text, channeling its communicative energies into proscribed responses. Pondering the problem of audience, radical poets are forced to recognize that reading, even reading conceived as a revolutionary event, occurs in institutional forums cross-sectioned by competing ideologies when not dominated outright by the very power structures the poem decries. Such reading experiences are infiltrated conspiracies, structures inhabited by the enemy in advance. No more than any author could Shelley simply look in his heart and write. He had to consider the Society for the Suppression of Vice, the system of lending libraries, the cost of books in relation to fluctuations in the economy and differences in printing costs (type, ink, and paper), publishers and the problem of introductions to them, the Reviews, differences in the values and education of his audience—and the ways such variables were affected by the broadest political and economic changes, the work of other writers, and the publication and proofreading difficulties attendant on sending work to London from abroad. Shelley's letters touch on all these matters. He despairs of the power of the booksellers, grows restive under the censure of reviewers, discusses the adaptation of printing style to audience, pays his own costs, advises Ollier on how to advertise, laments not having an audience, and knowingly dismisses the possibility of being prosecuted for *The Revolt of Islam* because its style and erudition left it "so refined and so remote from the conceptions of the vulgar" (*Letters* 1:579).[47] Romantic authorship was a complex social act requiring writers to find their way between invariably constraining options.

Yet nothing fettered Shelley's imagination so much as the language he used. The problem involved inherent verbal limitations—the very *idea* of language—but also the traditional meanings and conventions of nineteenth-century English. Shelley required a radical formalism. Disdaining to create his own system, as Blake's Los advocated, he could only plunder the verbal resources of English in an attempt to dislocate inherited meanings. The paradoxes of this enterprise often refashioned his "effort to be a radical poet" as "an aspiration towards a contradiction in terms."[48] Since iconoclasm presupposes icons, Shel-

---

[47] Consult the account of these matters in Ian Jack, *The Poet and His Audience* (Cambridge: Cambridge University Press, 1984), 90–116, and Charles E. Robinson, "Percy Bysshe Shelley, Charles Ollier, and William Blackwood: The Contexts of Early Nineteenth-Century Publishing," in *Shelley Revalued: Essays from the Gregynog Conference*, ed. Kelvin Everest (Totowa, N.J.: Barnes and Noble, 1983), 183–226.

[48] Cronin, *Shelley's Poetic Thoughts*, 7.

ley's adversarial rhetoric limits itself to recontextualizing maneuvers. He places words with a conservative import—"king," for example, as used in the anarchist apocalypse of *Prometheus Unbound* 4—in radical contexts designed to redefine them. Unfortunately, this strategy interrelates word and context as mutually constitutive antitypes, achieving polemical effects that are uncontrollably reversible. Monarchical words placed in republican contexts can nullify the redirective force of those contexts, after all, as easily as the opposite appropriation can occur. Shelley employs an antithetical rhetoric in which phrases and figures contest each other's power to determine meaning. He can thereby dramatize the clash of traditional authority and revolutionary energy as an aspect of style, but cannot mandate the outcome of that struggle.

In fact, Shelley's poetry often revalidates the conservatism that gives his radicalism its point of departure, and produces a deeply divided political vision. At times his poems can appear reactionary from the perspective of nineteenth-century class interests.[49] Shelley remained distrustful of the masses and fearful of populist violence. His liberalism was qualified by debts to subliminally elitist radical theory, such as Godwinian gradualism, with its hopes for an intellectually disseminated revolution. It was also qualified by the poet's inescapable obligations to literary and philosophical tradition. In its assumptions about truth and language, Shelley's poetry internalizes the hierarchical structures and institutional violence endemic to Western culture. Despite his avowed feminism, for instance, Shelley accepted models of poetic creation that regard the author as "a father, a progenitor, a procreator, an aesthetic patriarch whose pen is an instrument of generative power like his penis."[50] His sexual politics succumb to contradiction, consequently, as his poems reinvest genealogical and patriarchal norms in the egalitarian love they attempt to celebrate. All such contradictions complicate Shelley's aspirations to political influence by allowing the influence his poems attain to covertly support established authority. The pressure contradiction exerts on Shelley's radicalism ends by diverting love from worldly mediations to transcendent absolutes.[51] The apocalyptic drive of Shelley's late poetry

[49] As Donald H. Reiman argues in "Shelley as Agrarian Reactionary," *KSMB* 30 (1979): 5–15.

[50] Sandra M. Gilbert and Susan Gubar, *The Madwoman in the Attic: The Woman Writer and the Nineteenth-Century Literary Imagination* (New Haven: Yale University Press, 1979), 6.

[51] In *The Apocalyptic Vision in the Poetry of Shelley* (Toronto: University of Toronto Press, 1964), xi–xiv, 189–98, and elsewhere, Ross Woodman argues that Shelley's commitment to social reform gradually gave way to an apocalyptic desire for otherworldly

reflects the continuity of his idealism and politics as antitypical facets of a single desire. Confronted by the problems of political representation, and by his inability to command and redirect an audience, Shelley displaced his radicalism into idealized myths capable of accommodating it only because his radicalism was a displaced idealism from the start.

The apocalyptic reorientation of Shelley's poems signifies his growing political disillusionment. His invocations of death and transcendence should be construed principally as proleptic figures of a radical isolation. Privately experienced but publicly representative, this isolation is an unavoidable legacy of Romantic self-consciousness. It also prophesies the marginalizing of poetry and alienation of the artist in modern society. Shelley's alienation in 1821–1822 reflects the narcissism fundamental to mirroring, and exposes the problems of specular idealism as an agency of emotional and rhetorical closure. These paradoxes appear most clearly when passion and rhetoric converge in Shelley, in his representations of sexual experience as a metaphorical negotiation of antitypes. The following chapters will explore Shelley's rhetoric of Romantic love by concentrating on *Alastor*, *The Revolt of Islam*, *Prometheus Unbound*, *The Cenci*, and *Epipsychidion* as a poetic sequence organized around real or fantasized acts of sexual intercourse. The story these poems tell ends with Shelley's encrypting of imagination in *The Triumph of Life*. It begins with the alliance of eros, death, and solitude in *Alastor*, the title poem of the first volume Shelley published under his own name and, as such, the poem that truly initiated his career.

---

perfection. Versions of this argument can be found in Milton Wilson, *Shelley's Later Poetry: A Study of His Prophetic Imagination* (New York: Columbia University Press, 1959), 298, and in Wasserman, *Shelley*, 411–13, 443–44, 455–61.

Chapter 2

THE VANISHED BODY

"They whom thou spak'st of are no vision'ries,"
Rejoin'd that voice—"They are no dreamers weak,
They seek no wonder but the human face;

.   .   .   .

What benefit canst thou do, or all thy tribe,
To the great world? Thou art a dreaming thing;
A fever of thyself—think of the earth."
—Keats, *The Fall of Hyperion*

ALASTOR, Milton Wilson once remarked, "is the *Hamlet* of Shelley criticism."[1] Like Shakespeare's tragedy, Shelley's poem abounds in mysteries—enigmas concerning its structural integrity, the relation of its Preface to the poem proper, its attitude toward its protagonist, the identities and values of its dramatis personae,[2] and more. These ambiguities do not always promote controlled, Shakespearean complexity. *Alastor* is diffuse, sentimentally self-dramatizing, and so thematically "unsorted-out"[3] that each new critical reading, its virtues notwithstanding, can seem to shed more darkness than light by supplementing a medley already irreducible to consensus. But this sense of mysteries overmastering the poem's ordering and expressive powers only adds to its *Hamlet*-like interest. It suggests Shelley's initial encounter with the forces truly driving his imagination. *Alastor* appears so archetypally Shelleyan a text because here Shelley first formulates and explores his poetics of love. When the Poet encounters his reflection just

[1] Milton Wilson, *Shelley's Later Poetry: A Study of His Prophetic Imagination* (New York: Columbia University Press, 1959), 164.

[2] The dramatis personae of *Alastor* were first identified by Earl R. Wasserman in *Shelley: A Critical Reading* (Baltimore: Johns Hopkins University Press, 1971), 11–41. I refer to the poem's speaker as the Narrator and its protagonist as the Poet.

[3] As Frederick Kirchhoff writes, in "Shelley's *Alastor*: The Poet Who Refuses to Write Language," *KSJ* 32 (1983): 109. Kirchhoff challenges critical defenses of the text's inconsistencies as strategic ambivalence without supporting Raymond D. Havens' dismissal of *Alastor* as "confused" in "Shelley's *Alastor*," *PMLA* 45 (1930): 1098–1109. The most recent and useful overview of *Alastor* criticism is in Christopher Heppner, "Alastor: The Poet and Narrator Reconsidered," *KSJ* 37 (1988): 91–109.

> as the human heart,
> Gazing in dreams over the gloomy grave,
> Sees its own treacherous likeness there

$$(ll.\ 472–74),$$

the poem correlates specularity, eros, and death in a single visionary complex. Like the poems of Shelley's later years, *Alastor* also extends its interest in psychic mirrorings to formal reflection on its rhetorical strategies, thematizing figural structures as forms of desire. If most accounts of Shelley include *Alastor*, that is because the poem encapsulates his poetics and prophesies his career.

SHELLEY'S ROMANTIC ADAM

Shelley studies are still hampered by the poet's reputation for sky-larking optimism. While few contemporary readers angelize Shelley, many minimize his poetry's darker aspects, circumscribing the contagion of Shelleyan violence by attributing it to localized errors. Such defensiveness often informs readings of the deathliness of human desire in *Alastor*. These readings note the Poet's enervation, of course, but attribute it entirely to his rejection of all breathing human passion. The advantages of this attribution are obvious. It makes solipsism the scapegoat for the text's most disturbing implications. It permits destruction to arise not from eros but from narcissism, from an unfortunate but avoidable self-absorption rather than from the actual dawning of love within the Poet. And it reconciles the experiences of the poem's protagonist with certain elements of the Preface to *Alastor*, which initially praises the Poet but concludes by lamenting his "self-centred seclusion" (69).[4]

The ambivalence of the Preface is muted in the poem itself, however, for *Alastor* basically admires and sympathizes with its protagonist. Shelley's Poet by no means avoids error or guilt in his solitude; the poem surely makes that clear enough simply by conducting him to a narcissus-bordered "cove" (l. 405). Still, the Poet does not drown in these waters. His fate carries him to them, evoking Narcissus as mythic prototype, but beyond them as well, impelling him to a more complex, more typically Romantic ending. Fear of visionary autonomy recurs in Wordsworth, Coleridge, and Keats, as well as in Shelley, as an intrinsic part of the poetic project they embrace, an unavoidable legacy of the self-consciousness they explore. Reading

---

[4] Evan K. Gibson refuted Havens, and in effect redeemed *Alastor* for New Critical formalism, in part by reconciling the poem with its Preface in "*Alastor*: A Reinterpretation," *PMLA* 62 (1947): 1022–42, reprinted in *SPP*, 545–69.

Alastor as an object lesson in the necessity of socialization overlooks the poem's intimation that the imagination inherently resists socialization. Certainly the Poet is too isolated, but what determines his isolation? What logic, or justice, underlies the deathly conspiracy of solitude, imagination, and desire in this poem? If *Alastor* asks us to recognize the Poet's mistakes, it also insists that their debilitating consequences proliferate beyond his personal culpability, so that debility cannot be construed simply as the reflex of error. Shelley's protagonist is unfitted for life by what is finest in him, by weakness linked to strength as its inescapable obverse. The Poet must err, yet his error makes him a representative figure. It signifies a kind of fall and refashions him as a Romantic Adam.[5]

"The Imagination may be compared to Adam's dream—he awoke and found it truth."[6] Keats's famous comparison is virtually paradigmatic for the visionary romances of Shelley's era. It bears on *Alastor*, which echoes Milton, for instance, when the Poet "overleaps the bounds" (l. 207) even as Satan "overleap'd all bound" in entering Paradise (*Paradise Lost* 4.181). Shelley depends on Milton most strikingly, however, in appropriating entire narrative situations. In the passage Keats was remembering, Milton's Adam recounts his loneliness in Paradise, and God's promise to bring him "Thy likeness, thy fit help, thy other self, / Thy wish, exactly to thy heart's desire" (*Paradise Lost* 8.450–51). Adam then describes the creation of Eve:

> Mine eyes [God] clos'd, but op'n left the Cell
> Of Fancy my internal sight, by which
> Abstract as in a trance methought I saw,
>
> . . . .
>
> Under his forming hands a Creature grew,
> Manlike, but different sex, so lovely fair,
> That what seem'd fair in all the World, seem'd now
> Mean, or in her summ'd up, in her contain'd
> And in her looks, which from that time infus'd
> Sweetness into my heart, unfelt before,
> And into all things from her Air inspir'd

[5] For the motif of the Fall in *Alastor*, see Luther L. Scales, Jr., "The Poet as Miltonic Adam in *Alastor*," *KSJ* 21–22 (1972–1973): 126–44, esp. 134. In *Doubt and Identity in Romantic Poetry* (New Haven: Yale University Press, 1988), 171, Andrew M. Cooper stresses the revisionary aspect of Shelley's debt to Milton: "Unlike Adam's dream, the Poet's takes place in a fallen world."

[6] Keats's 22 November 1817 letter to Benjamin Bailey, in *The Letters of John Keats*, ed. Hyder Edward Rollins (Cambridge: Harvard University Press, 1958), 1:185. Andrew M. Cooper contends that Keats echoes the Preface to *Alastor* in this letter (*Doubt and Identity*, 31).

The spirit of love and amorous delight.
Shee disappear'd, and left me dark, I wak'd
To find her, or for ever to deplore
Her loss, and other pleasures all abjure.

(*Paradise Lost* 8.460-63, 470–80)

In *Alastor* the dreaming Poet's projection of the veiled maiden unmis-
takably evokes the creation of Eve. Both dreamers, Milton's Adam
and Shelley's Poet, see their identities duplicated in a female figure
of unsurpassed beauty. Both awake alone and dedicate themselves to
seeking the dream-figure. Just as Eve is Adam's "likeness," the veiled
maiden resembles the Poet, speaking in a poet's voice "like the voice
of his own soul" (l. 153). Most important, both dream sequences dra-
matize the birth of eros—for Adam, "The spirit of love" (*Paradise Lost*
8.477); for Shelley's Poet, "The spirit of sweet human love" (l. 203).
Taking Milton's creation of Eve as its point of departure, the dream
in *Alastor* offers a revisionary account of the psychological origins of
human desire.

In "On Love" emptiness recrystallizes as desire when the inwardly
insufficient self discovers its ideal counterpart: "A mirror whose sur-
face reflects only the forms of purity and brightness: a soul within
our soul that describes a circle around its proper Paradise which pain
and sorrow and evil dare not overleap" (474). This circle connotes a
God-like creativity, but also forms a barrier, an encircling wall that
delineates and protects through its power of exclusion. Defined by
their relation to everything they cannot admit, such paradises pre-
suppose their contraries at every moment. "Repression, then,
emerges as nothing less than the condition of identity in the psychic
order," yet "it produces the conditions of identity, that is of a certain
closure, only by *excluding*: that is, by installing a relation to exteriority
at the core of all that is enclosed."[7] So with Shelleyan eros: even its
name marks the "antitype" as antithetically constituted by the pain,
sorrow, and evil it supposedly nullifies, but that Shelley (instructively)
must mention even in describing it. Shelleyan desire continually re-
instates the forces threatening it through its structural dependence
on them.

Alastor joins "On Love" in conceiving the relation of self and anti-
type as a drama of doubling that binds love to a contrary it creates
through repression. The poem illustrates the gesture of negation by
which Shelleyan eros arises, for "the influx of sexual power experi-
enced in dream by the character the Poet," Leslie Brisman observes,

[7] Samuel Weber, *The Legend of Freud* (Minneapolis: University of Minnesota Press,
1982), 47.

"is founded on a repression."[8] Brisman speculates that the repressed psychic content may involve the Poet's sexual aggressions, his instinct to preserve the ego, or his subconscious awareness that fulfillment is delusory. All of these doubtless play a part. But what Shelley's Poet represses undeniably is the body, the female body in particular. Here we must attend to the role of the Arab maiden, who stole

> From duties and repose to tend [the Poet's] steps:—
> Enamoured, yet not daring for deep awe
> To speak her love:—and watched his nightly sleep,
> Sleepless herself, to gaze upon his lips
> Parted in slumber, whence the regular breath
> Of innocent dreams arose: then, when red morn
> Made paler the pale moon, to her cold home
> Wildered, and wan, and panting, she returned.
>
> (ll. 132–39)

Readers have condemned the Poet for spurning the Arab maiden, offering his neglect as justification for that punitive pursuit mentioned by the Preface ("the furies of an irresistible passion pursuing him to speedy ruin," 69) but conspicuously missing from the poem. In truth, the Arab maid "never exists as a real possibility for the Poet," Norman Thurston writes; "he never notices her. She never insists that he notice her. . . . after only ten lines in a poem of 720, she simply disappears, as if she had never been there."[9] Thurston is right: the Poet's lack of awareness of the maid hardly appears blameworthy as *Alastor* presents it. We may accept that point, however, and still find the Arab maiden dramatically functional, even crucial, for Shelley's poem.

Alastor presents and then abandons the maid to provide absence with a human face. Like a magician's assistant, she is introduced so she can vanish. Her disappearance merely shows the narrative reenacting what was already her fate in the Poet's psyche. But there she is not so much banished as displaced into the form of the veiled maid, who "appears in symbolic counterpoint to the Arab maiden," acting

---

[8] Leslie Brisman, *Romantic Origins* (Ithaca: Cornell University Press, 1978), 144.

[9] Norman Thurston, "Author, Narrator, and Hero in Shelley's *Alastor*," *SIR* 14 (1975): 121. Stuart M. Sperry rightly endorses this position in *Shelley's Major Verse: The Narrative and Dramatic Poetry* (Cambridge: Harvard University Press, 1988), 207 n. 20: "The fact is that, following the Poet's indifference to the Arab Maiden, the spirit of human love dispatches her second 'gift' to him less from deliberate malice than from a principle of compensation akin to emotional or psychological necessity. Similarly, the Poet should not be blamed (as he is by many critics) for neglecting the Arab Maiden, whom he not so much spurns as simply never sees and whose primary role is to dramatize his otherworldly longing and uniqueness." Also see Sperry, 208 n. 23.

as the visionary afterimage of a previous figure, the belated duplication of a potentially erotic object.[10] And only potentially erotic, for with Shelleyan desire, doubling alone eroticizes, so that the Arab maiden's ministrations remain passively watchful until repetition libidinally empowers them. The two female figures (the "maiden" and the "maid") are identified by their bending over the sleeping Poet, their love-stricken panting (ll. 139, 184), their "dark locks," and their clothing—if we allow the dream woman's "veil" an Oriental connotation. But such hints aside, only an ulterior connection between the human and dream maidens can explain the timing of the Poet's vision. Why does his amorous trance follow the incident with the Arab maiden so closely? The two episodes are narratively linked as cause and consequence. The Arab maiden's withdrawal functions as a precondition for the dream figure's appearance because in the dynamics of erotic idealization the antitype reconfigures denied energies. The *Alastor* Poet's love quest presumes a constitutive act of repression and organizes itself around a return of the repressed made possible by that act.

Unable to coincide with its original, it is a return that bequeaths eros the same failure. *Alastor* depicts the differential paradoxes of Shelleyan metaphor by denying love any possibility of unity. While *Alastor* presents the Poet's relation to the veiled maid as a variation of the self/antitype paradigm of "On Love," it also shows that the projected antitype projects its own complementary other. Bound as she is to the Arab maiden, the veiled maid becomes one aspect of a figure that oscillates between two poles. Even if the Poet could possess her (and he cannot) he would not transcend difference through a love where likeness completed the self. Rather, he would confront a specular impasse where every likeness would be divided between itself and its own reversed, mirroring likeness—engendering a "regress of consciousness," in Lisa M. Steinman's phrase, in which "for any image of a given mental activity there is always a further image to represent consciousness of that activity, suggesting an endless succession."[11] The possibility of such a regress explains the recurring reflexive imagery of *Alastor*—as if one mirroring demands others—but also underscores the structural heterogeneity of all objects of desire. Meta-

---

[10] Edward Strickland, "Transfigured Night: The Visionary Inversions of *Alastor*," *KSJ* 33 (1984): 151. Richard Holmes similarly believes that Shelley's portrait of the dream maiden "is clearly related to that of the Arab maiden. . . . She [the visionary maid] is in fact the same girl," in *Shelley: The Pursuit* (New York: Dutton, 1975), 303.

[11] Lisa M. Steinman, "Shelley's Skepticism: Allegory in 'Alastor,'" *ELH* 45 (1978): 264–65. For reflexive imagery in *Alastor*, see Wasserman, *Shelley*, 29–34, and William Keach, *Shelley's Style* (London: Methuen, 1984), 81–87.

phor seeks union but presupposes difference. This contradiction
ensures the incompletion of specular relations predicated on a meta-
phorical idealism. *Alastor* dramatizes this inescapable frustration
through the Poet's unsuccessful search, emphatically acknowledging
the differential logic of his longing for union.

Yet in *Alastor*, as in *Prometheus Unbound*, Shelley acknowledges in-
completion only to present it as derivative and inessential. This ide-
alization refashions the poem's quest as a glorious adventure only
gradually revealed as unsuccessful. In fact, the poem's elegiac closing
even depicts the Poet's failure as an ironic triumph, since his perse-
verance, as an index to greatness of soul, establishes him as "some
surpassing Spirit, / Whose light adorned the world around it" (ll.
714–15). Here difference legitimates rather than deconstructs the
holistic imperative of quests for likeness. *Alastor* accommodates dif-
ference to a metaphorically controlled dialectic that defines contrar-
ies as the complementary facets of a single, self-recuperative energy.
Shelleyan opposites dislodge and replace one another just as the neg-
ative makes possible the positive in "To a Sky-Lark":

> Yet if we could scorn
>   Hate and pride and fear;
> If we were things born
>   Not to shed a tear,
> I know not how thy joy we ever should come near.
>
> (ll. 91–95)

Desire needs "hate and pride and fear." Worldly limitation alone, re-
ducing the heart to a foul rag-and-bone shop, incites visions of limit-
less, compensatory fulfillment, so that without suffering, Shelley's
speaker declares, "I know not how thy joy we ever should come near."
If the same condition that permits nearness precludes possession,
and if desire must then fail, failure renews desire by recycling it to
limits it must reject once more. Shelley interrelates antitheses
through a mechanism of potentiality that makes each the transposed,
interconvertible form of the other.[12] In their mutual implication, the
phases of this cyclical dialectic share a covert identity. They enact
their dance of attraction and repulsion within a unity that circum-
scribes difference as desire's incentive, the rationale of its endless be-
coming.

In *Alastor* erotic dialectic centers on the traditional antagonism of

[12] See Daniel J. Hughes, "Coherence and Collapse in Shelley, with Particular Refer-
ence to *Epipsychidion*," *ELH* 28 (1961): 261–62, for the recuperative cycles of Shelleyan
potentiality. In *Alastor* Shelley coordinates repression and return as potentiality and
actuality are coordinated in his cohering, collapsing imagery.

body and spirit. Reminiscing in 1822, Shelley would remark, "one is always in love with something or other; the error, and I confess it is not easy for spirits cased in flesh and blood to avoid it, consists in seeking in a mortal image the likeness of what is perhaps eternal" (*Letters* 2:434). The Poet of *Alastor* makes precisely the opposite mistake. He looks not "for a copy of the vision in the actual world" but "for the pattern or original of the vision itself, the antitype."[13] Yet Shelley no sooner grants him these eternalizing aspirations than he imbues them with all they had sought to reject, sensuous mediation in particular. The Poet pursues a "Spirit" that *Alastor*, given his orgasmic encounter with her, defines as a vanished body from the start, deriving the supernal from sensual matrices—and Shelley elaborates on this irony, I will argue, throughout the latter part of the poem. *Alastor* insists on "the body's role in supplying the ground of consciousness," in Andrew M. Cooper's phrase,[14] so that transcendence can be conceived only in terms of the physical experience it would both supplant and restore in a finer tone. Seek spirit and you find the body. The Poet's rejection of sensuous mediation reverses itself to yield an immersion in the natural world where apparent signs of spiritual presence, like "two eyes, / Two starry eyes, hung in the gloom of thought" (ll. 489–90), may be no more than the twin horns of the fading moon (ll. 654–55). His search for absolute love returns him, by antithetical reflex, to sensuous images with a force proportionate to his original desire for unmediated ecstasy. The return of the repressed means the return of the body, which renews repression, and, in so doing, renews the entire cycle.

As the mechanism driving the Poet's quest, this interrelation of contraries permits *Alastor* to idealize temporality as a self-perpetuating continuum. Shelley parcels difference into sequential phases. He thereby suggests that the heart, to evade love's incompletion, will worship loss as a promise of recovery. *Alastor* dramatizes an amatory epiphany with the veiled maid and invokes Miltonic motifs and paradisal landscapes because the poem's erotic idealism requires a story of loss, of fall from a first into a second world. "To believe in a decisive moment of change from the one to the other," Lawrence Lipking observes, "is to dwell on the dream of an earlier, unproblematic golden age"[15]—the golden age *Epipsychidion* anticipates, and that *The Revolt of Islam* and *Prometheus Unbound* celebrate. From a Freudian

---

[13] Gibson, "*Alastor*," 549. Also see Steinman, "Shelley's Skepticism," 262.

[14] A. Cooper, *Doubt and Identity*, 2.

[15] Lawrence Lipking, "Life, Death, and Other Theories," in *Historical Studies and Literary Criticism*, ed. Jerome J. McGann (Madison: University of Wisconsin Press, 1985), 190.

perspective, such myths always "embody the ego's narcissistic effort to maintain the fiction of an undivided identity by constructing a narrative in which its heterogeneity assumes the form of a *loss*."[16] Heterogeneity is the truth of supplementarity between Shelleyan self and antitype, the truth of their incongruence. Desire continually struggles against this truth, resisting frustration by envisioning an origin in which all deferrals end. In *Alastor* this closure is death projected as the negative, or transposed, form of transcendence.

Only the logic of Shelleyan idealism, then, makes the Poet ask, "Does the dark gate of death / Conduct to thy mysterious paradise . . . ?" (ll. 211–12). His longing for unmediated rapture makes him gravitate toward the ultimate realities that frame life as both "the beginning impulse and . . . ultimate end of being,"[17] defining death as the coincidence of origin and end, self and antitype. Like the "fading coal" of Shelley's *Defence of Poetry*, the antitype's visitation inspires an effort to retrace the vestiges of an originary epiphany. This visionary nostalgia explains the geography of *Alastor*: whether the Poet's travels lead to the birthplace of humankind in the Indian Caucasus or the legendary site of the Garden of Eden near the western Caucasus, his destination remains the mythic origin.[18] Centered on the source, the Poet's yearning for death is regressive, a backward impulse "to embark / And meet lone Death" (ll. 304–5) in a reunion. The Poet's wanderings seem to narrate love in terms of succeeding moments in a forward-moving search. What the poet truly seeks is the reiteration of a prior event. As in Freud, repetition in *Alastor* performs a restorative, stabilizing function.[19] Repetition is the (spuriously) temporalized mode of Sameness. Shelley's representation of death as "a force inextricably bound up with love"[20]—the very seductiveness of oblivion in *Alastor*, the sensuous languor of death as consummation—confirms the poem's idealist premises. Here love turns deathward not as the last stage of an acceptance of process but as the unavoidable consequence of a rejection of process. Desire's compulsion to repeat, its fascination with an idealized origin, commits Eros to Thanatos.

After the fall, Eve advises Adam, "Let us seek Death" (*Paradise Lost*

---

[16] Weber, *Legend of Freud*, 25.

[17] Jerrold E. Hogle, *Shelley's Process: Radical Transference and the Development of His Major Works* (New York: Oxford University Press, 1988), 54.

[18] Donald H. Reiman discusses the Edenic mythography of *Alastor* in *Percy Bysshe Shelley* (Boston: Twayne Publishers, 1969), 37–38.

[19] See Freud's *Beyond the Pleasure Principle*, *SEF* 18:7–64.

[20] Bryan Cooper, "Shelley's *Alastor*: The Quest for a Vision," *KSJ* 19 (1970): 64. The "poet's death-longing is charged with an insistent erotic energy" for John C. Bean as well, in "The Poet Borne Darkly: The Dream-Voyage Allegory in Shelley's *Alastor*," *KSJ* 23 (1974): 67.

10.1001), but the thought of God's promised forgiveness dissuades the couple. *Alastor* lacks any such divine presence. Its one "spiritual" being remains the dream maiden who lures Shelley's Romantic Adam beyond life. The Poet's attraction to her reveals his special receptivity to powers inherent in eros. Only because death lurks in love do so many later Shelleyan poems join *Alastor* in tacitly or expressly urging lovers to "Die, / If thou wouldst be with that which thou dost seek!" (*Adonais*, ll. 464–65). The Poet does not seek death due to an error that (given his temperament) he could have avoided. He inherits his deathly quest as an irresistible compulsion simply due to the onset of desire. If his idealism proves excessive, it is the nature of idealism to intensify beyond limitation. We should pause before criticizing such intensities. Shelley's belief that "Power which strikes the luminaries of the world with sudden darkness and extinction, by awakening them to too exquisite a perception of its influences, dooms to a slow and poisonous decay those meaner spirits that dare to abjure its dominion" (Preface to *Alastor*, 69) can be construed as a variant of Blake's *Marriage of Heaven and Hell* dictum, "Those who restrain desire do so because theirs is weak enough to be restrained" (plate 5). By 1815 Shelley had "come to see that all love required some element of idealization," and that, "however dangerous the premise, the higher the love, the greater the idealization."[21] In *Alastor* love arises through an antitypical image constituted by negation, through a figure dependent on all it ostensibly negates and deathly in its repetitive compulsion. Only because this connection of narcissism and death remains a representative danger, a potential in all erotic idealization, is the Poet's fate "not barren of instruction to actual men" (Preface to *Alastor*, 69).

But not barren of instruction to poets above all. Shelley's choice of a poet as protagonist, and his investigation of a distinctly visionary rapture, anticipate the *Defence of Poetry* by making the lover and the poet of imagination all compact. In *Alastor* the dynamics of desire and imagination correspond so specifically that Shelley's specular self/antitype model acquires precise poetic correlatives. The paradigmatic value of mirroring for poetic vision can be inferred from individual passages, as when the Poet's

> wan eyes
> Gaze on the empty scene as vacantly
> As ocean's moon looks on the moon in heaven.
>
> (ll. 200—202)

---

[21] Sperry, *Shelley's Major Verse*, 26.

Yet a doubled relation between Poet and Narrator also underlies the structure of *Alastor*, which unfolds as an instance of authorial self-projection, a story of parallel doublings. Claiming that the "Narrator projects the Visionary, who in turn projects the Dream Maiden," recent criticism of *Alastor* finds in it "a rhetorical structure which is itself reflexive, self-infolded."[22] In calling this reflexive framing a "rhetorical structure," William Keach acknowledges how Shelley's treatment of doubling as an imaginative phenomenon unavoidably raises the issue of language. If "the entire poem is, in a sense, an inquiry about poetry,"[23] then the issue of language must become central, for while even savages have their dreams, poets alone "have employed language as the hieroglyphic of their thoughts" (*Defence of Poetry*, 483).

VISIONARY HIEROGLYPHICS

Shelley declares his interest in language in the crucial passage recounting the Poet's Manfred-like search for ultimate wisdom from engraved figures:

> Among the ruined temples there,
> Stupendous columns, and wild images
> Of more than man, where marble daemons watch
> The Zodiac's brazen mystery, and dead men
> Hang their mute thoughts on the mute walls around,
> He lingered, poring on memorials
> Of the world's youth, through the long burning day
> Gazed on those speechless shapes, nor, when the moon
> Filled the mysterious halls with floating shades
> Suspended he that task, but ever gazed
> And gazed, till meaning on his vacant mind
> Flashed like strong inspiration, and he saw
> The thrilling secrets of the birth of time.
>
> (ll. 116–28)

John Irwin argues that these "thrilling secrets" reveal the "narcissistic doubling that is the mythic origin of symbolization," for what the Poet

[22] Neil Fraistat, "Poetic Quests and Questioning in Shelley's *Alastor* Collection," *KSJ* 33 (1984): 168; Keach, *Shelley's Style*, 86. Other critics who view the poem's protagonist as a fictive projection of its narrator include Heppner, "Alastor," 99; Steinman, "Shelley's Skepticism," 258–61; Jean Hall, *The Transforming Image: A Study of Shelley's Major Poetry* (Urbana: University of Illinois Press, 1980), 29; Ronald Tetreault, *The Poetry of Life: Shelley and Literary Form* (Toronto: University of Toronto Press, 1987), 46; and Richard Cronin, *Shelley's Poetic Thoughts* (New York: St. Martin's Press, 1981), 89.

[23] Steinman, "Shelley's Skepticism," 256.

sees are "man-made shadow outlines, human doubles that have become 'wild images / Of more than man.' "[24] His absorption in these images prefigures his encounter with the veiled maid in her role as muse. The Poet's empathic meditation on them attempts to wrest linguistic meaning, to compel verbal articulation, from self-projections that carry his mind deathward, drawing it toward "dead men" and their primeval mysteries. As a model of language, these figures correlate doubling and death as an erotic poetics would demand. Thus it is only appropriate that the Poet's contemplation of them "leads him to Egypt and Abyssinia and to the origin of writing."[25]

Writing originates as hieroglyphics in *Alastor*. Pondering thoughts inscribed in shapes on the walls of ruins, the Poet ponders hieroglyphic carvings as the lost language of primal truth. Interest in hieroglyphics ran high in the eighteenth century and had been stimulated anew in the years preceding *Alastor*—first in 1802 by the arrival of the Rosetta Stone in England, and then by Thomas Young's 1814 claim to have translated its demotic text.[26] We can only speculate about Shelley's exact understanding of hieroglyphics, although certain ideas about them had become conventional. They supposedly signified occult spiritual mysteries, but placed those mysteries in a natural perspective. Until the work of Young and Champollion, hieroglyphic signs were considered pictographic, expressing concepts, Diodorus Siculus wrote, "by means of the significance of the objects which had been copied out and by the figurative meaning which practice had impressed on the memory."[27] Hieroglyphics consequently represented a "form of metaphorical thinking," a primordial language of nature "in which there was a necessary, emblematic connection between a sign and its referent."[28] Hieroglyphics offer an archaeological version of Coleridge's symbolic imagination, "which incorporating the Reason in Images of the Sense, . . . gives birth to a

[24] John Irwin, *American Hieroglyphics: The Symbol of the Egyptian Hieroglyphics in the American Renaissance* (New Haven: Yale University Press, 1980), 88.

[25] Irwin, *American Hieroglyphics*, 87.

[26] See John David Worthan's *The Genesis of British Egyptology, 1549–1906* (Norman, Okla: University of Oklahoma Press, 1971). Articles on hieroglyphics appeared fairly often in journals of the time and in the comparative mythographic studies that interested Shelley. With *Alastor*, his knowledge of hieroglyphics may have come principally from Volney's discussion of the origins and gradual mystification of the hieroglyphic nature symbolism in *Les Ruines*; see *A New Translation of Volney's Ruins*, intro. Robert D. Richardson (New York: Garland Publishing, 1979), 2:93–107.

[27] Cited by Don Cameron Allen, *Mysteriously Meant: The Rediscovery of Pagan Symbolism and Allegorical Interpretation in the Renaissance* (Baltimore: Johns Hopkins University Press, 1970), 109–10.

[28] Allen, *Mysteriously Meant*, 118; Irwin, *American Hieroglyphics*, 7.

system of symbols, harmonious in themselves, and consubstantial with the truths, of which they are the *conductors*."[29]

Such incorporated figures should induce cognitive syntheses that unite the mind and its object as self and antitype. Construed on these mediating grounds, reading would involve Shelley's protagonist seeing *into* the life of the signs he ponders, mentally cohabiting with them. Something like that certainly occurs, but can we call it "reading"? Reading decodes progressively. The Poet does not actually read these hieroglyphs; he understands them all at once, circumventing the mediation of physical inscriptions in a timeless interval: "meaning on his vacant mind / Flashed like strong inspiration, and he *saw*." In this flash the material world gives way to an Emersonian transparency of truth. Apparently, *Alastor* can preserve its model of understanding as the reader's symbiotic doubling of the author only by disdaining the mediation of language—thus "*speechless* shapes." The poem regards the gazing mind's involvement with graphic materiality as merely the surpassed stage of an ascent that proceeds toward spirit only by rejecting the body of the letter. Shelley once wrote that the "perfection" of sexual intercourse approximates "a total annihilation of the instinctive sense."[30] In *Alastor* the natural and sensuous dimensions of words require a similar annihilation of "sense," so that the Poet's pursuit of ultimate truths conveys him "beyond language"[31]— beyond the social and communicative agencies of language, certainly, but also beyond the limitations inherent in linguistic representation.

We can therefore understand why this passage so closely precedes the Poet's dream of his mirrored other. These linked episodes supply analogous instances, visionary and erotic, of a single imaginative process requiring repression of the body.[32] As in Shelley's representation of desire, *Alastor* initially idealizes linguistic repression as liberation from derivative constraints. If the body later assumes contrary roles through the poem's insistence on meaning as both immanent and transcendent, the veiled maid serves as the nexus of these contradictions. An erotic muse, the maid is a visionary hieroglyphic herself, a figure for figural language. Her veil represents what the Advertise-

---

[29] Coleridge, *The Statesman's Manual*, reprinted in *Lay Sermons*, ed. R. J. White, *CWC* 6:29.

[30] *A Discourse on the Manners of the Antient Greeks Relative to the Subject of Love*, in James A. Notopoulos, *The Platonism of Shelley: A Study of Platonism and the Poetic Mind* (Durham: Duke University Press, 1949), 410.

[31] Kirchhoff, "Shelley's *Alastor*," 118.

[32] See Strickland for a recent argument that *Alastor* "delineates an anti-mimetic myth of poesis as progressive disincarnation" in which the Poet seeks not "to redeem [matter] so much as evade it" ("Transfigured Night," 150, 159).

ment to *Epipsychidion* (alluding to Dante) terms *"veste di figura, o di colore rettorico"* (373), a vesture that must be withdrawn or become transparent if words are to convey truth. Her sensuous human form complements the veil as another vesture. Shelley presents truth as transparency of meaning when the Poet sees

> by the warm light of their own life
> Her glowing limbs beneath the sinuous veil
> Of woven wind,

(ll. 175–77)

and blood pulsing under layers of skin and flesh. We approach transparency again when the maid's unstable bodiliness seemingly dissolves into spirit. The idealism of *Alastor* centers on the binary opposition of body and spirit, and would have true illumination begin when the light of sense goes out.

Yet *Alastor* never fully accepts the negation of the corporeal, never completely surrenders the idea of meaning as immanence. The poem persistently treats body and soul as each other's double. Each provides the basis of the other's identity, so that spirit, like Poe's William Wilson, would destroy itself in murdering its other. Shelley acknowledges the interdependence of contraries in stressing the sensuousness of the veiled maid. By dissolving, she seems to invoke "the hues of heaven" (l. 197), but in fact offers the body as nature's "darkness visible" seen by the light of its own vital spark. She needs a language of nature ("Like woven sounds of streams and breezes," 155) just as the Poet needed a hieroglyphic language of nature to glimpse supernatural truth. The bodily qualities of the maid's words even gain in clarity as her passion intensifies:

> Soon the solemn mood
> Of her pure mind kindled through all her frame
> A permeating fire: wild numbers then
> She raised, with voice stifled in tremulous sobs
> Subdued by its own pathos: her fair hands
> Were bare alone, sweeping from some strange harp
> Strange symphony, and in their branching veins
> The eloquent blood told an ineffable tale.
> The beating of her heart was heard to fill
> The pauses of her music, and her breath
> Tumultuously accorded with those fits
> Of intermitted song. Sudden she rose,
> As if her heart impatiently endured
> Its bursting burthen: at the sound he turned,

And saw by the warm light of their own life
Her glowing limbs beneath the sinuous veil
Of woven wind.

(ll. 161–77)

Bodily vestures fade to windlike transparency *as* bodily longing
mounts. As Shelley's Poet (mis)understands it, this coincidence of in-
tensities signifies the moment of inspiration, when voice and song in-
terknit to make up "the only language which can hope to compre-
hend and communicate the truth."[33] Briefly it appears a holistic,
consubstantial value conveyed by the metaphoric harmony of body
and mind. At such moments *Alastor* seemingly shows truth resulting
when the light of sense and the light of heaven flow together.

Shelley's insistence on materiality as both surpassed and retained
in the representation of truth places an immense burden on lan-
guage. Unable to resolve its inherent ambivalence, the language of
Alastor ends by demystifying the Coleridgean symbol as a negotiation
of the sensory and eternal. The poem redefines reconciliation as con-
tradiction. As a figure of reconciliatory metaphor, the maid's impos-
sibly naturalized spirituality betokens an ideal inimical to language.
The narrator of *Alastor* can never quote the dream maiden or grant
her more than an untranslated "language strange" that, as with
Keats's La Belle Dame, conveys no human meanings. The poet seem-
ingly understands the maid's "talking" when he hears her voice as the
estranged echo of his own. Soon the "music" of her utterances "His
inmost sense suspended in its web / Of many-coloured woof and
shifting hues" (ll. 156–57). Surely this suspension of consciousness
connotes both its support and its abeyance—its submersion in a nat-
ural language legend-laden but unintelligible, a flow of expression
that becomes successively "wild," "strange," "ineffable," "intermitted,"
and abandoned, as the maiden's desire requires her to reject lan-
guage entirely. This rejection forbids any idealization of antitheses as
integral meaning. In *Alastor* desire "intensifies itself by frustrating its
own expression . . . [so that what] the poet envisions is his own desire
turning back on itself,"[34] and language performs a similar self-rever-
sion. The veiled maid's love both demands and precludes expression,
thrusting her toward "wild numbers" while provoking her voice to
stifle itself with every utterance.

This conflict refers to the metaphorical interplay of difference and
similitude in the relation of self and antitype. We may therefore con-
strue the rhetoric of *Alastor* as metaphor's revelation of its basic par-

[33] Thurston, "Author, Narrator, and Hero," 123.
[34] Keach, *Shelley's Style*, 83.

adoxes. Neil Fraistat has divided this formal revelation into two suc-
cessively synecdochic (or metaphoric, given Shelleyan metaphor's
holistic imperative) and metonymic phases.[35] The final phase be-
comes metonymic as the Poet's search for unity with the antitype—
indicating a "metaphoric imagination by which [he] will repeatedly
attempt to read the landscape as a projection of his mental state"[36]—
dissolves amid the contiguous images of his journey. The journey dis-
figures metaphor, accommodating it to metonymy but increasingly
toward allegory as well. For the Poet's quest requires him, as Evan
Gibson writes, to embark on a voyage undertaken in defiance of all
physical laws:

> When Shelley brings his poet to the shore of this vast sea and to the
> contemplation of death, he, apparently, changes his method of presen-
> tation. Before, he has introduced the youth and illustrated his character
> and attitudes in the world of the actual or at least the possible. . . . the
> happenings were a part of the actual life of the poet and not merely
> figures of speech in an allegorical system. However, from here on, the
> poem presents many physical impossibilities.[37]

This turn from "the world of the actual" signifies a turn from the
bounds of physical existence in the natural realm. Rhetorically, the
turn means abandoning the symbolic unity of sensuous image and
abstract idea for an allegorical predominance of idea over image, of
philosophical theme over narrative realism. Such allegorization, Gib-
son remarks, is required by death: "if death is the only possible area
of union with the vision, and if . . . Shelley intends to conduct the
poet into the realms of death, how else but by allegory may the ma-
terial be presented?"[38] We move, following the poem's disfigurative
patterning, from metaphor as the trope of doubling to allegory as the
trope of death.

   Yet the association of allegory and death signals Shelley's deter-
mined idealization of allegory. By 1822 allegory will emerge as the
master trope of Shelleyan eros, the demystified structure of its meta-
phorical poetics. Allegory of this sort enacts the relational, truth-de-
ferring displacements characterized by de Man as a "rhetoric of tem-
porality."[39] It is remarkable that even in 1815 the erotic energies of

---

[35] Fraistat, *Poetic Quests,* 164.

[36] Brisman, *Romantic Origins,* 144.

[37] Gibson, "*Alastor,*" 559.

[38] Gibson, "*Alastor,*" 560.

[39] Paul de Man, "The Rhetoric of Temporality," in *Blindness and Insight: Essays in the
Rhetoric of Contemporary Criticism,* 2d ed., rev. (1971; reprint, Minneapolis: University of
Minnesota Press, 1983), 187–228.

Alastor should force it beyond metaphor into a mode of allegory. This mode merely anticipates the authentic allegory of Shelley's later work, though, for the rhetoric of *Alastor* doubles its idealizing treatment of the psychology of desire. The veiled maid acts as a transcendental signified. Consequently, the poem's deferrals leave meaning, from the Poet's perspective, firmly centered on an origin left intact by the inability to represent or incarnate it. The allegory of *Alastor* trades temporal freedom and flux for an obsessional Sameness. Shelley's representation of time makes each passing moment of the Poet's quest, the poem's dramatic image of time unfolding, one more teasing vestige of presence, one more repetitive idol.

Alastor elides temporality by thematizing allegory as the transposed form of metaphor. With its exchanges of metaphor and allegory organized as a metaphorical economy, the poem's rhetoric gives rise to recuperative cycles. Demoting "the world of the actual," in Gibson's phrase, Shelleyan allegory ostensibly elevates ideas over images and events, which sacrifice their realism to the poem's scheme of abstract topoi. One might therefore expect the poem to abandon its sensuous poetics decisively in undertaking an allegorical voyage into death. Instead the allegorization of *Alastor* effects the return of sensuous contingency. The Poet's quest for permanence ironically devolves on extended scenic description: the imagistic triumph of nature occurs just where an "antinatural" allegory gains control of the plot. These descriptive passages are not mere psychic tableaux. Nor are they "pictures of nature for their own sake."[40] Similar complaints have been made about the Cumner Hills tableaux in Arnold's "The Scholar-Gipsy," where the gipsy wanders against another lavish natural background in something of the manner of Shelley's more fevered Poet. The wanderings of Arnold's protagonist, requiring a place, supply a rationale for the poem's natural settings, so that the gipsy comes to personify the perceptual and psychological availability of nature to

---

[40] Havens, "Shelley's "*Alastor*," 1109. When these passages are defended as thematically functional, their mental quality is usually stressed, as in Thurston's reading of the "last half of *Alastor* [as] an exhausting investigation into the involutions of a lonely mind" ("Author, Narrator, and Hero," 129). More recent versions of this argument occur in Heppner, who claims that the "gorgeous landscape has never really existed for [the Poet]" ("*Alastor*," 103), and Andrew M. Cooper, who writes that "*Alastor*'s narrative is gradually cut loose from its moorings in an assumed reality 'out there,' " and that this rejection of mimesis renders the latter stages of the Poet's journey "a voyage that evidently represents the continuation of his quest inside his mind" (*Doubt and Identity*, 178). These claims are perceptive but overstated. The Poet may ignore the natural setting, which increasingly serves as a landscape of consciousness, yet its sensuous immediacy is never wholly lost in Shelley's poem, in which language itself serves as a mooring inseparably connecting idea to image.

the narrator, and to the human imagination.[41] The landscape de-
scriptions of *Alastor* work a similar effect. They testify to the mind's
deep internalization of natural forms, colors, and rhythms, and to the
inseparability of natural beauty and imaginative power. Repress the
natural through allegory, *Alastor* implies, and sensuous images will
virtually inundate the language of poetry. But the dispersal of meta-
phorical oneness amid allegorical surrogates drawn from nature only
reenergizes the Poet's yearning for his mirrored likeness.

Alastor constrains allegory to a coincidence of origin and end with
the Poet's final intimation of his ideal:

> A Spirit seemed
> To stand beside him—clothed in no bright robes
> Of shadowy silver or enshrining light,
> Borrowed from aught the visible world affords
> Of grace, or majesty, or mystery;—
> But, undulating woods, and silent well,
> And leaping rivulet, and evening gloom
> Now deepening the dark shades, for speech assuming
> Held commune with him, as if he and it
> Were all that was,—only . . . when his regard
> Was raised by intense pensiveness, . . . two eyes,
> Two starry eyes, hung in the gloom of thought,
> And seemed with their serene and azure smiles
> To beckon him.
>
> (ll. 479–92)

Here desire comes full circle in a figure disdaining the sensuous me-
diations that left it "Lost, lost, for ever lost" (l. 209). But the lines also
imply that these mediating vestures alone rendered it imaginable.
Here is a radiance inexpressible without reference to the "bright
robes" it rejects and the limits it transcends. Shelley's lines create spir-
ituality by inverting natural form, by imagining the Poet's antitype as
the opposite of a being "clothed" by "the visible world." Language
must signify through relations of difference. The dream of perfectly
integrated opposites, of meaning beyond difference, exceeds verbal
possibilities, so that an unrenounced metaphorical idealism must suc-
cumb to silence. Eyes or stars, "gloom of thought" or actual twilight?
Shelley's spiritual figure occasions such questions not because it me-
diates disparate realms, but because it refuses a final, determinate lo-
cation. Rejecting allegorical deferrals in his fixation on the origin, the

---

[41] I have written on this aspect of Arnold's poem in "The Human Seasons: Arnold,
Keats, and 'The Scholar-Gipsy,' " *Victorian Poetry* 22 (1984): 247–62.

Poet must reject language. The poem therefore allows him speech
only on three occasions (ll. 280–290, 366–69, 502–14). All, appropri-
ately, are apostrophes to death, for death is the last refuge of a lin-
guistic idealism that insists on meaning as the closure of tenor and
vehicle, soul and body.

POLITICAL FORESHADOWINGS

Alastor banishes politics in order to concentrate on psychological and
rhetorical issues. This banishment resembles an act of repression,
and as such works to reinvest political concerns in Shelley's poem.
Even the most sublime Romantic poetry, we have learned, typically
includes a political subtext antithetically displaced as nature medita-
tion or visionary narrative. There is certainly reason to consider the
politics of the *Alastor* Poet's visionary quest. Yet even at a displaced
level, the politics of *Alastor* fails to achieve detailed thematic coher-
ence or to explain what seems imaginatively richest in the poem.
"The existential register is still somewhat more appropriate to em-
phasize than the historical one" in approaching certain texts, Paul Fry
cautions, and *Alastor* is one of them.[42] To place Shelley's poem in its
contemporary moment, we should turn from public events to more
expressly personal "historical" contexts.

   The summer of 1815 was a time of reminiscence and self-evalua-
tion for Shelley. The "Note on Alastor. By Mrs. Shelley" states that
"in the spring of 1815, an eminent physician pronounced that he was
dying rapidly of a consumption" and that this diagnosis encouraged
him "to turn his eyes inward" (*CW* 1:198). Her reference to a weight
of suffering incurred between 1813 and 1815, and related comment
that Shelley "at the time of doing [certain things] believed himself
justified to his own conscience" (*CW* 1:198), suggests a Shelley brood-
ing over the more painful complexities of retrospective justification.
The distressing experiences Mary had in mind can be inferred from
our knowledge of Shelley's life during this period. Foremost among
them in its relevance to *Alastor* is surely his abandonment of Harriet
for Mary. Back in England after his elopement, reviewing his life
from the prospect of death, Shelley had certain explanations to
make—to British society, the Court of Chancery, and his bewildered
family above all. How could he, Sir Timothy Shelley might well have
asked, forsake his inheritance and station for a woman, and three
years later forsake the woman too? The answer—both the epigraph
and Preface of *Alastor* ("nor fathers") stress it—lies with Shelley's

---

[42] Paul H. Fry, "History, Existence, and 'To Autumn,' " *SIR* 25 (1986): 211.

principled intention to follow love wherever (and to whomever) it led. Sir Timothy's response was an icy sarcasm: "P. B. has published a poem with some fragments," he informed his attorney, "and wants to find out one person on earth the Prototype of himself."[43] Viewed biographically, *Alastor* stands as the auto-elegy of a man determined to justify himself, to portray himself as his own greatest victim, to a hostile and misunderstanding world.

Alastor scarcely develops the political dimensions of this exoneration of desire. When later Shelleyan poems borrow and politicize aspects of *Alastor*, however, they point to the poem's political potential and underscore its importance for Shelley's career. Although composed sometime between mid-1818 and August 1819, "Athanase: A Fragment" returns to *Alastor* because, as Mary Shelley remarked, "the idea Shelley had formed of Prince Athanase was a good deal modelled on *Alastor*."[44] "Athanase" recasts the Poet—"a Youth, who, as with toil & travel, / Had grown quite weak & grey before his time" (ll. 8–9)—as a kind of Laon, the revolutionary hero of *The Revolt of Islam*. Like the protagonist of *Alastor*, Athanase "owned no higher law / Than love" (ll. 107–8), love that (in imagery reminiscent of *Alastor*) acted as "the shadow of a dream" pursuable only through the "dark stream" and "caverns underground" of the "soul's abyss," until it reached "A lair of rest" amid the "dim whirlpools of this dream obscure" (ll. 112–18). This fixating, futile love does not plunge Athanase into solitude, however. He accepts human society, even the intrusive gossip of his acquaintances, and, "Although a child of Fortune & of Power," deals with people equally, disdaining "Those false opinions which the hard rich use / To bind the world they famish for their pride" (ll. 37, 45–46). "Athanase" does not derive its protagonist's enlightened politics from his dedication to visionary desire. But the poem tacitly indicts the Poet of *Alastor* as a figure of social irresponsibility by showing how desire similar to his could be made humanly serviceable.

Rosalind and Helen addresses the politics of love more directly. Although begun at Marlow in 1817, this poem depicts a social ostracism that had victimized Shelley and Mary from at least 1814. In fact, *Rosalind and Helen* can be taken as an *Alastor* variation in which the questing Poet (Lionel) ends his travels and accepts an actual woman (Helen, acting as a surrogate Arab maiden), who survives him and recounts their life together as unmarried lovers. Identifying mar-

[43] As cited in Newman Ivey White, *Shelley* (New York: Knopf, 1940), 2:421.
[44] "Note on Prince Athanase. By Mrs. Shelley," *CW* 3:146. For "Athanase" I use the text established (and the title suggested) by Donald H. Reiman in *SHC* 7:110–60.

riage with other corrupt social institutions, the poem can present Lionel and Helen's illicit liaison as part of a larger iconoclasm. For Donald H. Reiman, *Rosalind and Helen* shows "that mutual sympathetic love between a man and a woman is at once the strongest support and the most valuable fruit of moral and social regeneration."[45] The poem also implies that a narrow-minded and unjust society can destroy such relationships. Although political disillusionment turns Lionel to love, he never embraces corrupt social conventions like matrimony. Immediately after Shelley's unmarried lovers consummate their relationship, the authorities imprison Lionel to nullify the threat he poses. When he succumbs to an *Alastor*-like obsession with death's beauty (*CW*, lines 1004–5) and dies, his death follows directly from the political oppression he suffered. Here the alienation of *Alastor* becomes politically resonant, its idealism including contempt for the limitations of restrictive social mores.

Alastor also anticipates the politics of later Shelley poems through its allusions to Wordsworth. Shelley's poetic development from 1814 to 1817 forced him to invoke, criticize, and disengage himself from his great Romantic precursors. "To Wordsworth" joins Mary Shelley's 14 September 1814 journal response to Wordsworth's *The Excursion* ("He is a slave")[46] in deploring the elder poet's conservative apostasy, while "Oh! there are spirits" laments Coleridge's emotionally withering imprisonment in dream. More pertinent here, though, are other poems that foreshadow *The Revolt of Islam* by tacitly censuring Wordsworth and Coleridge for slighting the sensuous. Neither "Mont Blanc" nor the "Hymn to Intellectual Beauty" concerns bodily love. But both correlate political criticism of the first Romantic generation with deference to the embodied aspects of human psychology. "Mont Blanc," for example, posits a dialectical tension between the mind's awareness of its own limitations and its inability to comprehend "vacancy"—its tendency to mythologize "Silence and solitude" as scenes

[45] Reiman, *SHC* 7:124. See Kenneth Neill Cameron, *Shelley: The Golden Years* (Cambridge: Harvard University Press, 1974), 253–55, for the relation of *Rosalind and Helen* to the Shelleys' personal lives, especially Mary's friendship with Isabella Baxter Booth.

[46] *The Journals of Mary Shelley*, ed. Paula R. Feldman and Diana Scott-Kilvert (Oxford: Clarendon Press, 1987), 1:25. Shelley's views of Wordsworth are conveniently summarized in Yvonne M. Carothers, "*Alastor*: Shelley Corrects Wordsworth," *MLQ* 42 (1981): 21–24. For Wordsworth's influence on *Alastor*, also see Paul Mueschke and Earl L. Griggs, "Wordsworth as the Prototype of the Poet in Shelley's *Alastor*," *PMLA* 40 (1934): 229–45; Wasserman, *Shelley*, 16–41; Reiman, *SHC* 7:121 n. 25; A. Cooper, *Doubt and Identity*, 176–77; and Hogle, *Shelley's Process*, 39–43, 46–57. Shelley's views of Coleridge are discussed by Joseph Raben, "Coleridge as the Prototype of the Poet in Shelley's *Alastor*," *RES*, n.s. 17 (1966): 278–92; and in Timothy Webb, "Coleridge and Shelley's *Alastor*: A Reply," *RES*, n.s. 18 (1967), 402–11.

involving eagles, dead hunters, wolves, and daemons ("Mont Blanc,"
ll. 68–72) and thus fall back on image making as a mode of thought.
The poem's Coleridgean model, the "Hymn Before Sun-rise, in the
Vale of Chamouni,"[47] suggests conversely that truth appears when
sensory realities vanish:

> O dread and silent Mount! I gazed upon thee,
> Till thou, still present to the bodily sense,
> Didst vanish from my thought: entranced in prayer
> I worshipped the Invisible alone.
>
> (ll. 13–16)

As a recasting of the "Immortality Ode," the "Hymn" similarly insists
on the naturalization of consciousness. Shelley's experience of tran-
scendence—"Sudden, thy shadow fell on me; / I shrieked, and
clasped my hands in extacy!" (ll. 59–60)—takes place beyond lan-
guage. The libertarian poet must reclaim such moments through
earthbound images and public discourse. Shelley's last stanza asks the
Power to "supply / Its calm" to his "onward life" (ll. 80–81). Yet that
plea follows lines that grant such calm (the serenity and harmony of
afternoon and autumn) to late phases of the day and season, leaving
the poet amid the natural cycles and mellow fruitfulness of earthly
existence. Wordsworth worships nature as a palimpsest of spirit in the
"Ode." Shelley embraces nature as a part of his humanity, accepting
mediated vision as the ground of his political aspirations.[48]

 Alastor combines Shelley's distrust of transcendence with a medita-
tion on human love. The result is an allusive critique of Words-
worthian emotion as disembodied. The echoes of Wordsworth in
Alastor reveal the incomplete assimilations typical of writers' early
work, and are less self-consciously controlled (and more admiring)
than is often assumed. The poem's ambivalence about Wordsworth-

---

[47] For Shelley's indebtedness to Coleridge in "Mont Blanc," see Tetreault, *Poetry of
Life*, 67–70, and Charles E. Robinson, "The Shelley Circle and Coleridge's *The Friend*,"
ELN 8 (1971): 269–74.

[48] In *The Visionary Company: A Reading of English Romantic Poetry*, rev. and enl. ed.
(Ithaca: Cornell University Press, 1961), 290–93, Harold Bloom alters my emphases to
argue that the "Hymn" criticizes Wordsworth for elevating the natural over the tran-
scendent. My sense of Shelley's response to the "Immortality Ode" in the "Hymn" con-
curs with William Keach's reading of Shelley's response to the "Ode" in *Alastor*. In
"Obstinate Questionings: The Immortality Ode and *Alastor*," *The Wordsworth Circle* 12
(1981): 37, 40, Keach contends that *Alastor* "is centrally about the failure of both pro-
tagonist and narrator to sustain through 'natural piety' a condition of 'beloved broth-
erhood' with 'Earth, ocean, air,' " and that Shelley "modelled on Wordsworth's his own
sense of the failure of an expanding consciousness to find resolution in nature's plen-
itude."

ian values cannot be separated into a nature-worshipping surrogate Wordsworth (the Narrator) and a nature-transcending surrogate Shelley (the Poet), as Earl Wasserman argued, for similarities linking the poem's two dramatic personae rule out that reading. To reconstruct the Wordsworthian matrix of *Alastor* we should follow Yvonne M. Carothers in regarding "Shelley's Narrator and Poet [as] aspects of a single consciousness" and the poem as a retrospective exercise interrelating past and present selves.[49] This approach locates the main Wordsworthian drama of *Alastor* in the plight of its questing Poet.

We must insist on the Poet as Shelleyan mask and grant the noble aspects of his longing for the absolute. Yet he both errs and personifies Shelley's Wordsworthian propensities—becoming an image of Wordsworth as the poet of solitude—and his errors correspond impressively with Shelley's reservations about Wordsworth. *Alastor* associates the self-deceptive dangers of the Poet's retreat into nature with Wordsworth's penchant for seeking motion and spirit in the natural world. Shelley's next volume, *The Revolt of Islam*, allots Cythna a diatribe against anthropomorphic mythmaking:

> "Some moon-struck sophist stood
> Watching the shade from his own soul upthrown
> Fill Heaven and darken Earth, and in such mood
> The Form he saw and worshipped was his own,
> His likeness in the world's vast mirror shown."
>
> (*PW*, ll. 3244–48)

The *Alastor* volume warns against such idealization by reprinting (with the title "Superstition") the section of *Queen Mab* that declares gods the unrecognized externalizations of human fear and need. Shelley reprinted "Superstition," Neil Fraistat suggests,[50] to contest Wordsworth's explanation of how primordial man "framed / For influence undefined a personal shape" by humanizing natural phenomena as Apollo, Diana, and other divinities (*The Excursion* 4.682–83, 847–87). For Wordsworth, skeptics who prize such mythic projections "as a mirror that reflects / To proud Self-love her own intelligence" (*The Excursion* 4.991–92) mistakenly ascribe them to human fantasy rather than the "infinite Being." For Shelley, such fictions remain mere reflexes of the human mind, shadows ideologically reified as power.

In this way *Alastor* criticizes Wordsworth's myth of nature by rede-

---

[49] Carothers, "*Alastor*," 27.
[50] Fraistat, "Poetic Quests," 180.

fining the nature of myth. The Poet's projection of the veiled maid confuses self and other so that, longing for ultimate truth, he willingly deifies a "spiritual" authority mistakenly believed to originate outside his mind. This spiritualizing impulse coordinates the psychology of tyranny with bodily repression. When *Alastor* condemns Wordsworthian mythmaking *and* associates it with desire that spurns physicality, the poem censures Wordsworth for preferring visionary isolation to human emotional ties. The Poet's unfulfilled immersion among sensuous images dramatizes nature's inability to substitute for human relationships. Love needs the body. When taken as an allusive polemic against Wordsworth, as acceptance of a nature that supposedly never betrays the heart that loves her, the Poet's journey unfolds as a misdirected displacement of eros from a human lover to rocks and stones and trees. The poem's ambivalence admittedly leaves this polemic shadowy. But that would motivate Shelley to define it more fully in 1817.

As always in Shelley, the textual politics of *Alastor* lies principally with his attempt to affectively reform an audience. He exhausts all his resources in that difficult endeavor. The poem establishes its Narrator as a surrogate reader, an interpreter who provides a dramatic locus for empathy. When the Narrator's reservations about the Poet end in a lament for his uncompromised dedication—"ah! thou hast fled! / The brave, the gentle, and the beautiful" (ll. 688–89)—we see a response right-thinking readers were presumably to emulate. The Preface, too, intercedes between the text and its audience. The numbers of prefaces addressed to a general readership in the Romantic era reflected both an increased democratization of reading and the writers' uncertainty about audience.[51] Prefaces were often written to bridge those differences in outlook that the loss of a hegemonic culture had produced. Just so, Shelley uses the Preface to *Alastor* defensively—to fill and compensate for lacunae in his poem, and to articulate views his narrative leaves too tenuous, such as the nature and extent of the Poet's "generous error" (69). The result is an introduction significantly at odds with the work it introduces. The Preface actually calls attention to problems it seeks to obviate. Shelley's effort to anticipate and disarm criticism by criticizing the hero's solitariness backfired when *The Eclectic Review* remarked that the poem's concern with a "morbid ascendency of the imagination. . . . could not be better illustrated" than by *Alastor* itself.[52]

[51] John F. Schell discusses the polemics (and contradictions) of Romantic prefaces in "Prose Prefaces and Romantic Poets: Insinuation and Ethos," *Journal of Narrative Technique* 13 (1983): 86–99.

[52] From the October 1816 review of the *Alastor* volume, reprinted in *The Unextin-*

The poem's failure to dictate its reception returns us to Shelley's political alienation. It is an alienation evident in the Poet's social displacement. Depending on whether we emphasize its culpable or admirable features, the Poet's isolating quest can appear to reflect the quietest retreat of Wordsworth's Solitary, disillusioned with the French Revolution, or the marginalizing of liberals during the conservative retrenchment of the Napoleonic years. In either case it signifies the radical poet's former or present withdrawal. The reader-response problems of *Alastor*, which exemplify such alienation, follow inevitably from the poem's interest in the politics of desire. Because Shelleyan texts envision the relation of author to reader as a variation of the relation of self to antitype, the Poet's encounter with the veiled maid prefigures the social question of the poem's readership. *Alastor* links love, reading, and (through the prophetic agency of poetry) social change as correlative aspects of its self/antitype paradigm. This correlation is the poem's political meaning.

When Shelley returns to the politics of desire in *The Revolt of Islam*, a revolutionary epic written in 1817, his return produces the same correlation of issues. The Dedication to *The Revolt*, for example, characterizes Shelley as a river-voyaging solitary seeking an antitype combining "all sympathies in one," accords Mary that role, then applauds her as the text's ideal reader. Her acts of love and reading occur as diverse forms of the same imaginative responsiveness: if *The Revolt* is ignored, the souls of Percy and Mary, "Two tranquil stars," will serve as lamps beaconing the future through their joint consolidation of the poem's truths. *The Revolt of Islam* corrects the excessive privacy of *Alastor*, but clearly continues the earlier poem's political interests in the body, the self/other dynamic, and the first Romantic generation. *The Revolt* thereby realizes the revolutionary potential of *Alastor* in distinctly Shelleyan fashion: by becoming its antitype.

---

guished Hearth: Shelley and His Contemporary Critics, ed. Newman Ivey White (Durham: Duke University Press, 1938), 107. Also see the reviews in the April 1816 *Monthly Review* and the May 1816 *British Critic* (reprinted in *The Unextinguished Hearth*, 105–6).

Chapter 3

EROS AND REVOLUTION

Love is not full of pity, as men say,
But deaf and cruel, where he means to prey.
—Marlowe, *Hero and Leander*

THE REVOLT OF ISLAM ends with the death and resurrection of Shelley's heroes, the revolutionaries Laon and Cythna. The dying Laon sees fire and smoke hurtle upward, hears a beautiful, oblivion-inducing music, and then wakes to "The warm touch of a soft and tremulous hand" (l. 4603).[1] This soft touch eases him into an afterlife that never bruises body to pleasure soul. Here a "Temple of the Spirit" (l. 4815) rises out of nature's abundance to marry the earthly and the eternal. As the "native home" of Genius (l. 570), the Temple also serves as a synecdoche of an imagination that seeks "the balance or reconciliation of opposite or discordant qualities" in a "double vision of man" oriented toward an "ideal of wholeness."[2] Shelley's insistence on meaning as the collocation of opposites accounts for the "system of correspondences" between Laon's and Cythna's experiences when separated, the evocation of Zoroastrian dualism, the equal roles assigned the public and private, and the narrative's myriad doublings and reenactments.[3] Such integrally linked repetitions stage the dialectical triumphs of a metaphorical idealism.

[1] I cite *The Revolt of Islam* as it appears in *PW*. In this chapter, ancillary materials are, when possible, also cited from *PW*.

[2] Douglas Thorpe calls "the temple within the poem . . . an image for the poem itself," in "Shelley's Golden Verbal City," *JEGP* 86 (1987): 217. The three quotations come respectively from Coleridge, *Biographia Literaria*, ed. James Engell and W. Jackson Bate, *CWC* 7:2.16; Brian Wilkie, *Romantic Poets and Epic Tradition* (Madison: University of Wisconsin Press, 1965), 113; and Stuart Curran, *Shelley's Annus Mirabilis: The Maturing of an Epic Vision* (San Marino: Huntington Library, 1975), 26. In "The Sexual Theme in Shelley's *The Revolt of Islam*," *JEGP* 82 (1983): 33, Stuart M. Sperry also emphasizes the copresence of antitheses in *The Revolt*: "Shelley's perspective arbitrates between the claims of optimism and pessimism, historical progress and mere alternation, the realm of the imaginative and ideal and that of human actuality."

[3] The quotation is from Richard Cronin, *Shelley's Poetic Thoughts* (New York: St. Martin's Press, 1981), 100. See Curran, *Shelley's Annus Mirabilis*, 28–29, for a brief discussion of narrative parallels in *The Revolt of Islam*; Kenneth Neill Cameron, "Shelley and Ahrimanes," *MLQ* 3 (1942): 287–95, for the poem's use of Zoroastrian dualism; and

Yet those victories seem spurious. *The Revolt of Islam* finally "lacks the dialectic it presupposes"[4] because it denies its tensive contraries equivalent energies. The antitheses of *The Revolt of Islam* revolve around the traditional opposition between spiritual and material— the latter appearing variously as history, woman, sexuality, and the body of the letter. Determined to recuperate materiality in egalitarian syntheses, Shelley glorifies the body, dramatizing sexual passion and even describing his versification as a body, or vesture: "I have simply *clothed* my thoughts," his Preface notes, in "the most obvious and appropriate language" (*PW*, 34, emphasis added). But in the end Laon and Cythna triumph because their physical demise, as it initiates a "winter of the world" (l. 3685), heralds a revolutionary springtime ordained from on high. By insisting on spirit as the controlling telos of political meaning, *The Revolt of Islam* presents history as alienated spirit in the process of returning to itself. This spiritual imperative leaves the body less enfranchised than subjugated. Instead of reorganizing opposites into partnerships of equals, the poem produces power relations that reinstate the authority Shelley opposes, rendering his "revolutionary epic . . . profoundly anti-revolutionary."[5] The political liberalism of *The Revolt of Islam* is enlightened, courageous, and praiseworthy. Praise demands understanding, however, and we will not understand the poem's ideological investments until we recognize its complicity with the hierarchical violence of Western culture.

THE EGOTISTICAL SUBLIME

The Revolt of Islam continues the imaginative struggle with the first Romantic generation that absorbed Shelley from 1814 through the summer of 1816. The poem has provoked comparisons with Southey and Coleridge,[6] but it presupposes a Wordsworthian model above all. In 1817, as Shelley fully realized, an epic on the contemporary political climate could be written only in the shadow of *The Excursion*. His Preface implies as much by addressing the influence of the French Revolution on the "literature of the age":

Deborah A. Gutschera, "The Drama of Reenactment in Shelley's *The Revolt of Islam*," *KSJ* 35 (1986): 111–25, for narrative repetition as a way of approximating the ineffable.

[4] Curran, *Shelley's Annus Mirabilis*, 30.

[5] P.M.S. Dawson, *The Unacknowledged Legislator: Shelley and Politics* (Oxford: Clarendon Press, 1980), 75.

[6] The most searching account of Shelley's obligations to the first Romantic generation in *The Revolt of Islam* can be found in Cronin, *Shelley's Poetic Thoughts*, 95–108.

The sympathies connected with that event extended to every bosom. The most generous and amiable natures were those which participated the most extensively in these sympathies. . . . But, on the first reverses of hope in the progress of French liberty, the sanguine eagerness for good overleaped the solution of these questions, and for a time extinguished itself in the unexpectedness of their result. Thus, many of the most ardent and tender-hearted of the worshippers of public good have been morally ruined by what a partial glimpse of the events they deplored appeared to show as the melancholy desolation of all their cherished hopes. Hence gloom and misanthropy have become the characteristics of the age in which we live, the solace of a disappointment that unconsciously finds relief only in the wilful exaggeration of its own despair. (*PW*, 33)

Shelley's Preface condemns Byronic self-absorption—the political irresponsibility so memorably lampooned in the figure of Peacock's Mr. Cypress: "Sir, I have quarrelled with my wife; and a man who has quarrelled with his wife is absolved from all duty to his country."[7] The conservative apostates of the first Romantic generation nonetheless remain Shelley's chief target. In *The Excursion* Wordsworth's Wanderer defines the Solitary's despondency as the inevitable reflex of his excessive hopes for the French Revolution (4.260–72). The Wanderer exchanges revolutionary zeal for traditional faith in God and nature. Shelley's Preface attacks this conservative apologetics for its circumscription of love. By 1817 the quietist pronouncements of Southey, Coleridge, and Wordsworth had more and more accredited "the private and the public life with separate and incompatible virtues,"[8] betraying love as "the sole law which should govern the moral world" (Preface to *The Revolt of Islam*, *PW*, 37).

A combination of circumstances brought Coleridge, Southey, and Wordsworth to the forefront of Shelley's thinking at the time of *The Revolt of Islam*. These circumstances exacerbated Shelley's dissatisfaction with the role his precursors accorded the body. Coleridge had recently published both the *Biographia Literaria*—which Richard H. Haswell considers a major influence on the holistic aesthetics of *The Revolt of Islam*[9]—and the *Statesman's Manual*. There Coleridge's faith in the Bible as historical prophecy allowed him to blame "the revolution and fearful chastisement of France" on a "spirit of sensuality and

[7] Thomas Love Peacock, *Nightmare Abbey* (Harmondsworth: Penguin Books, 1969), 99. Also see Charles E. Robinson, *Shelley and Byron: The Snake and Eagle Wreathed in Fight* (Baltimore: Johns Hopkins University Press, 1976), 60–68.

[8] Cronin, *Shelley's Poetic Thoughts*, 102.

[9] Richard H. Haswell, "Shelley's *The Revolt of Islam*: 'The Connexion of Its Parts,'" *KSJ* 25 (1976): 99–102.

ostentation," on "restlessness, presumption, sensual indulgence, and the idolatrous reliance on false philosophy in the whole domestic, social, and political life of the stirring and effective part of the community."[10] Restated so decisively, Coleridge's moralistic traditionalism would have struck Shelley as inexcusable.

Southey's political provocations verged on slander. The year 1817 was the turning point in Shelley's relations with Southey, whose *On the Rise and Progress of Popular Disaffection* appeared in the April *Quarterly Review*. The thinly veiled personal references in this article characterize Shelley as the prototype of those "literary adventurers who choose their part in political warfare" from a naïveté and arrogance that "make them believe that they are wiser than their elders, and capable of reforming the world," when they are in fact dealing "in scandal, sedition, obscenity, or blasphemy, whichever article may be most in demand, according to the disease of the age."[11] Even more offensive, and unfair, was Southey's pointed reference to "moral suicide," a phrase tacitly blaming Shelley for Harriet's death at a time when his domestic affairs, as Southey himself later observed, were matters of "public notoriety."[12] Shelley's sensitivity to criticism of his sexual ethics and his concern over the "league of incest" rumors already circulating (for which he also blamed Southey) help to explain both the idealizing defense of himself and Mary in the Dedication to *The Revolt of Islam*, and the note he appended to his *Laon and Cythna* Preface: "The sentiments connected with and characteristic of this circumstance [the protagonists' incestuous love], have no personal reference to the Writer" (*CW* 1:247 n. 1).

In the summer of 1817, Shelley would have pondered Wordsworth from a related viewpoint. Here we must credit Hazlitt's role in the reception and understanding of Wordsworth's poetry. Hazlitt and Shelley met through Hunt and saw each other socially on several occasions in 1817, though they never became friends. Shelley found Hazlitt's theory of moral sympathy particularly "welcome and exciting," Dawson argues, "for it provided a link between his own poetic enterprises and permanent principles of human action."[13] More pertinent to *The Revolt of Islam* were Hazlitt's *Examiner* essays, particularly

[10] Coleridge, *The Statesman's Manual*, reprinted in *Lay Sermons*, ed. R. J. White, *CWC* 6:33–34.

[11] Robert Southey, *On the Rise and Progress of Popular Disaffection*, *Quarterly Review* 16 (1817): 540, 541, 539. Kenneth Neill Cameron discusses the impact of this article on the relationship of Shelley and Southey in "Shelley vs. Southey: New Light on an Old Quarrel," *PMLA* 57 (1942): 489–512.

[12] The two quotations are from Southey, *Rise and Progress*, 539, and Southey's letter to the editor of *The Courier*, 8 December 1824, as cited by Cameron, "Shelley vs. Southey," 494.

[13] Dawson, *Unacknowledged Legislator*, 236.

his review of *The Excursion*.[14] Although this review had appeared in
1814, it would have remained alive for Shelley in 1817 because he
was particularly interested in Wordsworth, because the critical stance
toward the elder Romantics maintained by *The Examiner* through
1817 confirmed (and recalled) the basic viewpoint of the review, and
because it had attracted considerable attention, both on its own ac-
count and for gossip circulating about Wordsworth's reaction to it.[15]
Hazlitt's comment that *The Excursion* lacked any "lively succession of
images or incidents," as well as "the pomp and decoration and scenic
effect of poetry,"[16] probably stands behind the various Romance af-
finities of *The Revolt of Islam*—Shelley's claim to offer a story "diver-
sified with moving and romantic adventures," a "succession of pic-
tures" depicted in Spenserian stanzas selected in part for their
"brilliancy and magnificence" (Preface, *PW*, 32, 35). With Hazlitt's ac-
count of Wordsworth firmly in mind, Shelley devotes *The Revolt of
Islam* to a poetics of the verbal body, to an aesthetic sensuousness in-
tended as an affront to Wordsworthian precedent. But the influence
of Hazlitt's review extended well beyond this formal and stylistic is-
sue.

"Observations on Mr. Wordsworth's Poem The Excursion" repre-
sented a watershed in Hazlitt's career. It was his "first attempt to ex-
plain the workings of the sympathetic imagination in literary crea-
tion."[17] It also concluded with a stirring defense of the ideals of the
French Revolution, which soon became the essay's best-known sec-

[14] Michael Henry Scrivener argues for Shelley's indebtedness to Hazlitt's article on
Coriolanus in *Radical Shelley: The Philosophical Anarchism and Utopian Thought of Percy
Bysshe Shelley* (Princeton: Princeton University Press, 1982), 120–22. The *Coriolanus*
piece appeared in the 15 December 1816 edition of *The Examiner* and claimed, as Scrive-
ner writes (120), that the "natural tendency of poetry is to foster authoritarianism, a
love for tyrannical power, and a contempt for the people," so that *Laon and Cythna* took
shape in part as "a practical attempt to counter Hazlitt."

[15] The gossip was later recounted by Hazlitt in "Reply to Z," in *The Complete Works of
William Hazlitt*, ed. P. P. Howe, centenary ed., 21 vols. (London: J. M. Dent & Sons,
1930–1934), 9:3–10. Briefly, the story concerns Wordsworth's feigned indifference to
a postage-due review he received (and for which he grudgingly paid), his initial (and
transparently egotistical) enthusiasm when he found it complimentary, and his subse-
quent rage when he discovered that its author was Hazlitt, whom he could not tolerate.
Shelley alludes mischievously to this story in *Peter Bell the Third*: "All these Reviews the
Devil made / Up in a parcel, which he had / Safely to Peter's house conveyed. / For
carriage ten-pence Peter paid— / Untied them—read them—went half mad" (ll. 488–
92). *Peter Bell the Third* also shows Hazlitt's continuing influence on Shelley's view of
Wordsworth in lines 293–312.

[16] Hazlitt, "Observations on Mr. Wordsworth's Poem The Excursion" and "The
Same Subject Continued," *Complete Works* 4:112, 120.

[17] Herschel Baker's comment, in *William Hazlitt* (Cambridge: Harvard University
Press, 1962), 343.

tion. For Shelley as well as Keats, however, it was Hazlitt's conceptions of sympathy and egotism that proved more significant. In *The Excursion*, Hazlitt argued,

> An intense intellectual egotism swallows up every thing. Even the dialogues introduced in the present volume are soliloquies of the same character, taking different views of the subject. The recluse, the pastor, and the pedlar, are three persons in one poet. . . . The power of [Wordsworth's] mind preys upon itself. It is as if there were nothing but himself and the universe. He lives in the busy solitude of his own heart; in the deep silence of thought. . . .
>
> . . . The philosophical poet himself, perhaps, owes some of his love of nature to the opportunity it affords him of analyzing his own feelings, and contemplating his own powers,—of making every object about him a whole length mirror to reflect his favourite thoughts, and of looking down on the frailties of others in undisturbed leisure, and from a more dignified height.[18]

Criticizing an egocentrism that subjectively appropriates objective data in the very act of seeing, Hazlitt ties Wordsworthian egotism to the unrelieved artistic austerity of *The Excursion* and to the social isolation of its characters, arguing that the Solitary's failure to love repeats itself in his creator's willingness to inhabit the "solitude of his own heart." But Hazlitt also ties Wordsworth's emotional enervation to his political apostasy. Loss of feeling and loss of republican ardor become complementary aspects of a single moral failure.

Shelley's epic similarly condemns the sexual politics of the egotistical sublime. *The Revolt of Islam* implies that Wordsworth's poetry celebrates a love so morally rarefied as to seem a mere ethical abstraction. The moral love of Shelley's poem is embodied in the sensual attachment of Laon and Cythna. Noting the erotic qualities of the Greek pastoralists, the *Defence of Poetry* comments that corruption typically "begins at the imagination and the intellect as at the core," and moves on "through the affections into the very appetites" because "poetry ever addresses itself to those faculties which are the last to be destroyed" (493). The body therefore represents a repository of revolutionary potential, and sensuality a political weapon. The eroticism of *The Revolt of Islam* belongs to what Marilyn Butler terms the "Cult of the South"—a polemical poetics that achieved its clearest formulation at Marlow in 1817, and that reproved the ascetic conservatism of Wordsworth and Coleridge. This cult employed a mytho-

---

[18] Hazlitt, "Observations," 113, 117.

graphic syncretism valued partly for its paganism, its discovery of a key to all mythologies in the allegorization of a universal sexual myth:

> The crucial fact about the classicism of Shelley and Peacock is that it does evolve into paganism—not so much an aesthetic as an ideological cult, an interpretation of man's oldest beliefs which stresses first that they are inventions, and second that they belong to a natural rather than a supernatural order. What is more—a significant advantage in a propaganda war—the cult of sexuality is celebratory and joyous; it shows up in its most unfavourable light the authoritarian, ascetic and life-denying tendencies of Hebraic Christianity. . . . [Among the second Romantic generation] the glorification of sexual love has become an accepted challenge to orthodoxy over its whole range of influence, cultural, moral, and political. Behind *Don Juan* is the unwritten manifesto of Marlow.[19]

Also behind *Don Juan*, as Byron delighted in pointing out, stand the Lake Poets: Coleridge's Kantian flutterings, Wordsworth's "rather long" *Excursion*, and both Southey's dull narratives and "Satanic school" attacks on the "lasciviousness" of Byron and Shelley.[20] Byron's epic returns fire on several fronts, but the frank carnality of *Don Juan* in itself castigates the elder poets' moral primness. The earlier Romantics were increasingly considered vulnerable to criticism on sexual grounds. Hazlitt merely clinched the point when he observed of Wordsworth's *Lyrical Ballads*, "it does not appear that men eat or drink, marry or are given in marriage."[21] In *Peter Bell the Third* (1819) Shelley makes Peter a surrogate Wordsworth, and censures him as a "Male prude," "a formal Puritan / A solemn and unsexual man" (ll. 331, 550–51):

> But from the first 'twas Peter's drift
> To be a kind of moral eunuch
> He touched the hem of Nature's shift,
> Felt faint—and never dared uplift
> The closest, all-concealing tunic.
>
>   (ll. 313–17)

The glorification of sensual love in *The Revolt of Islam* subtly reproves Wordsworth for the same sexual timorousness treated comically in

---

[19] Marilyn Butler, *Romantics, Rebels, and Reactionaries* (New York: Oxford University Press, 1982), 131, 137.

[20] Southey introduced this phrase in the preface to his 1821 *Vision of Judgement*, reprinted in *Byron: The Critical Heritage*, ed. Andrew Rutherford (New York: Barnes and Noble, 1970), 179–81.

[21] Hazlitt, "On Burns, and the Old English Ballads," *Complete Works* 5:131. In the preceding sentence of this lecture, Hazlitt writes that "in Mr. Wordsworth there is a total disunion and divorce of the faculties of the mind from those of the body; the banns are forbid, or a separation is pronounced from bed and board—*a mensâ at thoro*."

Peter Bell the Third. With *The Revolt of Islam*, Shelley's reaffirmation of the principles underlying the French Revolution would have required some ethical defense of sexual freedom. Jacobinism had been repeatedly denounced for its "abandoned love of sensual pleasure"[22] since the time of Burke's *Reflections*.

Read in its contemporary context, the sexual passion of Laon and Cythna counters the politics of Wordsworth's sublime egotism. Such were Shelley's intentions, in any event. As soon as we reconstruct the epic's polemical purposes, however, we confront their inefficacy. After it has received due credit for censuring egocentrism, *The Revolt of Islam* remains as egotistical as any Wordsworthian poem. "The book is full of humanity," Leigh Hunt granted, "and yet it certainly does not go the best way to work of appealing to it, because it does not appeal to it through the medium of its common knowledges."[23] Shelley's epic is elitist in its erudition, remote in its idealism, and (despite his disclaimers) persistently didactic—for the poem's repeated violations of simple plausibility themselves effect a potent didacticism. The resultant ironies are entirely systematic. If reading *The Revolt of Islam* means tracing interrelated contradictions to the assumptions underlying them, this process had best begin with the work's divided attitudes toward sexuality and language.

SEXUALITY AND POWER

Shelley's representation of sexuality in *The Revolt of Islam* ostensibly follows from the Platonism of canto 1. There the transformation of Woman and Serpent into "a bright and beautiful shape, which seems compounded of both," as Leigh Hunt wrote,[24] depicts love as a force that reassembles the Aristophanic androgyne of *The Symposium*. This sublime oneness once more characterizes Shelleyan eros as a harmonizing agency. But *The Revolt of Islam* also recognizes the alliance of sexuality with aggression, which lends the poem's dream narratives a truly disturbing garishness. Critics usually explain this psychosexual violence as the early phase of a developmental scheme in which Shel-

[22] See the chapter so entitled in Isaac Kramnick, *The Rage of Edmund Burke: Portrait of an Ambivalent Conservative* (New York: Basic Books, 1977), 151–57.

[23] From Hunt's three-part 1818 review of *The Revolt*, reprinted in *The Unextinguished Hearth: Shelley and His Contemporary Critics*, ed. Newman Ivey White (Durham: Duke University Press, 1938), 123. Also see Hunt's inference of the poem's critical pertinence to the Lake School (*Unextinguished Hearth*, 120–21). For the ideological implications of the elitism and dogmatism of *The Revolt of Islam*, see Curran, *Shelley's Annus Mirabilis*, 29–32; Wilkie, *Romantic Poets*, 137–38; and Jerrold E. Hogle, *Shelley's Process: Radical Transference and the Development of His Major Works* (New York: Oxford University Press, 1988), 100–102.

[24] Hunt, in White, *Unextinguished Hearth*, 118.

ley's characters (principally Laon) gradually outgrow their inner flaws. The poem's negative and positive images of desire accordingly mark the inception and conclusion of a redemptive movement.

Shelley initiates this movement with Laon's dream of dark "shapes" at once motivating and impeding his flight with Cythna (ll. 1122–52). Awakening from this nightmare to find Othman's soldiers abducting her, he kills three of them. Stuart M. Sperry comments that

> Behind the incidents Laon recounts one can sense the adolescent boy's experience of guilt and disgust in facing the full implications of sexual maturity and divergence from the opposite sex and the fear of confronting the new power of such feelings as lust. . . . [Laon's acts of murder signify his] unthinking recourse to powers he must learn to forswear. Nevertheless the striking way in which the moral theme emerges from the crisis in Laon's sexual development has gone unregarded, even though the principal elements of violence—Laon's "small knife" as against the warriors' swords—are manifestly phallic. Logically the episode argues, with an incisiveness that reveals much of Shelley's intuitive understanding of the human psyche, that aggression is the inevitable outgrowth of masculinity.[25]

Laon's phallic violence, for Sperry, is only the catalyst of the protagonists' progress toward "a deeper relationship free from guilt and fear."[26] Shelley's hero is helped on his way by the fatherly Hermit of canto 4. But the redemptive process begins with Laon's tribulations in canto 3, particularly the subconscious revelations symbolized by his dreams:

> Methought that grate was lifted, and the seven
>   Who brought me thither four stiff corpses bare,
> And from the frieze to the four winds of Heaven
>   Hung them on high by the entangled hair:
>   Swarthy were three—the fourth was very fair.
>
> (ll. 1324–28)

The fourth corpse is Cythna's, while the three "swarthy" ones represent the murdered soldiers. The dream symbolically conflates Laon's aggressions toward them with his passion for Cythna to suggest that "the misconceiving principle of self . . . had, in effect, murdered her by murdering them."[27] The hero's "recognition of the fourth corpse as 'Cythna's ghost,' " Richard H. Haswell adds, signifies his "awareness of his blindness."[28] From this perspective, Laon's moral regen-

[25] Sperry, "Sexual Theme," 41.
[26] Sperry, "Sexual Theme," 49.
[27] E. B. Murray, " 'Elective Affinity' in *The Revolt of Islam*," *JEGP* 69 (1968): 573.
[28] Haswell, "Shelley's *The Revolt of Islam*," 85.

eration appears in his pacifism during the warfare at the Golden City, while his sexual redemption appears in his climactic, well-earned reunion with Cythna.

Yet the reunion of Laon and Cythna is itself a brief phase of a larger progression to willed, violent death. When Laon and Cythna embrace their martyrdom, *The Revolt of Islam* characterizes the body as the site of aggressions that can be redirected (even turned against the body itself) but not outgrown. The sexual thematics of *The Revolt of Islam* are by no means wholly redemptive. Ambivalence suffuses Shelley's third canto, which "defines the impulse to incest," John Donovan writes, "as arising from those depths of our nature where the good and the bad are not readily separable."[29] Just so, Laon's attack on Othman's soldiers links masculinity and domination integrally. His immediately previous dream of sitting with Cythna "to taste the joys which Nature gave" had been disturbed by "foul and ghastly shapes" prefiguring the imperial soldiery (ll. 1125, 1149). Recounting that dream, Laon describes an intensification of submerged energies nearing the surface of consciousness, until he suddenly finds himself holding Cythna and flying "through the air and over the sea," as

> through the darkness spread
> Around, the gaping earth then vomited
> Legions of foul and ghastly shapes, which hung
> Upon my flight; and ever, as we fled,
> They plucked at Cythna—soon to me then clung
> A sense of actual things those monstrous dreams among.
>
> (ll. 1147–52)

This emission fantasy engenders a horrified recoil from the sexual scene depicted.[30] But Laon's revulsion hardly overrules the libidinal, wish-fulfilling component of the dreamwork: the orgasm and the guilt are equally elements of his psyche. When the threatening shapes originating in Laon's psyche abduct Cythna in dream, and then Othman's dusky soldiers abduct her in fact, we confront a psychomachia where Laon plays all the roles. These abducting shapes, as surrogate selves, show Laon's libidinal energies intensifying until they generate the aggressions from which he ironically tries to protect Cythna. His

[29] John Donovan, "Incest in *Laon and Cythna*: Nature, Custom, Desire," *Keats-Shelley Review* 2 (1987): 57. While emphasizing Laon's role in producing the sexual violence of the poem, this essay also regards that violence as ultimately transcended: Laon's "chains can be loosed when he has recognized the violent and anarchic aspect of his desire for Cythna," so that the protagonists' erotic consummation signifies a "sacred action whose ritual accomplishment redeems defeat" (58, 77).

[30] In *The Interpretation of Dreams*, Freud remarks that "in men flying dreams usually have a grossly sensual meaning," in *SEF* 5:394.

psychosexual violence arises not with his resistance to the soldiers but with their appearance. As tyranny's minions, moreover, the soldiers symbolically link Laon with Othman, signifying his internalization of the patriarch's appropriative sexuality. For Laon, transcendence of erotic violence will require a transcendence of patriarchy.

The purgatorial scenes that follow heighten Laon's complicity with the forces of erotic violence. In a passage in canto 3 anticipating Prometheus with the Furies, the bound Laon falls into a sleep "Which through the caverns dreary and forlorn / Of the riven soul, sent its foul dreams to sweep" tumultuously through him until he "descried / All shapes like [his] own self, hideously multiplied" (ll. 1299–1300, 1313–14). These "foul dreams" are the "foul . . . shapes" of the previous dream enacting a return of the repressed. In moving from such self-images to the four corpses suspended from the tower, three of them corpses of the slain guards, Shelley implies that they too function as Laon's psychic personae. Their presence haunts the scenes that, teaching Laon the horror of aggression, supposedly turn him to a saving pacifism. Here is the revelatory moment, his recognition of Cythna:

> A woman's shape, now lank and cold and blue,
>   The dwelling of the many-coloured worm,
> Hung there; the white and hollow cheek I drew
>   To my dry lips—what radiance did inform
>   Those horny eyes? whose was that withered form?
> Alas, alas! it seemed that Cythna's ghost
>   Laughed in those looks, and that the flesh was warm
> Within my teeth!—A whirlwind keen as frost
> Then in its sinking gulfs my sickening spirit tossed.

(ll. 1332–41)

E. B. Murray justly remarks that "the Gothic extravagance of [this] vision should not overshadow the fact that Shelley is allowing his lover to embrace the loved one in dream."[31] Laon's embrace signifies desire-as-violence. In Freudian theory, cannibalism usually connotes an urge for sexual incorporation typical of the initial, oral stage of psychosexual development, a stage quite commonly characterized by a "fusion of libido and aggressiveness."[32] Laon's erotic epiphany preserves the violence of his earlier erotic fantasies by relocating it.

Such relocation testifies to a guilt both deeply rooted and extraor-

---

[31] Murray, " 'Elective Affinity,' " 573.

[32] As J. LaPlanche and J.-B. Pontalis write in *The Language of Psycho-Analysis*, trans. Donald Nicholson-Smith (New York: Norton, 1973), 55.

dinarily complex, as in Victor's analogous dream in *Frankenstein*, which Mary, with her husband's assistance, completed during the summer of 1817:

> I thought I saw Elizabeth, in the bloom of health, walking in the streets of Ingolstadt. Delighted and surprised, I embraced her; but as I imprinted the first kiss on her lips, they became livid with the hue of death; her features appeared to change, and I thought that I held the corpse of my dead mother in my arms; a shroud enveloped her form, and I saw the grave-worms crawling in the folds of the flannel.[33]

Victor embraces Elizabeth in order to hold the mother, and then recoils in a self-loathing displaced onto the woman. Laon embraces his own violence as the price of possessing Cythna. With the flying dream Laon had attempted to sublimate his erotic interest in her by eluding the phallic soldiers personifying his sexual aggressions—thus the trajectory of heavenly ascent. In the dream of eating Cythna, Laon's subconscious again projects a fantasy of sexual intercourse requiring the proximity of the "stiff," libidinally potent bodies, dead themselves but symbols of psychic forces alive within Laon. His necrophagic dream brazenly displays the affinity of eros and death. Yet it also accepts the presence of images of male aggression as a precondition for sexual enjoyment of the woman. By no means do the early cantos of *The Revolt of Islam* idealize erotic catharsis in their portrayal of Laon.

The vagaries of power that structure Laon's sexuality recur with Cythna too. Although "Cythna is shown as a near-perfect heroine with less to learn than Laon,"[34] her errors merely perpetuate violence more subtly. When Laon discovers Cythna bound by the soldiers, he declares,

> I started to behold her, for delight
>   And exultation, and a joyance free,
> Solemn, serene and lofty, filled the light
>   Of the calm smile with which she looked on me:
>   So that I feared some brainless ecstasy,
> Wrought from that bitter woe, had wildered her.
>
> (ll. 1171–76)

Cythna's exultation and delight lend her anticipation of the harem a voluptuous edge. She wills her victimization out of a sense of moral mission as truth's "chosen minister" (l. 1179), certainly, but we can

---

[33] Mary Wollstonecraft Shelley, *Frankenstein; or, The Modern Prometheus*, ed. James Rieger (1974; reprint, Chicago: University of Chicago Press, 1982), 53.

[34] Gutschera, "Drama of Reenactment," 121 n. 12.

detect in it her indulgence of a stereotypically feminine passivity, the masochistic obverse of Laon's sadism. If his resistance to Othman seems excessively ruthless, Cythna's seems excessively pliant. Her pliancy is a form of innocence. She naively underestimates her degradation because she has a purely hypothetical understanding of violence. Cythna's brutalization teaches her

> what a loathsome agony
> Is that when selfishness mocks love's delight,
> Foul as in dream's most fearful imagery
> To dally with the mowing dead—that night
> All torture, fear, or horror made seem light
> Which the soul dreams or knows, and when the day
> Shone on her awful frenzy, from the sight
> Where like a Spirit in fleshly chains she lay
> Struggling, aghast and pale the Tyrant fled away.
>
> (ll. 2875–83)

Cythna's narrative of her rape recalls Laon's hallucinatory dalliance with the dead. The sufferings of Shelley's protagonists are opposed and complementary: for Laon, the woman is dead; for Cythna, the rutting Othman is dead. But the centrality of death in both scenes reconfirms the bonds among Othman's predatory sexuality, Laon's anguished dream, and Cythna's imprisonment.

Cythna's liberation requires her to discard female passivity to save herself and advance the emancipation of women. She enjoys a success with this endeavor noteworthy enough for Nathaniel Brown to praise *The Revolt of Islam* as "the most powerful feminist poem in the language."[35] Cythna first achieves a feminist heroism by surviving her underwater imprisonment. Othman has her carried to an underwater cave by "a green and wrinkled eunuch" and "a wretch from infancy / Made dumb by poison" (ll. 2895, 2898–99). These "slaves" enact the tyrant's intention to negate her sexuality and her language, her powers of bodily and imaginative creation. When the dark Ethiop embraces Cythna and plunges down to the underwater cavern, Shelley glances back at the "swarthy" phallic soldiers and flying embrace of canto 3, depicting a symbolic rape that returns Cythna to the womblike matrices of her own womanhood. Othman reduces Cythna from woman to child. In the cave, she must reaffirm her womanhood: "Cythna's test is essentially an initiation into sexual maturity and motherhood and a symbolic working through of the dangers

---

[35] Nathaniel Brown, *Sexuality and Feminism in Shelley* (Cambridge: Harvard University Press, 1979), 181.

they pose."[36] This "working through" requires her to discover the creative autonomy of her own mind so that she can live within the conviction of her freedom and dignity.

Cythna must overcome the theft of her child—a symbol of the body's natural fecundity—and move from natural to mental priorities in achieving identity. Shelley emphasizes her progress when she frees the slave ship of canto 8 with her eloquent rhetoric, and soon afterward assumes her role as Laone, the revolution's prophetess. By allotting her this role, *The Revolt of Islam* can even appear to grant Cythna a heroism more compelling than Laon's. Carlos Baker certainly found it more compelling:

> The central agent of unification is the heroine, Cythna. She serves throughout the poem, even when she is not present, as a positive dynamic force, a kind of matrix of revolution, and is very obviously the apple of Shelley's revolutionary eye. By comparison, Laon is a mere shadow, a bearer of news, an observer and reporter, more acted upon than acting. The force of her personality and her capacity for leadership result in partial success for her campaign. She faces down Othman, enslaver and hater, and temporarily establishes emancipation and love.[37]

Baker's points are well taken. Cythna starts a revolution already triumphant when Laon arrives at the Golden City. When mercenary armies defeat the rebels and endanger Laon himself (ll. 2487–96), Cythna bravely rescues him. She suddenly appears, brandishing a sword, on "A black Tartarian horse of giant frame" (l. 2499), a symbol of martial activism reminiscent of *The Giaour* and of Byronic adventure and energy.

Unfortunately the saving act that empowers her heroism also ends it. Laon's return and nearness to Cythna—the very proximity of the masculine will—debilitates her. During the few days of their reunion, Cythna becomes a hapless Dickensian heroine, always about to swoon, always appearing "most pale, / Famished, and wet and weary" (ll. 2812–13), while Laon takes the "horse of giant frame" and the risks of leaving their sanctuary. Despite Shelley's feminist creed, his poem can award Cythna an initiative activism only in Laon's absence. The union of Laon and Cythna supposedly serves as Shelley's model of revolutionary desire. Yet his protagonists consummate their love amid the desolation and debris of the revolution's failure, and there is a disconcerting logic to that apparent coincidence. Laon's arrival at

[36] Sperry, "Sexual Theme," 46.

[37] Carlos Baker, *Shelley's Major Poetry: The Fabric of a Vision* (Princeton: Princeton University Press, 1948), 81.

the Golden City accompanies the resurgence of Othman because eros can fulfill itself only under the auspices of a triumphant male power in *The Revolt of Islam*.

By screening the alliance of power and sexuality in its overt love theme, *The Revolt of Islam* fails to trace libidinal aggressions to their matrices. Later, *Prometheus Unbound* will pursue that trail to the familial antagonisms of tragic myth. *The Revolt of Islam* adumbrates similar familial topoi in passing, however. Canto 6 introduces the figure of the woman Pestilence, whom Cronin calls "Cythna's antitype," a character in whom "the ideal has projected its own antithesis."[38] This dark double aligns Cythna with maternity. Once the mother of "two babes—a sister and a brother" (l. 2768) much like Laon and Cythna as originally conceived by Shelley—the woman Pestilence forces "her burning lips" to Laon's in proof of a specifically feminine sexual violence. These kisses derive their aggression from family romance, however, for they are above all maternal kisses. *The Revolt of Islam* includes a shadowy Oedipal theme by associating Laon and Othman as competitors for Cythna, rivals for the prerogatives of fatherhood. Ambivalence toward paternity explains the appearance of the Hermit, who functions as Othman's double, allowing the father's dissociation into threatening and benevolent figures. This dissociation makes Laon's filial resistance to Othman the hallmark of his filial loyalty to the Hermit. Through such evasive strategies Laon can "transcend oedipal emotions and achieve adulthood without triumphing over the father so violently as to generate guilt."[39] But attempts to circumvent guilt in *The Revolt of Islam*, as in Laon's refusal to sanction the people's execution of Othman, reenfranchise paternal power and exchange one form of violence for another.

The partnership of eros and violence also accounts for Laon and Cythna's curiously suicidal execution. It seems "evident from the first that Laon is inviting just such a disaster as occurs," Carlos Baker com-

---

[38] Cronin, *Shelley's Poetic Thoughts*, 106.

[39] William Veeder, *Mary Shelley & Frankenstein: The Fate of Androgyny* (Chicago: University of Chicago Press, 1986), 129. Also pertinent here is Murray's claim (" 'Elective Affinity,' " 578) that during her rape Cythna's spirit "refused to accept the imprint of [Othman's] evil character," so that the child she bears in the subaqueous cave is "at once the fruit of her spiritual communion (in the one mind) with Laon and her physical rape by the Tyrant." This genealogy privileges spirit over body, allowing Laon to assume the role of father while avoiding sexual intercourse. A full-scale Oedipal reading of the Othman-Cythna-Laon triad would make Cythna a mother-figure for Laon by pursuing Dawson's observation that the *Quarterly* identifies "Cythna with Mary Shelley, but it seems more likely that Shelley modelled his heroine on Mary's mother, Mary Wollstonecraft" (*Unacknowledged Legislator*, 71 n. 1).

ments,[40] while Cythna disdains any attempt to rescue her lover, preferring to "woo" death "With smiles of tender joy" (ll. 4565–66). The actual moment of death achieves the finer "music of a breath-suspending song" like the song of Keats's nightingale, a music "Which, like the kiss of love when life is young, / Steeps the faint eyes in darkness sweet and deep" (ll. 4597–99). Clearly Shelley's lovers pursue death "to complete their mutual ecstasy."[41] The consummation luring them simply diverts the violence of the body against itself in a last self-destructive gesture. Canto 12 celebrates the body's annihilation as the apotheosis of Shelleyan eros. The climactic position of this celebration demonstrates that desire exhausts its propensities for aggression when it exhausts itself. Only those dark inclinations, and the fears they incite, explain why *The Revolt of Islam* consistently seeks to elide the body—why the negation of corporeality provides Shelley's poem its standard of truth and fulfillment.

SUBTLER LANGUAGE

The Revolt of Islam, Wilkie wrote, "not only preaches but is *about* preaching."[42] The poem names language as one of tyranny's habitations (l. 389) and explores the politics of rhetoric by using the metaphor of the body to link sexuality and language. The contradictions of Shelley's sexual theme thereby recur in his treatment of words. While his demotion of the body associates meaning and spirit, any poetics adequate to the poem's revolutionary purpose presupposes a commitment to the body of the letter. Shelley again tries to negotiate these antithetical aims by making them poles in a dialectic. As the worldly fate of Laon and Cythna promotes deathless ideals, the poem's linguistic allegiances to body and spirit cohere as complementary aspects of a reconciliatory poetics. Such holistic imperatives, which typify Romantic aesthetics, organize the metaphorical idealism of *The Revolt of Islam*. Cronin rightly points out, for example, that Shelley's imagery attempts to harmonize opposites:

> The central images of Shelley's poem express his concern to merge the public and private; dungeons and chains are now physical impediments, now mental fetters. Cythna's cave is a real prison, but in line 3101 it becomes a metaphor for her mind. An unstable relationship between the literal and the metaphoric is, in the terms of Shelley's poem, a badge of

[40] Baker, *Shelley's Major Poetry*, 81.

[41] So Alex Comfort claimed, in *Darwin and the Naked Lady: Discursive Essays on Biology and Art* (London: Routledge and Kegan Paul, 1961), 82.

[42] Wilkie, *Romantic Poets*, 139.

mental strength. The poem is designed to drive together the world of public event and of private imagining, to represent the one as the product of the other.[43]

Shelleyan tropes characteristically seek to abrogate the distinction between contraries. As with the poem's sexual theme, however, the unities that result are disguised hierarchies.

The hierarchical structure of power emerges only gradually in *The Revolt of Islam*. The educative developments of Laon and Cythna proceed as each explores the possibility of a language abrogating difference. Their experiences can be read as allegories of imaginative renewal, as can the trials of Prometheus and Asia in acts 1 and 2 of *Prometheus Unbound*. When Laon attacks Cythna's abductors in canto 2, he embraces a violence corresponding to Prometheus' hatred of Jupiter. Both heroes must absolve themselves of hate by liberating their imaginations. For Laon that involves immersing his mind in literary and philosophic tradition. Shelley returns Laon to the cultural sources of the imagination through the tutelary Hermit, a character fittingly reminiscent of Godwin, Wordsworth, and Coleridge, all of them so important to Shelley's own intellectual and artistic growth. Although lacking in passion—"I am cold," he admits (l. 1560)—the Hermit has preserved vital cultural traditions. Living "In converse with the dead, who leave the stamp / Of ever-burning thoughts on many a page" (ll. 1478–79), he personifies revolutionary potential:

> "Yes, from the records of my youthful state,
>   And from the lore of bards and sages old,
> From whatsoe'er my wakened thoughts create
>   Out of the hopes of thine aspirings bold,
>   Have I collected language to unfold
> Truth to my countrymen; from shore to shore
>   Doctrines of human power my words have told,
> They have been heard, and men aspire to more
> Then they have ever gained or ever lost of yore."
>
>   (ll. 1513–21)

The Hermit needs Laon as literary tradition needs individual talent to actualize its promise. But in canto 3 Laon desperately needs the Hermit. As Shelley's poet-figure, Laon has to learn the Godwinian

---

[43] Cronin, *Shelley's Poetic Thoughts*, 103. Donovan's interpretation of Laon and Cythna's reunion stresses "the contraries that structure the psychology of their meeting," but takes them as evidence of "a conception of the sacred whose essence it is to comprehend opposites in a relation of positive equilibrium" ("Incest," 77).

language of political gradualism in order to enlighten and control the masses assembled at the Golden City.

As Laon must return to tradition, Cythna must return to nature, so their reconciliation can fashion an educated imagination from which poetry comes "as naturally as the Leaves to a tree."[44] With Cythna, Shelley exchanges the Hermit's Yeatsian tower for an underwater cave. There Cythna recovers from madness to be reborn as the "prophetess of Love." The cave contains "A fountain round and vast" (l. 2931); the imprisoned, pregnant Cythna similarly feels her child stirring "in the fountains of my life" (l. 2970). Carrying a baby in her womb, Cythna is herself carried in a kind of womb. This womb acts as a synecdoche for nature, which *The Revolt of Islam* persistently feminizes: inhabiting "the wide earth's maternal breast," men are necessarily "sons of one great mother" (ll. 976, 817). Cythna's return to nature reacquaints her with the bodily essence of her womanhood, the affective and natural life of the female body.

The education in language she undergoes in the cave stresses the materiality of signification. Cythna's memories of the cultural and intellectual values that Laon personifies no doubt shape her development. Her "self-education depends upon her already possessing a language," William Keach comments, yet "as her mind grows it also fashions a language partly its own," mutually accommodating tradition and self, spirit and body.[45] It is nonetheless bodiliness that Shelley emphasizes. Cythna's experiments with signs allegorize the emergence of language from nature, the origination of words as "imitations of natural objects" (*Defence of Poetry*, 481). Only the loss of her child, her maternal link to nature, prompts Cythna's compensatory creation of a "subtler language." This creation begins with the "inarticulate" converse of her infant (ll. 3010–18) and with the eagle who visits her. The eagle sympathetically infers Cythna's wish that the Nautilus be spared, but cannot grasp her more complex request for help in escaping: "long in vain I sought," she says, "By intercourse of mutual imagery / Of objects, if such aid he could be taught" (ll. 3087–89). Cythna then gains wisdom by "rifling" her cave—by exploring the cave conceived as a physical place—until its symbolic connection to "One mind, the type of all" (l. 3104) becomes clear and her progression from natural to universal understanding can complete itself.

[44] Keats's phrase, in *The Letters of John Keats*, ed. Hyder Edward Rollins (Cambridge: Harvard University Press, 1958), 1:238.

[45] William Keach, *Shelley's Style* (London: Methuen, 1984), 39. Also see Lloyd Abbey's comments on the mentalistic, self-reflexive status of Cythna's "subtler language" in *Destroyer and Preserver: Shelley's Poetic Skepticism* (Lincoln: University of Nebraska Press, 1979), 38.

Now she requires a language adequate to her perceptions:

> "And on the sand would I make signs to range
>   These woofs, as they were woven, of my thought;
> Clear, elemental shapes, whose smallest change
>   A subtler language within language wrought:
>   The key of truths which once were dimly taught
> In old Crotona;—and sweet melodies
>   Of love, in that lorn solitude I caught
> From mine own voice in dream, when thy dear eyes
> Shone through my sleep, and did that utterance harmonize."
>
> (ll. 3109–17)

These lost truths are Pythagorean (as the Crotona reference indicates). They probably found their way into *The Revolt of Islam* through Thomas Moore's "The Grecian Girl's Dream of the Blessed Islands," where Pythagoras admits that

>   whate'er his dreamy thought
> In mystic numbers long had vainly sought,
> The One that's form'd of Two whom love hath bound
> Is the best number gods or men e'er found.
>
> (ll. 53–56)[46]

Like Moore's Grecian girl, Shelley's Cythna intuits a version of the ideal, androgynous paradigm envisioned in canto 1. She achieves this intuition through the agency of the body, learning truth from characters inscribed in sand, from a temporalized language of nature. Shelley accords these material signifiers a constitutive role in the production of truth, even as Asia avows the priority of language to thought in *Prometheus Unbound* (2.4.72). Here the role of language as the agency of subtler, more abstruse ideas is linguistically "wrought" (written), engendered by changes in the "elemental shapes" themselves. The body of the letter remains crucial to the liberation of spirit and truth.

To all appearances, Cythna's imaginative renewal complements Laon's, pairing nature with culture in one more antithesis bridged by the harmonizing aesthetics of Shelley's epic. Here is a poem, to borrow a Shelleyan phrase from 1819, in which the imagination assumes

[46] I cite Moore's poem from *The Poetical Works of Thomas Moore* (New York: D. Appleton and Co., 1853), 145. In *Shelley's "The Revolt of Islam"* (Salzburg: Institut fur Englische Sprache und Literatur, Universität Salzburg, 1972), 40–42, James Lynn Ruff argues that this poem influenced cantos 1 and 12 of Shelley's poem, and notes that Shelley was reading Moore in 1817 and twice requested his publishers to submit *The Revolt of Islam* to Moore's judgment.

"flesh for the redemption of mortal passion" (Preface to *The Cenci*, 241), a poem which valorizes a parity of body and spirit imaged in the equality of Laon and Cythna, whose erotic passion blends "two restless frames in one reposing soul" (l. 2658). Recalling Shelley's sexual treatment of the body, however, we must eventually ask just how equal the constituent terms of its syntheses are. Often "even the potentially neutral concept of opposition also turns into a hierarchy, because it is impossible ever to be entirely disinterested and one element must be primary and the other secondary."[47] In fact, relations of ascendancy and abjection proliferate in *The Revolt of Islam*, for the poem includes disapproval of the sensual complicities of language as part of its cultural legacy. In *The Statesman's Manual*, Coleridge allows "Images of the Senses" an incarnating role in his notion of a symbolic imagination, yet disdains "the dead letter" of allegorical veils and falsehoods.[48] By evoking such contexts, *The Revolt of Islam* acquiesces to a Pauline denigration of the body, which resists recuperation into any unitive equilibrium, and which finally cripples the poem's metaphorical idealism.

Metaphor empowers tenor over vehicle, type over antitype, as meaning's controlling referent. Such power disrupts the relation of Laon and Cythna as idealized complements contributing equally to meaning-as-union. This subversive force increases with the allegorizing tendency of Shelley's characterizations. Although tentative, the protagonists' divergent allegorical roles are recognizable enough to be a matter of critical consensus: Laon and Cythna represent "male and female principles, the man being the visionary and the woman the human voice of his poetic insights"; there is "a persistent identification of Laon with the rational faculties and Cythna with the affective powers"; "Laon's discursive knowledge is complemented by Cythna's intuitive knowledge."[49] As such comments indicate, Cythna prefigures the Asia of *Prometheus Unbound* by bearing gifts emotional and instinctive. Her "young heart" can wage war against oppression when she can barely sustain "conscious thought" because "conscious thought" is not her forte. If she instructs Laon at all, it is typically "in the visions of her eloquent sleep / Unconscious of the power" by which those dreams become "intelligible thought" (ll. 966–68, 969). Through such intuitive wisdom, Cythna endows Laon's "purpose with a wider sympathy" (l. 984). She becomes the body's champion

[47] Margaret Homans, *Women Writers and Poetic Identity: Dorothy Wordsworth, Emily Brontë, and Emily Dickinson* (Princeton: Princeton University Press, 1980), 36.
[48] Coleridge, *Statesman's Manual*, 29–30.
[49] Wilkie, *Romantic Poets*, 141–42; Haswell, "Shelley's *The Revolt of Islam*," 87; Cronin, *Shelley's Poetic Thoughts*, 98.

too. So Shelley implies by returning her to the womb of nature while Laon recovers in a tower connoting intellectual tradition. In fact, Cythna's association with the body follows inevitably from Shelley's feminization of nature—his depictions of nature as maternal—which reflexively naturalizes the feminine.

Linked with nature in contrast to mind and spirit, Cythna and her powers of speech play a secondary role in *The Revolt of Islam*. Cythna's heroism can temporarily make her appear Laon's equal. Her equality nonetheless suffers from Laon's return, as we saw, and from Shelley's feminine psychology. Cythna constructs her identity by an empathic adaptation to Laon. She studies his face, "Watching the hopes which there her heart had learned to trace" and seeking, as she informs him, "by most resembling thee, / So to become most good and great and free" (ll. 945, 1021–22). Laon remains Shelley's sole poet-figure. His words are stirring prophetic utterances, Cythna's address to the slave traders merely a public relations *coup*. For while Cythna becomes an effective rhetorician, her message is never her own. She can act as a "prophetess of Love," she tells Laon, only when her lips "rob thee of the grace thou wearest, / To hide thy heart, and clothe the shapes" that inhabit *his* visions (ll. 3641–43). In all of these ways, "Cythna exists less as an autonomous being than as a reflection of Laon."[50] "As mine own shadow was this child to me" (l. 874), Laon comments, designating Cythna the diminished duplication of a prior term and the representative of a second sex.

Despite Shelley's feminist allegiances, the cultural context of *The Revolt of Islam* leaves its linguistic premises and practice sexually biased. Laon's poetics are similarly sexist. His inspiration descends from the immortal realm that frames *The Revolt of Islam*, so that his words function as the medium of what *Adonais* calls

> the one Spirit's plastic stress [which]
> Sweeps through the dull dense world, *compelling* there,
> All new successions to the forms they wear.
> (ll. 381–83, emphasis added)

In their spiritual power, these words incarnate an imperialist Logos. Laon's language becomes the very "type of appropriative language" by acting "to identify otherness as self, to appropriate objects and transform them into subject."[51] His poetry forces empathy from the members of his audience, wrenching their minds into identity with his own:

[50] Veeder, *Mary Shelley & Frankenstein*, 55.
[51] Homans, *Women Writers*, 37.

These hopes found words through which my spirit sought
　To weave a bondage of such sympathy,
As might create some response to the thought
　Which ruled me now—and as the vapours lie
　Bright in the outspread morning's radiancy,
So were these thoughts invested with the light
　Of language: and all bosoms made reply
On which its lustre streamed, whene'er it might
Through darkness wide and deep those tranced spirits smite.

(ll. 802–10)

Here communication comes about as an effect of power. Ruled by the ideals he serves, Laon influences auditors by ruling in turn: his "strong genius . . . / . . . compels all spirits to obey" (ll. 1546–47). Persuasion is conquest: selecting "Words which were weapons" (l. 842), Laon exercises verbal skills by which, he declares, "all things became / Slaves to my holy and heroic verse" (ll. 933–34).[52]

As this telling phrase implies, the heroism of such verse resides in its attunement to the spirit. Laon's poetic vocation is a holy war committed to a transcendent universalism that relegates the body of the letter to the first stage of a supernal ascent. Meaning exists as the transparency of one consciousness to another when physical vestures are erased. Laon's prophetic power lets him speak directly to the minds of his listeners, appealing to an innate love superimposed layerings cannot extinguish. So Cythna's "subtler language" worked a progression from material inscription to ideal revelation, ending with the "One mind." So with the structure of The Revolt of Islam as a whole: the eternalizing frame of Shelley's poem, which provides the narrative site of Laon's tale, dramatizes a movement of language from spirit to body (the earthly fortunes of the protagonists) and back again. Shelley never alludes to this frame in the intermediate cantos. As a result, we never see Cythna taking over the narrative from Laon to relate her own experiences; she speaks only through Laon's Romantic ventriloquism. Bracketed within Laon's act of narration, Cythna's words exist at one further remove from spirit—the traditional association of woman with the body of nature and the "dispensation of death" effectively denying her any voice at all in the regions of eternity.

---

[52] Wilkie, Romantic Poets, 139–41, treats the rhetorical contradictions of Shelley's poem. In The Poetry of Life: Shelley and Literary Form (Toronto: University of Toronto Press, 1987), 113, Ronald Tetreault similarly notes that "Laon's oratory is too often modelled on the very relationship of dominance and submission which he is rebelling against."

As a model of the poem's affective strategies, Laon's domination of language replicates itself in Shelley's relation to his audience. Here we return to the authorial elitism Leigh Hunt deplored, and to the egocentrism of the poem's scenes of reading. *The Revolt of Islam* begins by introducing its despairing poet to a woman, clearly a muse, who commands the Coleridgean "boat of rare device" that transports the poet to the Temple of the Spirit (l. 325). Through a complex series of symbolic transferences, the poet's empathic connection with her is communicated to Laon and Cythna, who become his true inspiration: "They pour fresh light from Hope's immortal urn," he is told. "A tale of human power—despair not—list and learn!" (ll. 647–48). *The Revolt of Islam* unfolds narratively through this auditor's listening. He therefore acts as a surrogate reader. Since *The Revolt of Islam* makes him a surrogate author, it opens by guaranteeing itself a coincidence of reader and writer, decreeing a necessarily sympathetic audience projected in the author's own image.[53] By depicting the poet himself as the poem's ideal reader, Shelley risks reducing art to that "dialogue of the mind with itself" Matthew Arnold termed the hallmark of Romantic alienation.[54]

Shelley takes considerable political risks too. He deliberately gave *The Revolt of Islam* a "character so refined and so remote from the conceptions of the vulgar" to avoid censorship: the government, he assumed, "would hesitate before they invaded a member of the higher circles of the republic of letters" (*Letters* 1:579). But this defensiveness necessarily recognizes the powers it seeks to neutralize, incorporating conservative values in the poem and minimizing its revolutionary potential. Shelley's elitist epic reconfirms class divisions by the restrictive claims it makes on its highly select readership. In fact, representation reestablishes hierarchies throughout the poem. Even his glorious revolution reifies what it denies through its very recourse to language and symbol. The populace storms the Golden City and rears an "Altar of the Federation," "a marble pyramid / Distinct with steps," thronged with female choirs, and occupied at its summit by the veiled Laone "upon an ivory throne" (ll. 2072, 2076–77, 2106).

---

[53] Tetreault remarks that "the failure to exploit the narrator to instruct the reader's response is one of the missed opportunities of the poem, unless the very passiveness of the narrator in listening to Laon is meant to serve as a model. . . . By deferring to Laon, the narrator provides an unfortunate model for the way the reader is expected to defer to the author in this poem" (*Poetry of Life*, 111).

[54] Matthew Arnold, "Preface to the First Edition of *Poems*," reprinted in *The Poems of Matthew Arnold*, ed. Kenneth Allott (London: Longman's, Green and Co., 1965), 591. Pointing to Shelley's interest in the advertising of his poem, Donald H. Reiman emphasizes the poet's hopes, defensive disclaimers notwithstanding, of reaching a large audience with *The Revolt of Islam*, in *SHC* 5:393.

Laone's (temporary) enthronement affronts egalitarian ideals and en-
sures her demotion. "Even as this spectacle attempts to critique mo-
narchical empires, the way the Revolution did, by inversely employ-
ing the throne-centered stagecraft of what it opposes," the effort
undermines itself by "the raising of an ego-ideal for a new society to
pursue."[55] The poem's rhetorical assumptions systematically promote
the reactionary oppression they appear to struggle against—mascu-
line authority and the patriarchal social order created in its image—
because language signifies hierarchically. Metaphor prevails, but only
by violently yoking a lower term to a higher. In *The Revolt of Islam* all
appearances of parity and harmony are the ideological mystifications
by which power reproduces itself in whatever opposes it.

UNCERTAIN PRIORITIES

The Revolt of Islam concludes as it began. This circuitous journey en-
acts a phenomenology of history in which politics remains the deriv-
ative (antitypical) form of transcendence. As in *Alastor*, these circular
returns thematize the priority of metaphor, assigning history—as the
field of temporal contingency and allegorical difference—to an inter-
mediate phase in Unity's emanation away from and back to itself.
This metaphorical circumscription of allegory is an effect of power
contested, however futilely, by the poem's subplot. The idealism of
The Revolt of Islam insists on Laon and Cythna's triumph: if they die
while Othman reigns, history's ability to adapt itself to spirit is merely
postponed. Time is of little moment from the perspective of eternity.
Yet materiality's vehicle-like adaptation of itself *to* the ideal-as-tenor
alone guarantees the preeminence of spirit in Shelley's metaphorical
idealism. The pyramidal scenes of *The Revolt of Islam*—moving from
Spirit's Temple, to revolution's altar, to death's pyre—manifest a pro-
gressive warping of spirit by historical intransigence, undermining
Shelley's privileging of the ideal. *The Revolt of Islam* shows how the
substitutive identity of self and antitype renders causal priority un-
certain in all metaphorically conceived models of historical change.

Since Shelley's poem sidesteps this problem, it manifests itself as an
alternation of conflicting assumptions. Ambivalence of this sort is
fundamental to *The Revolt of Islam*. The poem begins as a *"beau idéal*
as it were of the French Revolution" (*Letters* 1:564) and ends as the
story of another failed revolution. This paradox can be easily ex-
plained—*The Revolt of Islam* simply displays the prematurity of de-
mocracy in France—but the explanation finally explains too little.

[55] Hogle, *Shelley's Process*, 100.

Shelley's intention was indeed "to account for the failure of the
French Revolution," as Stuart M. Sperry writes, but also "to rebuke
the revulsion and despair of his contemporaries by reaffirming the
imaginative ideals of millennial fulfillment."[56] *The Revolt of Islam*
never reconciles these related but discrete purposes. We cannot argue
that the poem *had* to show an uprising that shared the French Revo-
lution's self-destructiveness. Why should Shelley be constrained by
the historical record in that regard when his text strays from it in
countless others? Why does the poem subordinate revolutionary de-
sire to reactionary fact as vehicle to tenor, instead of just the reverse?
Why not *correct* historical precedent by representing millennial tri-
umphs?

In theory imagination mediates "the eternal, the infinite, and the
one" in *The Revolt of Islam* as in *A Defence of Poetry* (483). The moral
will, similarly, enjoys priority over political events. "Shelley," Mary
wrote, "believed that mankind had only to will that there should be
no evil, and there would be none" ("Note on Prometheus Unbound.
By Mrs. Shelley," *PW*, 271). This is simplistic, but less so than it may
appear. William Godwin, Shelley's chief radical mentor, advocated re-
form produced by the dissemination of enlightenment from a chosen
few, and *The Revolt of Islam* works from Godwinian premises.[57] God-
win's understanding of the process of reform duly recognized the rel-
ative inefficacy of individual conversion. At one point in *Political
Justice* Goodwin asks rhetorically, "May it not be found, that the at-
tempt to alter the morals of mankind singly and in detail is an erro-
neous and futile undertaking; and that it will then only be effectually
and decisively performed, when, by regenerating their political insti-
tutions, we shall change their motives and produce a revolution in
the influences that act upon them?"[58] Yet Godwin's belief in human
beings as effective agents of change and his atomistic conception of
social organization tended to counteract his insistence on the prece-
dence of institutional reform. This tendency becomes even more pro-

[56] Stuart M. Sperry, *Shelley's Major Verse: The Narrative and Dramatic Poetry* (Cam-
bridge: Harvard University Press, 1988), 43.

[57] See the accounts of Godwin's influence on Shelley in Scrivener, *Radical Shelley*, 3–
21, and Dawson, *Unacknowledged Legislator*, 76–99. Shelley agreed with Godwin, as
Dawson writes (108, 109), that "since opinion is so powerful a determinant of man's
social existence it follows that all political reform must begin with a reform of opinion,"
or "transformation of man's consciousness." While Shelley regarded "moral and polit-
ical reform as the mutually supporting elements of an unending dialectic" (Dawson,
192), his poetry privileges the causal power of the reformed self.

[58] William Godwin, *Enquiry Concerning Political Justice and Its Influence on Morals and
Happiness*, ed. F.E.L. Priestley (1793; reprint, Toronto: University of Toronto Press,
1946), 1:5.

nounced in Shelley's poetry because his affective purposes led him to emphasize the political efficacy of the individual will. Readers would never alter their values unless convinced, by authors, that values can produce significant change in social events and institutions; thus Prometheus *wills* Jupiter's downfall. In *The Revolt of Islam* Shelley's allusions to the deterministic force of the historical process are nods to mundane contingencies that qualify Spirit's telic design without dominating it. His view of the relation of imagination to historical progression assigns causal priority to mental categories and the enlightened individual.

Why then does the rebellion of the Golden City fail? Or, given Shelley's commitment to the historical fate of the French Revolution as a model, why did that rebellion fail? It failed, in Shelley's view, because action preceded the inner moral revolution that provides social reform its only secure basis—even as Shelley's fictional revolt collapses because "it is only sustained by the individual genius of the hero and heroine, not by the assimilation of their principles into 'general knowledge,' and thus the final reaction is inevitable."[59] Revolution requires the right moment. But again, how can there be wrong moments when the prophetic poet legislates the historical process? If society's resistance to change proves powerful enough to undermine the ideals promulgated by Laon and Cythna, then doesn't that very fact indicate a more complex reciprocity in the relation of mind and history? Shelley's political intelligence would not allow him to overlook the social conditioning of imaginative possibilities. The Preface to *The Revolt of Islam* specifically deplores the artistic impact of a reactionary mood. Yet Shelley continually dedicated his poetry to "beautiful idealisms" with an assimilative power like that of the "flowering isles" of his "Lines written among the Euganean Hills":

> We may live so happy there,
> That the Spirits of the Air,
> Envying us, may even entice
> To our healing Paradise
> The polluting multitude;
> But their rage would be subdued
> By that clime divine and calm . . .
> They, not it, would change; and soon
> Every sprite beneath the moon
> Would repent its envy vain,
> And the earth grow young again.

(ll. 352–58, 370–73)

[59] Dawson, *Unacknowledged Legislator*, 69.

The failure of Laon and Cythna's revolutionary program, however complex, implies that polluting multitudes can destroy paradisal possibilities. It reverses Shelley's causal faith to intimate the priority of collective force to individual ideals, of history to imagination.

Because *The Revolt of Islam* thematizes history as spirit's vesture, historical priority arises as a materialist possibility. It intimates the analogous possibility of the priority of letter to spirit in Shelley's aesthetics. His images of poetic creation in *The Revolt of Islam* had occasionally assumed genealogical and corporeal forms. During the revolution's brief triumph, Laon is declared "The parent of this joy" (l. 1876), even as Shelley urged Byron to become "the parent of greatness" by writing on the French Revolution (*Letters* 1:507). Imagery of gestation—"Truth's deathless germs" "sleeping in the soil" (ll. 3670, 3676)—informs Cythna's famous anticipation of "Ode to the West Wind." The creative force of Cythna's inscriptions in sand and the earthliness of Shelley's postmortal realm betray a similar sensuousness. If the revolutionary eroticism of *The Revolt of Islam* succumbs to idealism, that idealism succumbs to a residual bodiliness, and it is difficult to say which properly comes first. Shelley's epic never interrogates the reversible potential of its hierarchies. *The Revolt of Islam* never asks if the material vestiges of its postmortal realm, like the remnants of a subjugated people, are evidence of a spirit that validates itself only by assimilating opposition to its own nature. By no means can the poem ask if such assimilation implies a notion of incorporation that is itself irreducibly bodily. It cannot ask if those material vestiges hint that supernal ideals, like the Freudian ego, are bodily projections, the reflexes of an antecedent and constitutive materiality.

Later poems will not only ask but answer these questions. Shelley's inability to pose them in 1817 reflects his still growing understanding of his own metaphorical idealism. *The Revolt of Islam* grants his idealism supremacy while also exposing its hidden fractures, rifts dividing meaning against itself. Material vestiges in an ideal realm can as easily imply spirit's mastery of the body as spirit's dependence on it. Such traces invariably suggest both at once. Since masters need slaves, any apparent priority of one element can be metaleptically reversed to reveal the (just as reversible) priority of its antithesis. The precipice on which Shelley's idealism totters, then, will not be the tendency of its unitive models to erect hierarchies. The contradictions addressed by *The Triumph of Life*, for instance, predicate neither the priority of spirit to body nor the body's actual priority to spirit. They involve rather the tendency of the higher and lower terms in those hierarchies to replace each other in an indeterminate and endless oscillation.

If at times *The Revolt of Islam* seems to fear bodily violence, it fears indeterminacy more. In idealizing the reciprocity of body and spirit as a substitutive equilibrium, *The Revolt of Islam* neutralizes the threat of chaos through metaphor. Such a temporary solution controls contradiction through impositions of force, but resolves nothing. Ironically, the metaphorical idealism of *The Revolt of Islam* becomes especially precarious because the poem includes a postmortal realm where likeness supposedly achieves perfected closure. Fully understood, even that court of last appeal represents an internally differentiated alternation of meanings, neither of which can be reduced to the other except through an exercise of power. The poem will not fully assent to this fracturing of eternity into time, of unity into difference, because Shelley still understands temporal difference as a barrier to truth. A similar elision of temporality arises in *Prometheus Unbound* as the counterplot of its anarchist celebration of becoming. Unlike *The Revolt of Islam*, *Prometheus Unbound* dramatizes the successful overthrow of tyranny. But it resembles *The Revolt of Islam* in showing that even the most "beautiful idealisms of moral excellence" (Preface to *Prometheus Unbound*, 135) cannot banish violence from language, love, or politics.

Chapter 4

THE UNBINDING OF METAPHOR

For know there are two worlds of life and death:
Which thou henceforth art doomed to interweave
—*Prometheus Unbound*, manuscript variant

ALLEGORY, Theresa M. Kelley writes, "is one of two competing yet cooperative modes" of figuration especially prevalent in Romantic poetry.[1] Competing, because the other mode, symbolism, grants the congruence of figure and referent, while allegory denies that congruence, dispersing symbolic Meaning into a succession of differential meanings. Cooperative, because these contrary powers are interdependent, with each functioning as the ground of the other's possibility. This interdependence prompts an alternation that never entirely assimilates either mode to the other. Yet whenever these figurative modes occur together (and they always do) allegory necessarily prevails. The figural oscillations of Romantic poetry are ultimately allegorical, since any unresolved difference, even the mere fact of two poles, can only signify a failure of the symbolic imperative. It is as true for texts as for critics that "the irreducible difference between the subjectivist and the objectivist, symbolist and allegorist, reflects the ineluctable priority of allegorical discourse."[2]

To read an allegory such as Shelley's *Prometheus Unbound*, we must follow Kelley's lead in attending to its rhetorical oscillations. We must certainly credit its release of transferential energies beyond closure.[3] But we must also watch for the possibility that such a poem, by its very inclusion of a symbolic imperative, will ideologically repress its own allegorical logic. The antitheses of Romantic allegory open it to idealization as a substitutive equilibrium empowering metaphor over

[1] Theresa M. Kelley, "Proteus and Romantic Allegory," *ELH* 49 (1982): 624.

[2] Jerome C. Christensen, "The Symbol's Errant Allegory: Coleridge and His Critics," *ELH* 45 (1978): 643.

[3] This aspect of *Prometheus Unbound* is discussed by Daniel J. Hughes, "Potentiality in *Prometheus Unbound*," *SIR* 2 (1963): 107–26, reprinted in *SPP*, 603–20; Ronald Tetreault, *The Poetry of Life: Shelley and Literary Form* (Toronto: University of Toronto Press, 1987), 169–96; and Jerrold E. Hogle, *Shelley's Process: Radical Transference and the Development of His Major Works* (New York: Oxford University Press, 1988), 167–202.

allegory. Shelley will acknowledge the priority of the allegorical in his darker poetry, above all in *The Triumph of Life*. The "beautiful ideal-isms" of *Prometheus Unbound* forestall a similar acknowledgment. The play's allegorizing is constrained by a nostalgia for symbolic media-tions, a nostalgia presenting love's triumph as a restoration of unity. Shelley's ambivalence toward allegory as a "rhetoric of temporality," in de Man's famous phrase,[4] emerges when Prometheus and Asia consummate their nuptials in a cave where, themselves unchanged, they witness the endless ebbing and flowing of the world from an eternal center. This elision of change undermines Shelley's represen-tation of the historical process and the possibilities of revolution. My reading of *Prometheus Unbound* will move to its political ironies. But it will begin with the poem's erotic impasse, a dilemma inherited from Greek tragedy and reconceived as a problem of Romantic rhetoric.

EROS AND TRAGEDY

The sublime joy of *Prometheus Unbound* arises in part from its trans-figuration of eros. Shelley's lyrical drama employs the "Biblical figure of the exile, return, and marriage of the bride" to realize "the human need for love to fulfill what is incomplete and to reintegrate what has been divided, both in the individual psyche and in the social order."[5] The bridal masque of act 4, a "celebration of the rebirth of sexual-ity,"[6] puts to rest any doubts about the erotic dimensions of this love. Shelleyan eros underlies the liberating promise of Promethean myth, but also its "dark underside" and "potential for either hope or de-spair."[7] As the reflex of Jupiter's subjugation, Shelley's erotic apoca-lypse is enfranchised by a violence that can be displaced as irony but never transcended.[8] The poem's visionary ironies seemingly occur by design. The Preface to *Prometheus Unbound* reconfirms Shelley's ide-

[4] Paul de Man, "The Rhetoric of Temporality," in *Blindness and Insight: Essays in the Rhetoric of Contemporary Criticism*, 2d ed., rev. (1971; reprint, Minneapolis: University of Minnesota Press, 1983), 187–228. I am indebted to this essay for my ideas of irony, allegory, and Shelleyan metaphor, which I again find to be driven by a holistic (or synecdochic) imperative symbolic in the Coleridgean sense.

[5] M. H. Abrams, *Natural Supernaturalism: Tradition and Revolution in Romantic Litera-ture* (New York: Norton, 1971), 299.

[6] Stuart M. Sperry, *Shelley's Major Verse: The Narrative and Dramatic Poetry* (Cam-bridge: Harvard University Press, 1988), 117.

[7] Sperry, *Shelley's Major Verse*, 75.

[8] There is still reason to quote G. M. Matthews' observation, "With astounding una-nimity, critics have contrived to find that Jupiter's overthrow is an essentially peaceful process. . . . Nevertheless, it must be allowed that a dispute which eclipses the sun and shakes the planets (possibly even the Milky Way) has its claim to seriousness," in "A Volcano's Voice in Shelley," *ELH* 24 (1957): 218.

alism while cautioning that the play expresses it selectively. "Beautiful idealisms of moral excellence" were "hitherto" his artistic object, and might be again—in a "history of . . . the genuine elements of human society," presumably the feelings and principles the Preface mentions just previously (135). Yet Shelley dissociates *Prometheus Unbound* from that projected "history" by remarking that it would hardly take "Aeschylus rather than Plato" as its model (Preface, 135).

Beginning with Aeschylus, *Prometheus Unbound* begins with tragedy, and proceeds toward the cosmic harmonies of act 4 by gradually transvaluing its tragic beginnings. Shelley acknowledges tragic precedent often enough for his story to unfold against an almost archetypally tragic background. Unsatisfied with appropriating *Prometheus Bound*, he borrows the Furies of the *Oresteia*. Unsatisfied with borrowing from Aeschylus, he also evokes Euripides: in cursing Jupiter, Prometheus invokes the same

> robe of envenomed agony;
> And . . . crown of pain
> To cling like burning gold round [his] dissolving brain,
>
> (1.289–91)

with which Medea murdered her rival for Jason's love. Shelley's evocation of Sophocles is more subtle. After Jupiter's fall, the liberated family of *Prometheus Unbound* gathers to seek a forest retreat near a temple which, as the Earth tells her unbound son, was once called by

> Thy name, Prometheus; there the emulous youths
> Bore to thine honour through the divine gloom
> The lamp, which was thine emblem.
>
> (3.3.168–70)

We can readily understand why this temple should represent Plato's Academy; Plato personifies Prometheus' educational legacy to humankind. But it is not to the temple that the Titan retires. Curiously, he goes instead to the nearby woodland cave, to "the sacred grove at Colonus" with its fissure reputedly leading to the underworld.[9]

[9] Edward B. Hungerford, *Shores of Darkness* (New York: Columbia University Press, 1941), 197. Milton Wilson touches on *Oedipus at Colonus* in connection with *Prometheus Unbound* in *Shelley's Later Poetry: A Study of His Prophetic Imagination* (New York: Columbia University Press, 1959), 44–45. For Shelley's interest in classical tragedy, see Timothy Webb, *The Violet in the Crucible: Shelley and Translation* (Oxford: Clarendon Press, 1976), 80. For Shelley and Aeschylus, see Bennett Weaver's thorough "*Prometheus Bound* and *Prometheus Unbound*," *PMLA* 64 (1949): 115–33, and James R. Hurt's "*Prometheus Unbound* and Aeschylean Dramaturgy," *KSJ* 15 (1966): 43–48, which views Shelley's poem in relation to the entire *Oresteia*.

The choice of Colonus as the site of transcendence rests on its Sophoclean associations as the setting for Oedipus' apotheosis. Shelley stages Prometheus' retirement, in the light of Sophoclean precedent, as a similar triumph over Oedipal guilt. The Oedipal dimensions of *Prometheus Unbound* reflect both its classical legacy and its contemporary interests. Blake's remarkable account of Urizen, Enitharmon, Orc, and the "Chain of Jealousy" (*The Book of Urizen*, plates 18–19) is merely the clearest example of Oedipal configurations that recur in Romantic representations of revolution and sexuality.[10] Responding to moralistic censure of the incestuous rape of *The Cenci*, Shelley himself cited precedents in "Sophocles, Massinger, Voltaire, & Alfieri," and remarked of his critics, "Good heavens what wd. they have tragedy" (*Letters* 2:200)—as if some form of incestuous aggression were fundamental to tragedy. *Prometheus Unbound* merely makes those aggressions Oedipal. Basic to the Promethean myth in Aeschylus was the castrating warfare waged by God against Titan. Shelley appropriates this myth for Romantic tragedy by compounding its generational rivalry with the Oedipal thematics of Sophocles. The poem's Oedipal subplot emerges as soon as we ask why Prometheus empowers Jupiter.

The orthodox answer refers Prometheus' acts to discontent with golden age primitivism (2.3.34–46). While seeming to stress the crucial opposition of Saturn and Prometheus, this explanation slights it by ignoring its extension in the warfare of Saturn and Jupiter. For Jupiter is "only the dark shadow of Prometheus," an alter ego who enacts wishes the ego consciously disclaims.[11] The crimes of Jupiter represent the acts of Prometheus at one symbolic remove. To understand why Prometheus empowers Jupiter, then, we need only consider what the tyrant of Olympus actually does: Jupiter overthrows the patriarch. Mediated through Jupiter's symbolic murder of Saturn, Prometheus' displaced parricide asserts the rights of the son in the face of patriarchal tyranny.[12] Jupiter's characterization of himself

[10] For the representation of Oedipal violence in Romantic art and literature, consult Ronald Paulson, *Representations of Revolution (1789–1820)* (New Haven: Yale University Press, 1983), 8 and elsewhere; Michael Henry Scrivener, *Radical Shelley: The Philosophical Anarchism and Utopian Thought of Percy Bysshe Shelley* (Princeton: Princeton University Press, 1982), 201–6; and Peter L. Thorslev, "Incest as Romantic Symbol," *Comparative Literature Studies* 2 (1965): 41–58.

[11] Earl R. Wasserman, *Shelley: A Critical Reading* (Baltimore: Johns Hopkins University Press, 1971), 258. There is widespread critical agreement on this point.

[12] Psychoanalytic readings of *Prometheus Unbound* have focused primarily on the father-son relations of Prometheus, Demogorgon (the "fatal Child" [3.1.19] begotten by Jupiter's despotism), and Jupiter himself, instead of seeing Prometheus and Jupiter as the passive and aggressive impulses of a guilty filial consciousness that has already de-

as the father is a wishful self-legitimation that Prometheus rightly finds suspect: "Heaven lowers under *thy* Fathers' frown," he tells Mercury (1.409, emphasis added). As Asia's cosmological narrative shows, the Titanic viewpoint insists on Saturn as father, no less so for his defeat and absence. In engineering that defeat, moreover, Prometheus unleashes the forces of appetitive sexuality: the God of Olympus, as our one glimpse of him sufficiently shows, is a God of rape (3.1.36–44). Prometheus and Saturn fight for sexual preeminence. Freud's remark that "the shape and movements of a flame suggest a phallus in activity" glosses Prometheus' theft of fire as sexual revolt, a wresting of phallic prerogatives from father to son.[13]

Seen in this light, Prometheus' punishment terrifies him with his own sexual fantasies, unrecognizably transposed as external aggression. Phallic glaciers pierce him with their spears, and his subconscious ("The ghastly people of the realm of dream") mocks his bound impotence (1.31, 37–38). His binding by Jupiter reflects the fixating power of Oedipal guilt. The repression-and-displacement through which Prometheus cedes Jupiter the power to act re-creates him as Prometheus' diabolical double. "But since the figure of the double is an unconscious projection of the ego in its fixated state," John T. Irwin remarks, and "since the double, as the repressed, returns from an area that lies outside control of the conscious will, . . . then the double in its character of an involuntary repetition evokes that very danger of the overruling of the son's will by an alien force (the castrating father) that repression had tried to avoid."[14] Jupiter repre-

---

feated the primal father Saturn. See, for example, William H. Marshall, "The Father-Child Symbolism in *Prometheus Unbound*," *MLQ* 22 (1961): 41–45. In *Mary Shelley & Frankenstein: The Fate of Androgyny* (Chicago: University of Chicago Press, 1986), 148, William Veeder comes closest to my approach when he argues that, for Shelley, "the 'son' is *two* men, who reflect his contradictory responses to father. Prometheus is the Percy of Agape who, as son, is oppressed by fathers yet remains as perfect in love as they are sunk in evil. Then, since the 'son' in the Greek myth is not Prometheus, the actual offspring of Thetis can express the homicidal rage of Eros. . . . Demogorgon does the dirty work and keeps Prometheus' hands clean." For me, Prometheus is a son enormously imperfect in love, and it is Jupiter who does the real dirty work by deposing Saturn, the Titanic patriarch.

[13] Freud's contention, from "The Acquisition and Control of Fire," in *SEF* 22:190. Leon Waldoff also quotes this phrase in "The Father-Son Conflict in *Prometheus Unbound*: The Psychology of a Vision," *Psychoanalytic Review* 62 (1975): 79–96. Opinions on the affinities of Freud and Shelley differ: Nathaniel Brown calls them "superficial at best" in *Sexuality and Feminism in Shelley* (Cambridge: Harvard University Press, 1979), 42, while Kenneth Neill Cameron claims that Shelley's ideas about sexual psychology anticipate Freud in several respects, in *SHC* 2:612.

[14] John T. Irwin, *Doubling and Incest/Repetition and Revenge: A Speculative Reading of Faulkner* (Baltimore: Johns Hopkins University Press, 1975), 92.

sents "the great Father's will" (1.354) in *Prometheus Unbound* because he personifies Prometheus' guilty projection of the father's retributive violence. Prometheus reconfirms Jupiter's power with every refusal to internalize and confront his own Oedipal aggressions. As the reflex of that refusal, the punishment of Prometheus brings back the castration anxieties attendant on filial rebellion. Since devouring his sons is the mythic patriarch's preferred way of nullifying the sexual threat they pose, Prometheus undergoes "a symbolic castration"[15] whenever Jove's eagle devours his heart.

Outlined against a myth of libidinal energies crippled by guilt, Shelley's exploration of eros joins *Oedipus the King, Hamlet,* and *The Brothers Karamazov* in disclosing the archetypal dangers besetting father and son. For Shelley, as his choice of Prometheus implies, these dangers are inherent in social organization. The Promethean story mythologized the origins of human culture, as Asia's account of Prometheus insists (2.4.59–99), implicating civilization in Oedipal discontent. The most impressive analogues of *Prometheus Unbound*, consequently, may be the cultural meditations of Freud's last years. Both Freudian and Shelleyan myth depict civilization beginning with sexual guilt and instinctual renunciation. In *Totem and Taboo* sons organize to contest the primal father's monopolizing of women, successfully kill him, and find themselves wracked by guilt, which they appease "by resigning their claim to the women who had now been set free."[16] This appeasement signifies a concession to the love intermixed with filial hatred of the father. The ambivalence of Freudian identification clarifies the Titan's psychic dissociation into his passive (Promethean) and aggressive (Jupiterean) personae. Ambivalent identification explains why that division confirms rather than dissipates his guilt, since it signifies the very form taken *by* his guilt.

Freud's notion of belated remorse also explains why Prometheus' banishment from Asia happens *after* Saturn is overthrown. The socializing role of guilt accounts similarly for the metamorphoses of the mother in *Prometheus Unbound.* Guilt socializes by mandating displacements, easing Oedipal intensities by distributing the maternal icon among mutually associated female figures. With *Prometheus Unbound* these redistributions begin with Shelley's elevation of Earth over Thetis as his hero's nominal mother. This mythographic transference can seem to enhance the Oedipal aspects of Prometheus' insurrection against Saturn. Saturn's traditional consort is Ops, a harvest deity associated with Rhea, herself a nature goddess "hardly distinguishable

---

[15] Waldoff, "Father-Son Conflict," 85.
[16] Freud, *Totem and Taboo, SEF* 13:143.

from Ge (the Earth)."[17] Shelley's text rechannels Promethean desire
for Earth into Jupiter's will to power, his real and prospective domin-
ion over "this Earth / Made multitudinous with [his] slaves" (1.4–5).
But the poem also refashions Promethean Oedipalism as the Titan's
desire for Asia as the earthly Spirit's "Mother, dearest Mother"
(3.4.24). Asia's generative presence, which fosters growth in the nat-
ural world, associates her with Shelley's maternal Earth, and "in most
genealogies of the Titans, Asia is not Prometheus' wife but his
mother."[18] Since Jupiter anticipates his child's momentary birth
(3.1.46–50), even Thetis has apparently reached the term of her
pregnancy, appearing as a figure of ghostly, liminal motherhood
forestalled by Jupiter's blighting proximity.

The mother's metamorphoses signify the problem of *Prometheus
Unbound*—broadening and confirming the text's Oedipal pattern-
ing—while also harboring a solution, for they establish the possibility
of sublimation, of displacing erotic attachments into surrogate forms
and nonviolent registers. The renovation of human sexuality in *Pro-
metheus Unbound* depends on libidinal displacements that are the psy-
chic correlatives of metaphor. Patriarchal violence is metaphor gone
wrong, the wrenching of all vehicles to a single tenor, a single signi-
fied. The liberation of Prometheus from the fixating guilt of act 1
presupposes a reconstitution of metaphor, a reconnection of self and
antitype as complementary. The Titan's quest is to rewrite family ro-
mance by metaphorically assimilating mutual surrogates into the re-
deemed family of act 3. In its inclusive harmony the familial love of
Prometheus Unbound 3 is a social analogue of the reconstellated Andro-
gyne of Plato's *Symposium*. In the "androgynous union" of Asia and
Prometheus, Ross Woodman notes, "Shelley finds his ultimate image
of the One," and "the archetype of [the poem's] social, moral and
political revolution."[19] And the poem stages the Titan's union, as de
Man has written in another context, "as a substitutive movement in
which self and other constantly exchange their identity, as if they
were a single androgynous being whose identity could not be de-
ranged by the internal transfers of attributes."[20] Love begins in *Pro-*

[17] Sir Paul Harvey, *The Oxford Companion to Classical Literature*, rev. ed. (1937; reprint,
Oxford: Oxford University Press, 1984), 363.

[18] Stuart Curran, *Shelley's Annus Mirabilis: The Maturing of an Epic Vision* (San Marino:
Huntington Library, 1975), 45. Ross Woodman remarks that "the suggestion that the
Earth is Asia's veil which can, at least momentarily, be lifted to reveal their identity
makes Asia both wife and mother," in "The Androgyne in *Prometheus Unbound*," *SIR*
20 (1981): 245 n. 16.

[19] Woodman, "Androgyne," 236, 225.

[20] Paul de Man, *Allegories of Reading: Figural Language in Rousseau, Nietzsche, Rilke,*

metheus Unbound with the Oedipal matrices of tragic myth but moves to metaphor as the agency of erotic renewal.

METAPHOR AND METAMORPHOSIS

Shelley's idealization of metaphor in *Prometheus Unbound* presumes its metamorphic power. He envisions the "dialectics of likeness and difference"[21] fundamental to metaphorical constructs as a self-differing potential by which metaphor can displace its identity (without loss) through surrogate forms. *Prometheus Unbound* stages these displacements as an allegorizing of metaphor but locates allegory, as the language of difference, *within* the compass of metaphor's tropical emanations. The allegorizing of metaphor operates as a figural corollary of the poem's self-recuperating cycle of coherence and collapse.[22] Oscillating between self and other, similitude and difference, Shelley's rhetoric of Romantic love begins with desire's thirst for "its likeness" ("On Love," 473). Since love's object is unrealized, and love's fulfillment prospective, Shelleyan desire extends metaphor into prolepsis. When the effort to realize desire quickly exhausts image after successor-image—in typically Shelleyan fashion—we see metaphor succumbing to metonymy, dispersing "likeness" through progressively unlike appositives. When difference achieves antithesis—when joyful eyes "burn through smiles that fade in tears" (2.1.28)—Shelley's figural sequence reaches its apogee and yields to the gravitational pull of metalepsis, returning to the unassuaged desire from which the language of love originates. This rhetorical dynamic is empowered by chiasmus. Shelley treats allegory as a figure of the difference latent in metaphor. The metamorphoses of metaphor involve its oscillation between antithetical phases conceived as each other's transposed (chiasmal) complement: metaphor enters the allegorical modality by

---

and Proust (New Haven: Yale University Press, 1979), 212. De Man is describing the relationship of Julie and St. Preux in *La Nouvelle Héloïse*.

[21] Paul Fry, *The Reach of Criticism* (New Haven: Yale University Press, 1983), 163.

[22] For the mutually recuperative circlings of actuality and potentiality in Shelley, see Daniel J. Hughes's comment that Shelleyan epiphanies are organized "as a series of fading coals leading to an over-all structure which, like the phoenix, rises from its ashes," in "Coherence and Collapse in Shelley, with Particular Reference to *Epipsychidion*," *ELH* 28 (1961): 262; Hughes, "Potentiality," 604–5, 618–20; and William Keach, *Shelley's Style* (London: Methuen, 1984), 79–80, for Shelleyan reflexive imagery as illustrating "an act of mind in which something is perceived as both . . . itself and something other than itself," and in which "the signifying function of a phrase or clause turns back on itself, and its doing so marks an 'operation of the human mind' that couples analysis or division (as an aspect is separated from the idea to which it belongs) with synthesis or reunion (as the separated or divided aspect is re-identified with that same idea)."

turning itself inside out and, as a reflex of that reversal, is then re-reversed.

This figural patterning recurs in the imagery and structure of *Prometheus Unbound*. Shelley's triumph of love starts with metaphorical coincidence, proceeds as metaphor liberates its allegorical counter-potential, and ends in allegory—allegory not as ungrounded errancy but (again) as a metaphorically grounded energy. Some of the enigmas of act 1 resolve themselves as soon as we understand its concentration on metaphor. Why must the curse be repeated? Why must the phantasm of Jupiter be called to reproclaim it? The curse presents love's lapsing as a problem of language, yet that hardly explains such elaborate machinery.[23] To grasp the rhetorical logic of act 1 we must note what Prometheus' imprecation presupposes. Shelley needs the curse because the curse itself requires (and allows) a ghostly speaker, requiring in turn a world of the dead as a dramatic postulate making Jupiter's ghost possible. From the opening scene Shelley's interest in metaphor commits his poem to a myth of two worlds:[24]

> —Ere Babylon was dust,
> The Magus Zoroaster, my dead child,
> Met his own image walking in the garden.
> That apparition, sole of men, he saw.
> For know, there are two worlds of life and death:
> One that which thou beholdest, but the other
> Is underneath the grave, where do inhabit
> The shadows of all forms that think and live
> Till death unite them, and they part no more;
> Dreams and the light imaginings of men
> And all that faith creates, or love desires,
> Terrible, strange, sublime and beauteous shapes.
>
> (1.191–202)

As a matrix of potentiality, this spectral realm is as crucial for repetition of the curse, and so for the role Shelley assigns language, as the concept of the unconscious is necessary for the return of the re-

[23] For language in *Prometheus Unbound*, consult the treatments of "voice" in Angela Leighton, *Shelley and the Sublime: An Interpretation of the Major Poems* (Cambridge: Cambridge University Press, 1984), 73–100, and Susan Hawk Brisman, " 'Unsaying His High Language': The Problem of Voice in *Prometheus Unbound*," *SIR* 16 (1977): 51–86; for the language of the dead, see Norman Thurston, "The Second Language of *Prometheus Unbound*," *PQ* 55 (1976): 126–33.

[24] P.M.S. Dawson offers an especially detailed explanation of why the poem's various subterranean settings are actually diverse perspectives on the same place, and why there are thus only two worlds, in *The Unacknowledged Legislator: Shelley and Politics* (Oxford: Clarendon Press, 1980), 126.

pressed. Yet Earth stresses similitude in describing the relationship of these two worlds. They are each other's antitypical reflection. Shelley's shadow-world stands to the life-world as spirit to letter when "spirit" signifies vacuity requiring completion through embodiment. Love's loss has re-created the poem's mythic cosmos as a broken metaphor.

As love's champion, Prometheus confronts a challenge described most succinctly in the two cancelled lines of the epigraph to this chapter: "For know there are two worlds of life and death: / Which thou henceforth art doomed to interweave."[25] *Prometheus Unbound* pursues that interweaving by conjuring up Jupiter's phantasm. The ensuing encounter stages a triumph of metaphor when the specular dialectic of self and other defers to the Titan's identification with his dark double. "Neither the eye nor the mind can see itself," Shelley declared in the *Defence of Poetry*, "unless reflected upon that which it resembles" (491). Nor, of course, can love be vitalized except through the self's discovery of its likeness to an anti-image. What we witness at the beginning of act 1 are the first stirrings of a reconstitution of desire by metaphor. In the *Defence of Poetry*, Shelley lamented the ossification of "vitally metaphorical" language marking "the before unapprehended relations of things" into codified signs fixed in their abstractness (482). Seen in this light, the language of the dead is simply dead language, and the curse, unpronounceable until death intrudes into life, a rhetoric of hatred responsible for affixing Prometheus to the unliving summit of his mountain. The Titan's plight illustrates an instance when, as Hogle argues, "the socialized psyche must . . . be forced back into the shifting depths of metaphor from which it came, else the same mind will fabricate ways to enchain itself."[26]

So Jupiter's repetition of the curse prompts the regeneration of desire in *Prometheus Unbound* because the repetition tropes the return of metaphor. Epitomizing metaphor-in-action, it forges a connection between "before unapprehended" realms, invoking the resemblance of disparate beings and worlds. The curse scene provides Shelley a node of metaphoric coincidence in which shadow and substance, the visage and voice of Jupiter and the utterance of Prometheus, achieve dramatic unification. Shelley underscores the resulting catharsis of hatred, moreover, by transferring the language of hate to Jupiter's ghostly surrogate. For by this transfer hatred is made to curse itself, and responsibility for the Olympian tyrant's fall is seemingly dis-

[25] Cited from *Shelley's "Prometheus Unbound": A Variorum Edition*, ed. Lawrence John Zillman (Seattle: University of Washington Press, 1959), 143.
[26] Jerrold E. Hogle, "Shelley's Poetics: The Power as Metaphor," *KSJ* 31 (1982): 185.

placed, as an effect of morally vitalizing resemblance, from Prome-
theus to Jupiter.

The rest of act 1 is also metaphorically organized. Mercury can
function as mediator between the main antagonists because in his role
as psychopomp he connects riven worlds and because he is tradition-
ally associated with language, Shelley's mediating agency. The Furies
are obviously specular phenomena. "So from our victim's destined
agony," one confesses, "The shade which is our form invests us
round, / Else are we as shapeless as our Mother Night" (1.470–72).
"Whilst I behold such execrable shapes," Prometheus exclaims, "Me-
thinks I grow like what I contemplate / And laugh and stare in loath-
some sympathy" (1.449–51). The consoling Spirits that follow also
represent specular powers because they "do not merely replace the
Furies—they *are* the Furies in another form."[27] When they too vanish,
Panthea takes over. Panthea is the "shadow" of Asia (2.1.70), her re-
flection in a lower, sensuous register,[28] and the "shadow" of Prome-
theus as the soul of Asia's life (2.1.31). Panthea is the shadow-point
at which Asia and Prometheus coincide emotionally, the latent con-
nection between them.

This connection enables Panthea's intercession, so that *"Prometheus
Unbound* moves from its masculine first act to its feminine second act
in terms of a highly characteristic Shelleyan *desire*"[29]—characteristic,
that is, in its metaphorical structure. Through Panthea's journey to
the scene of Asia's exile, the triumphs of act 1 engender in act 2 their
own antitypical fulfillment. Shelley stages this carrying-across as a
transference of dreams. Panthea arrives at Asia's vale as the bearer of
two dreams, the first a dream she remembers and relates, the second
a dream she has forgotten, which Asia eventually reconfigures. As
with the phantom of Jupiter, these dreams represent intrusions of
potentiality into life, or of the unconscious into consciousness. The
mediations they effect are again linguistic: "Lift up thine eyes," Asia
tells Panthea, "And let me read thy dream" (2.1.55–56). The sisters'
dream-reading—as each ponders the mirror of the other's eyes—cre-
ates a specular encounter in which words permit psychic coincidence.
Asia reads Panthea's dream by immersing herself in her sister's con-
sciousness. What ensues is the interpenetration of a diviner nature
through Panthea, what William H. Hildebrand calls an "intersubjec-

[27] Dawson, *Unacknowledged Legislator*, 115–16.

[28] As Curran observes, *Shelley's Annus Mirabilis*, 47–49.

[29] Daniel J. Hughes, "Prometheus Made Capable Poet in Act One of *Prometheus Un-
bound*," *SIR* 17 (1978): 11.

tive . . . meeting of presences in and through the formulative agency of the symbol."[30]

Panthea initiates this sharing through dream one, a vision of Prometheus erotically transfigured. Her responsiveness to love now stimulated, Asia tells Panthea, "oh, lift / Thine eyes that I may read his written soul," to which Panthea replies, "what canst thou see / But thine own fairest shadow imaged there?" (2.1.109–10, 112–13). The shadow connecting Prometheus and Asia bursts into actuality as a grey and golden "shape," the body of the signifier running off and crying, "Follow, follow!" (2.1.131). Reciprocal exchanges follow, beginning with Panthea's identification of the shape as her "other dream." At that point "It disappears" from Asia's mind, oscillating rapidly to Panthea, who reclaims it with self-consciousness sufficient for the narration of its content. To Panthea's dream-story, Asia replies,

> As you speak, your words
> Fill, pause by pause my own forgotten sleep
> With shapes.

(2.1.141–43)

Asia's memories identify the Oceanides' dreams as vectors converging on a single point: Panthea's vision of the words "*O follow, follow!*"; Asia's vision of the words "*O follow, follow, follow me!*" (2.1.141, 159). The final dream is a single shared dream. Reconstructing it together, the sisters discover the resemblance of their emotional lives.

From this achievement eros sweeps through the dull, dense world of *Prometheus Unbound*, compelling all new successions to its own metaphorical form. Asia passes the duplicative power on to Demogorgon, a specular oracle who answers questions by converting them, reflexively, "into the answers that the terms of the questions already assumed before the answers were given."[31] Demogorgon overthrows Jupiter, creating a harmony apparent in the urbane gossip of Apollo and Oceanus (intimating a reconciliation of Titanic and Olympian regimes), in the newfound freedoms of human society, and finally in Shelley's cosmic apotheosis. This "unity without produced by a series

---

[30] William H. Hildebrand, "Naming Day in Asia's Vale," *KSJ* 32 (1983): 196–97. My understanding of these scenes relies on Tilottama Rajan's "Deconstruction or Reconstruction: Reading Shelley's *Prometheus Unbound*," *SIR* 23 (1984): 317–38.

[31] Hogle, *Shelley's Process*, 189. Frederick Pottle similarly remarks that Demogorgon answers Asia only "in her own terminology and at the level of her own understanding," in "The Role of Asia in the Dramatic Action of Shelley's *Prometheus Unbound*," in *Shelley: A Collection of Critical Essays*, ed. George M. Ridenour (Englewood Cliffs, N.J.: Prentice-Hall, 1965), 138.

of unities within"[32] everywhere organizes the Promethean apoca-
lypse. Triggered by the command "Unite!" events occur as variations
on the Titans' weaving of "harmonies divine, yet ever new, / From
difference sweet where discord cannot be" (4.80; 3.3.38–39). The
world's visual emblem is unifying reflection—the "Heaven-reflecting
sea," the "lovely forms" of paired, berry-eating halcyons "imaged [in
water] as in a sky," the Promethean temple mirrored on the "un-
erasing waves" of a bordering pool (3.2.18; 3.4.83; 3.3.160). This
world's emotional principle is the desire by which "a lover or chame-
leon / Grows like what it looks upon" (4.483–84). Of course, the met-
aphorical chain reactions of *Prometheus Unbound* occur as interrelated
vehicles of the Titans' marriage as causal tenor. Even Shelley's danc-
ing Earth and Moon merely "enact a macrocosmic and hermetic anal-
ogy to the union of Titan and nymph."[33]

Yet these concentric analogies release complementary allegorical
energies. The poem's narrative carries metaphor into an allegorical
register most clearly with Shelley's turn to Demogorgon. If "Demo-
gorgon's mighty law" (2.2.43) shows a resurgence of metaphor, that
arises as a subsequent complication, for we meet Demogorgon as met-
aphor's disfiguration, as allegory incarnate. He briefly serves Asia as
the glass in which she sees herself darkly, but he refuses to enter the
fire-inlaid chariot she drives to Prometheus. He goes a different way,
driving to the difference beyond harmony dramatized in his battle
with Jupiter. Rhetorically, Demogorgon signifies catachresis as alle-
gorical errancy concentrated explosively in a single figure. Entering
mythological tradition through the scribal miscopying of "demiurge,"
he inescapably connotes the disfiguration of creative order by sheer
randomness. Despite his oracular solemnity, Demogorgon deflects
questions and withholds truths when we first meet him, acting as an-
titruth, antiform, a black hole into which certainties vanish amid im-
agelessness.

With allegory comes temporality. To all appearances, Demogor-
gon's advent corroborates de Man's contention that "the prevalence
of allegory always corresponds to the unveiling of an authentically
temporal destiny."[34] The risen world of *Prometheus Unbound* affirms a
transferential deferral of presence, unbinding energies inimical to

[32] Hogle, "Shelley's Poetics," 182.

[33] Harold Bloom, *Shelley's Mythmaking* (1959; reprint, Ithaca: Cornell University
Press, 1969), 139. The flowering of the moon also makes her into an image of the
earth. James B. Twitchell notices Shelley's assumption "that inner and outer, psyche
and cosmos, can work in harmonious metaphor" in "Shelley's Metapsychological Sys-
tem in Act IV of *Prometheus Unbound*," *KSJ* 23 (1974): 32.

[34] De Man, "Rhetoric," 206.

constraint or closure. These energies wield "the force of self-destroy-
ing swiftness" (4.249) because their own trailing off into oblivion re-
energizes their swiftness. They create a cosmos utterly committed to
"Haste, oh haste," where words outspeed "the blast; / While 'tis said,
they are fled," where reborn natural elements are driven "By the
Storm of delight, by the panic of glee," and where the two chief cel-
ebrants are surrounded by the moon's "ebbing light" and spheres
whirling "Over each other with a thousand motions" (4.21, 36–37, 44,
208, 247). The defeat of Jupiter, "the King of Hours" (4.20), merely
frees life from the burden of the past, for the passage of his funeral
procession—comprising "dead Hours" and "many a cancelled year"
(4.13, 11)—leaves fresh Hours present to sing in chorus with the
"Spirits of the human mind" (4.81). This "mystic measure" (4.77) em-
phasizes temporalized harmony. However "Ceaseless and rapid and
fierce and free," the poem's depiction of time forces "Chaos" to "flee"
from the mind's approach, leaving a universe where "Love rules,
through waves which dare not overwhelm, / Forcing life's wildest
shores to own its sovereign sway" (4.163, 144–46, 410–11).

Love's assimilation of oceanic flux to "its sovereign sway" reimposes
a metaphorical rule. Temporal harmonies arise due to Shelley's sense
of metaphor and allegory as cooperative and complementary—arcs
of the metamorphic cycle discussed earlier. The Promethean apoca-
lypse presupposes the ability of metaphor to marry even "eternity
and change," a power the *Defence of Poetry* specifically claims for imag-
ination (505). Demogorgon assures Asia, "Fate, Time, Occasion,
Chance and Change? To these / All things are subject but eternal
Love" (2.4.119–20). Just so, Asia's apotheosis as Love forestalls tem-
poral process, as the Spirit of the Hour observes:

> The sun will rise not until noon.—Apollo
> Is held in Heaven by wonder—and the light
> Which fills this vapour, as the aerial hue
> Of fountain-gazing roses fills the water,
> Flows from thy mighty sister.
>
> (2.5.10–14)

Prometheus Unbound suspends time as a wedding gift to its reunited
spouses.[35] The poem by no means denies temporality or death: Pro-

---

[35] Shelley borrows this motif from the reunion of Odysseus and Penelope: for the
hero's homecoming Athena "slowed the night / when night was most profound, and
held the Dawn," so that the lovers might go "into that bed so steadfast, loved of old, /
opening glad arms to one another" (*Odyssey* 23.246–47, 299–300). The resurgence of
metaphor promotes eternality because, for Shelley, "time is merely the variable rela-
tionships made possible by the fracturing of unity into diversity" (Wasserman, *Shelley*,

metheus' query, "What can hide man from Mutability?" (3.3.25), is
purely rhetorical. Instead Shelley correlates time and eternity as vari-
ant forms of one another, staging an apocalypse that reconciles pro-
cess and stasis as tenor and vehicle of an egalitarian unity. Since act 4
is metaphorically constituted as the cosmic reflex of a timeless Titanic
lovemaking, Shelley's great wheel of time revolves around a still cen-
ter that anchors becoming in being as tenor anchors vehicle in truth.
For all its affirmation of process, *Prometheus Unbound* concedes the
priority of the eternal. No other point so clearly betrays the willed
idealism of Shelley's figural dialectic. In moving from the Oedipal
impasse of the poem's beginning to its valorization of metaphor, we
have moved from the initial problem to its apparent solution. We
must now attend to the problem of the solution.

PLOTTING HISTORY

Shelley's faith in the complementary interaction of allegory and met-
aphor idealizes power's self-concealment. Since these figural orders
trade places within a substitutive economy weighted toward meta-
phorical unity, they are not equal partners. If Shelley cannot dispel
the subversive power of allegorical deferrals, he can minimize it by
presenting metaphor as the source of his drama's values. Allegory
undermines without nullifying. It unveils the inner fractures of Shel-
leyan idealism without transforming it into unrecognizable otherness.
A transformation of that kind would signify allegory's transcendence
of relation, so that the liberation of allegory from vestigial metaphor-
ical ties would occur only as it became impossible to speak of allego-
ry's liberation *from* anything that was not an aspect of itself—which
immediately returns the question to metaphorical criteria of correla-
tion, self-reflexivity, and identity. Allegory's implication of metaphor
gives misrepresentation an opening. And *Prometheus Unbound* seizes
this opportunity by systematically occluding the temporal force of al-
legory. Since allegorizing remains the figural strategy of philosophi-
cal anarchism, Shelley's equivocal treatment of allegory results in po-
litical contradictions throughout acts 3 and 4. Incongruities skew the
poem's representation of the historical process as well. These latter
contradictions point to the enchaining of time in Shelley's drama.
   The metaphorical idealism of *Prometheus Unbound* promotes a spu-
rious temporalizing of value. When Shelley presents the erotic double
as antitype, or other, he empowers chiasmus as the source of energy
and change. Activated by a visually reversed image, Shelleyan desire

359). For the time scheme of *Prometheus Unbound*, see Carlos Baker, *Shelley's Major Po-
etry: The Fabric of a Vision* (Princeton: Princeton University Press, 1948), 108 n. 44.

seeks a transposition of self into other, a cross-substitution of terms modelled on chiasmus as the figure of mirroring in its reversible symmetry.[36] In *Prometheus Unbound* the poetics of history are similarly structured because the poem envisions desire as the motive force of political renewal. Unfortunately, Shelley's chiasmal model falters in explaining temporality. It accounts for time by once more dividing presence into potentiality and actuality. The result is a cyclical alternation in which any phase exhausts itself, like a Yeatsian gyre, only by evoking its opposite. So conceived, temporal difference arises solely within the presupposition of a metaphorical total form. Metaphorically controlled, Shelleyan chiasmus submits identity to otherness—to allegory as the trope of temporal difference—only after restricting allegory to an intermediate position within metaphor's dialectical emanation away from and back to itself. *Prometheus Unbound* elides real temporality by dramatizing the oscillations of the Same between obverse forms of itself. Shelley can thereby idealize changefulness as liberated energy without having to account for attrition, destruction, or loss. The metamorphic pattern of Shelleyan rhetoric, with chiasmus as the trope triggering reversal, makes time a derivative epiphenomenon.

Shelley's equivocal treatment of time and history in *Prometheus Unbound* explains the dual role given Demogorgon. Fry notes the "doubleness" of time in Shelley's poetics: in the *Defence of Poetry* "the single word, *Time*, indicates eternity in some places and temporality in others."[37] *Prometheus Unbound* illustrates this doubleness almost definitively when Demogorgon, who denominates himself "Eternity," also declares himself to be Jupiter's "child" (3.1.52, 54). The paradox can be explained, but leaves a certain awkwardness in "that Demogorgon, previously an abstract force outside time, now becomes historically specified: he becomes a revolutionary power within the world of time, liable to be consumed by the future as he has consumed the past."[38] Demogorgon personifies historically located political changes. The "spells" he gives humankind to prevent despotism's reawakening—strung-together abstractions like "Gentleness, Virtue, Wisdom," "Life, Joy, Empire and Victory" (4.562, 578)—are variations on the "sacred watchwords" of the French Revolution, "Truth, liberty, and

[36] Chiasmus frames objects "in such a way as to allow a reversal of their categorical properties, and this reversal enables the reader to conceive of properties that would normally be incompatible . . . as complementary" (de Man, *Allegories*, 40). These remarks are pertinent to Shelley's poetics precisely because, as de Man remarks on the same page, "a particularly clear and concrete instance of such a structural reversal would be, for example, the specular reflection."

[37] Fry, *Reach of Criticism*, 159.

[38] Rajan, "Deconstruction," 319.

love!" (1.648, 651). Yet Demogorgon also embodies an atemporal Ultimate. His identity as "Eternity is necessary if the Promethean resolution is to have some kind of transcendental guarantee and not to be a purely local event."[39] Demogorgon allows Shelley to idealize history—that "record of crimes & miseries" (*Letters* 1:340)—by rooting temporal contingency in immutable truth, in "the eternal, the infinite, and the one" (*Defence of Poetry*, 483).

These last realities enter time through the imagination: higher power shapes the lower realm through the mediating activity of "vitally metaphorical" creativity as "the principle of synthesis" (*Defence of Poetry*, 482, 480). *Prometheus Unbound* assumes a phenomenology of time. "Time is our consciousness of the succession of ideas in our mind," Shelley stated in the notes to *Queen Mab*, adding that "If, therefore, the human mind, by any future improvement of its sensibility, should become conscious of an infinite number of ideas in a minute, that minute would be eternity" (*CW* 1:156–57). Since "nothing exists but as it is perceived" ("On Life," 476), an utter plenitude of consciousness would reconstitute the phenomenal world as an eternal moment. As a reintegration of sundered psychic complements, the reunion of Prometheus and Asia symbolizes just such eternity—timelessness as a figure of love, of mind and hours singing in unison. Properly understood, allegory argues that "the now cannot be produced except out of its relation to the non-now," so that "the present is primordially divided by the *retentional trace*."[40] By metaphorically binding allegory, Shelley's act 4 can appropriate the theocentric images of cosmic music and the circle of perfection for a retuning of the skies that makes the "infinite sphere . . . nothing now but the field encompassed by human consciousness."[41] In this humanistic apocalypse the revolving energies of act 4 mark time's effort to stand still by going fast enough. Shelley agnostically reconfigures "the Platonic or Christian idea of time as a succession of nows grounded in the stasis and infinite eternity of a God to whom all times are co-present."[42] And his elision of temporality-as-loss rests on an ontological privileging of mind and spirit.

[39] Rajan, "Deconstruction," 320. Bloom claims, similarly, that "Demogorgon, the dialectic of history, rises from the abyss and *stops* history," in "The Internalization of Quest-Romance," in *Romanticism and Consciousness: Essays in Criticism*, ed. Harold Bloom (New York: Norton, 1979), 22, emphasis added.

[40] John Brenkman, "Narcissus in the Text," *Georgia Review* 30 (1976): 319.

[41] Georges Poulet, *The Metamorphoses of the Circle*, trans. Carley Dawson and Elliott Coleman in collaboration with the author (Baltimore: Johns Hopkins University Press, 1966), xxvii.

[42] J. Hillis Miller, "Georges Poulet's 'Criticism of Identification,' " in *The Quest for Imagination*, ed. O. B. Hardison, Jr. (Cleveland: Press of Case Western Reserve University, 1971), 215.

The derivation of time from consciousness recurs in the political drama of *Prometheus Unbound* as the derivation of revolutionary change from the individual will. However unacknowledged its legislations, the mind makes history happen. Prometheus' turn to pity, and then to Asia, extends an antecedent psychic renovation into the sphere of public events and deposes Jupiter. This narrative serves as Shelley's metaphorical plot of history—metaphorical in that it conceives causality as the transmission of resemblance, the form and consequence of metaphor carrying inner to outer. This plotting of history reflects Shelley's sense of "the necessity for a mental and moral revolution in the people as a prelude to any political change," his conviction that "it was no use regenerating the institutions of society until man had regenerated himself."[43] The poem's notion of social renovation again relies on Godwinian gradualism, a model that explains reform as the ripple effect of mental enlightenment. While Shelley recognized the necessary priority of institutional to personal change in some political situations,[44] the affective aspirations of *Prometheus Unbound*, its effort to influence its readership, presupposed the causal power of the will. Critics defer to Shelley's myth of internalized and individualized power whenever they refer Jupiter's deposition to the Titan's spiritual purification.

But the action of *Prometheus Unbound* cannot be psychologically circumscribed. Readings of the poem as an inclusive allegory of consciousness balk at Demogorgon, "who stands ultimately outside the mental action of the drama,"[45] but leave Prometheus' self-renewal equally mysterious. If, Stuart M. Sperry asks,

Shelley intended his first act to dramatize man's powers of self-regeneration through inward recognition, repentance, and reform, why did he do his work so badly? Granted that the act describes the hero's change of heart, from hatred toward love, why is that movement so halting and

[43] Dawson, *Unacknowledged Legislator*, 66; Timothy Webb, *Shelley: A Voice Not Understood* (Atlantic Highlands, N.J.: Humanities Press, 1977), 121.

[44] Harry White, in "Relative Means and Ends in Shelley's Social-Political Thought," *SEL* 22 (1982): 613–31, argues for the realistic flexibility of Shelley's political views, which accepted violence as a necessary cause or accompaniment of change in certain circumstances, and which often noted the need for reforming social institutions *before* individual moral improvement could ensue. The implication is that apparent contradictions in Shelley's politics merely reflect the different contexts in which he judges political events and values. Unfortunately, the careful discriminations between historical situations and their political possibilities formulated in Shelley's prose break down in his poetry. *Prometheus Unbound*, for instance, combines Prometheus' moral self-renovation with Jupiter's violent deposition. We cannot absolve Shelley's poems of such ideological contradictions by appealing to distinctions drawn in his prose.

[45] Ross Woodman, *The Apocalyptic Vision in the Poetry of Shelley* (Toronto: University of Toronto Press, 1964), 108.

unfocused? . . . Why is that process so spasmodic and inscrutable? Why does it not more fully illuminate the grounds for change within Prometheus himself?[46]

Sperry's answer is that the grounds of change lie not with Prometheus but with necessity: "Prometheus is not the instigator of his own transformation but rather the first manifestation of a larger change working throughout the entire universe."[47] The historical action of *Prometheus Unbound* features an allegorical counterplot that exchanges love for Demogorgon's violence.[48] Demogorgon figures history as necessity, an incompletely comprehensible process unresponsive to the individual will and allegorical in its decentered interrelation of contending forces. The interaction of will and necessity in *Prometheus Unbound* offers alternative historical explanations. As with the play's rhetorical thematics, the metaphorical and allegorical plots of history are presented as complementary aspects of a continuous truth. Shelley's metaphorical idealism envisions their congruence "by suggesting a universal necessity that can fulfill itself only with the cooperation of the human will and spirit."[49]

Sperry's reading shows how tenuous the internalization of causality becomes in *Prometheus Unbound*. But Shelley's allegorical plot remains subordinated to its metaphorical obverse despite the dubieties of the Titan's change of heart. The two plots of history diverge when Asia and Demogorgon take separate chariots to apocalypse. Yet their difference, merely *as* difference, both signifies "the ineluctable priority of allegorical discourse"[50] and permits allegory's displacement by the thematic and dramatic emphases of Shelley's play. Act 1 marginalizes the operation of necessity through its dramatic focus, which centers on the causal efficacy of metaphorical agents and scenes. When the timing of events links Promethean catharsis with Jupiter's downfall, the poem actively encourages inferences of causal connection. In retrospect, those inferences may appear simplistic, but they are just reactions to the suggestive power of Shelley's unfolding action. We read responsively, rather than err, in construing the motivational force that dramatic context lends Prometheus' introspective triumph. The

[46] Sperry, *Shelley's Major Verse*, 76.

[47] Sperry, *Shelley's Major Verse*, 78.

[48] For the idea of two historical plots in Shelley's poem, see John Rieder, "The 'One' in *Prometheus Unbound*," *SEL* 25 (1985): 775–800. I am greatly indebted to this article, but regard the individualist interpretation of *Prometheus Unbound*, which Rieder attributes to a tradition of critical misreading, as a legitimate reading of the poem's prevailing if conflicted self-presentation.

[49] Sperry, *Shelley's Major Verse*, 95.

[50] Christensen, "Symbol's Errant Allegory," 643.

poet's refusal to dramatize the growth of forgiveness in Prometheus alters nothing. Shelley merely dissociates forgiveness from the antecedent stages of its growth to insist on it as a dramatic *moment*, an epiphanic now, and to reclaim love-as-miracle for a myth of presence.

This causal myth erases historical conflict and contingency by conceiving "change as the pre-given substitute of one steady-state for another."[51] The respect Shelley deserves for his political commitments cannot absolve his poem from the charge that "its central absence is the concept of revolution and of the figuration of any sort of human activity."[52] The banishment of time in *Prometheus Unbound* finds its clearest illustration in the text's inability to represent history as a materialist or class dialectic. Shelley's individualist conception of political change, from the viewpoint of socialist theory, merely reifies power's self-representations. It evokes the timeless vistas of myth to reformulate bourgeois ideology. Prometheus' repentance reconstitutes him as Nietzsche's ethical man, a good citizen capable of promising because he can remember, an individual who, believing himself the origin of his actions, opens himself to the contractual exploitations of an industrial state. "The crux of this individualism," as Rieder comments, "is its atomization and disintegration of class, economic, and political relations into psychological and moral perspectives, with the result that class, economic, and political structures are reified into the Nature within which human nature enjoys its freedom," codified as intrinsic rights and internalized identity.[53] This individualist ethos is basic to Shelley's visionary humanism. The allegorical plot of *Prometheus Unbound* exposes the contradictions of Promethean myth, the conservative ties of Shelleyan idealism, without ceding that myth to historical becoming. Shelley's deepest emotional sympathies inhabit the cave of Prometheus and Asia. It is another "still cave of the witch Poesy" ("Mont Blanc," l. 44), a privileged interiority where imagination's rule allows lovers to say, "ourselves unchanged" (3.3.24).

POLITICAL IRONIES

The poem's transcendent longings follow from its inability to reconcile its two historical plots. This inability refers to Shelley's under-

---

[51] Dana Polan, "The Ruin of a Poetics: The Political Practice of *Prometheus Unbound*," *Enclitic* 7 (1983): 39. In *Prometheus Unbound* "the diachronic vanishes as the play becomes a veritable monologic and synchronic unveiling of one moment of discourse after another," so that "the text can have no real conception of change, of history" (Polan, 38).

[52] Polan, "Ruin," 35.

[53] Rieder, "The 'One,'" 794.

standing and use of language. The fissure in his plotting of history redefines the relation of allegory and metaphor as a contradiction that can be hidden but not resolved. As a result, contradictions suffuse the politics of acts 3 and 4, ironies testifying to the paradox of constitutive repression. The poem's rhetoric belongs to a tradition in which "the effacement of the signifier in speech is a condition of the idea of truth," as Jonathan Culler succinctly puts it, and in which speech supplies writing its model.[54] In *Prometheus Unbound* as in *The Revolt of Islam*, poetic figures negate the material signifier so as to privilege an ideational signified. Whenever metaphor assimilates vehicle to tenor, repressing difference to express meaning, we witness the Laon-like violence of Shelleyan rhetoric. The particular problems of an adversarial rhetoric merely exacerbate this dilemma, hastening the repressed's return. Represent anarchism as the reflex of Jupiter's downfall, as despotism's transposed form, and you make "revolutionary society depend on Jupiter for its identity even in his absence."[55] For it can "be assumed as a maxim that no nation or religion can supersede any other without incorporating into itself a portion of that which it supersedes" (*Defence of Poetry*, 496).

The linguistic basis of political contradiction surfaces in the play's monarchical tropes. Linked to essentialist criteria by divine right, monarchy looks to metaphor as the figure of individualized power, and opposes the necessitarian allegory located, as a historical force, amid the nameless masses. Thus the deposed king returns invisibly as soon as Shelley's circumvention of history marginalizes the people. Shelley enfranchises humankind through power withheld from them by ideologies prejudiced against the populace as a social body. In the radical culture of Shelley's day "it was an unquestioned assumption that the poor were to be represented and led," Scrivener comments, and "this bias is reinforced in Shelley's case by the nature of his idealism, which elevates spirit over the bodily and terrestrial, and eternity over temporality."[56] The uncultured masses are rife with sons of Orc whose restless sexual energies bode ill for order. For Shelley, Demogorgon is indeed Demosgorgon, the people-monster,[57] his fearfulness reflecting Shelley's distrust of the swinish multitude. We owe "the curiously tentative quality of mankind's regeneration" in act 3 to the poem's wary emotional distance from actual people.[58] Shelley's

---

[54] Jonathan Culler, *On Deconstruction: Theory and Criticism after Structuralism* (Ithaca: Cornell University Press, 1982), 108.

[55] Rieder, "The 'One,' " 796.

[56] Scrivener, *Radical Shelley*, 199.

[57] As Paul Foot suggests, in *Red Shelley* (London: Bookmarks, 1984), 194.

[58] Lloyd Abbey, *Destroyer and Preserver: Shelley's Poetic Skepticism* (Lincoln: University of Nebraska Press, 1979), 60.

celebration of Man—"Man, oh, not men!" (4.394)—tellingly shifts from the social populace to an idealized abstraction of human nature. The incongruities of a leveling drama "written only for the elect" (*Letters* 2:200) explain why *Queen Mab*, not *Prometheus Unbound*, became the anthem of the Chartist movement.

The banishment of the masses from Shelley's plot recurs in the rhetoric of *Prometheus Unbound*. Reading the politics of *Prometheus Unbound* becomes an exercise in reading contradiction because Shelley's phrasing recuperates what it resists. His effort to articulate libertarian values obligates him to residually conservative words, in part because of his adversarial stance, in part because "latent in language is a rhetoric which works covertly to secure approval for established social institutions."[59] *Prometheus Unbound* can only advocate the toppling of kings through monarchical diction and elitist conventions. Hence Mother Earth's account of redeemed mankind as

> a chain of linked thought,
> Of love and might to be divided not,
> Compelling the elements with adamantine stress—
> As the Sun rules, even with a tyrant's gaze,
> The unquiet Republic of the maze
> Of Planets, struggling fierce towards Heaven's free wilderness.
>
> (4.394–99)

Shelleyan liberation enchains people by a pairing of "love and might" encoded in the poet's linguistic options, in the traditional associations of "rule" and "tyrant," for example. As metaphors for power, such words both invite and prevent their assimilation to radical tenors. Delineated through conflict, these tenors disclose the "secret sympathy between Destruction and Power, between Monarchy and War" (*A Philosophical View of Reform*, CW 7:53). Due to them, ideological contradiction ramifies through the phrasing of Shelley's poem.

These contradictions are fundamental, despite arguments to the contrary. P.M.S. Dawson has argued that Shelley redeems the language of rule by discriminating between psychological and extrinsic authority, so that his negatives work as a perfectible language celebrating freedoms still unrealized.[60] Yet Shelley's myth of causality—

---

[59] Richard Cronin, *Shelley's Poetic Thoughts* (New York: St. Martin's Press, 1981), 5. Cronin's phrase refers to Bentham's linguistic theory, but he proceeds to make the same point about the politics of language in Shelley. Shelley's recognition that "*words are the very things that so eminently contribute to the growth & establishment of prejudice*" (*Letters*, 1:317) dates from 1812 at the latest.

[60] See Dawson for a defense of Shelley's use of monarchical diction as noncontradictory (*Unacknowledged Legislator*, 88–94, 113–21). Dawson's argument seeks to refute Cronin's account of Shelley's adversarial poetics, which concludes that, "in struggling

his attribution of political renovation to renovations in the consciousness of Asia and Prometheus—presupposes an intimate continuity of psychological and extrinsic orders. Besides, distinctions between inner and outer rule merely divide Shelley's model of authority into obverse complements: each remains a form of rule inherently misplaced in a world of anarchism. Redefinitions of man as

> Sceptreless, free, uncircumscribed—but man:
> Equal, unclassed, tribeless and nationless,
> Exempt from awe, worship, degree,—the King
> Over himself

(3.4.194–97)

can leave relatively little redefined. When the Spirit of the Hour describes millennial harmony "in a manner that evokes the old world that has been destroyed far more vividly [than] it suggests the new," then "the reader, while supposedly being offered a perfect world, is actually experiencing the world as it is."[61] Negative constructions such as "Sceptre*less*" and "*un*classed" conjure up scepters and classes, reconfirming the status quo by inscribing Shelley's apocalypse with the icons it would smash. At best, a phrase like "Sceptreless" looks Janus-faced toward both the monarchical past and the democratic future. It wanders between two worlds as a reflex of the transitional struggles of nineteenth-century politics. It surrenders "Man" to kingship just as the forces of political reaction co-opted revolutionary agendas throughout the Europe of Shelley's day.

When the politics of style reintroduce rule in Shelley's anarchist world, *Prometheus Unbound* seemingly verges on commonplaces. Any sufficiently subtle, flexible idea of authority will introduce a form of authority into any human relationship. True enough, but that is precisely Shelley's point, and his poem makes it new by discovering it everywhere. Violence is rarefied, but acquires an insidious danger when relocated in the structures of language. The Oedipalism of Promethean myth allowed Shelley to trace social aggression to psycholog-

---

against the emotive power of language, the radical poet can succeed only in diverting, not in destroying that power. He will therefore be forced into troublesome paradoxes" (Cronin, *Shelley's Poetic Thoughts*, 13). Scrivener, *Radical Shelley*, 175–80, joins Cronin in stressing the inconsistency of political doctrine and rhetoric in *Prometheus Unbound*. For Shelley's negatives, also see Timothy Webb, "The Unascended Heaven: Negatives in *Prometheus Unbound*," in *Shelley Revalued: Essays from the Gregynog Conference*, ed. Kelvin Everest (Totowa, N.J.: Barnes and Noble, 1983), 37, for the view that Shelley's relational constructions (consisting of positive and negative elements, such as *un*ascended) suggest rather than subvert "the possibility of a realm in which the seemingly negative is caught up, transformed, redeemed, or even regenerated, by some higher reality."

[61] Cronin, *Shelley's Poetic Thoughts*, 159; Scrivener, *Radical Shelley*, 179.

ical matrices. He proceeds to attribute psychological aggression to language by acknowledging the linguistic determination of consciousness:

> Language is a perpetual Orphic song,
> Which rules with Daedal harmony a throng
> Of thoughts and forms, which else senseless and shapeless were.
>
> (4.415–17)

Depending on language, consciousness depends on a variously gross or muted violence. The dynamism of act 4, so welcome after the Utopian passivity of act 3, consistently dramatizes energies empowered by their tensions. The vestiges of authority and aggression in *Prometheus Unbound* 3 and 4 are not subtleties hardly weighing in the balance given the poem's emphatic optimism. They are indices to the virtual omnipresence of violence in a verbally configured world. Shelleyan metaphor redistributes power but never transcends it.

Even in the poem's first acts, stagings of likeness consolidate themselves only by repressing their allegorical counterparts. Allegory then returns to disperse the unities that exclude it. With Prometheus and the phantasm of Jupiter, for example, we overhear the curse at a threshold where Prometheus' words, sayable in the real world but unsayable in its shadowy counterpart, reconfirm the barrier between them. Prometheus' determination to "recall" the curse divides meaning. Since "recall" can signify to remember (to summon into presence) or revoke (to banish into absence), the curse cannot be univocally recalled.[62] It illustrates a structural model in which all terms, however variously defined, will at every moment signify both themselves and their negations. The irreconcilable criteria governing meaning-as-recollection cannot be determinably negotiated, for the curse *refers*: it is a statement meaningful insofar as it accurately repeats a prior statement missing from both Shelley's poem and Prometheus' memory. The utterance that initiates apocalypse in act 1 exists as an aporia available only through questionable versions of itself. Otherness similarly imbues the poem's psychological drama. Pondering Jupiter, Prometheus ponders a mirror reflecting him in a reversed image that, as in the formulations of recent psychoanalytic theory, demonstrates the state of differing-from-itself fundamental

---

[62] Shelley's "recall," like the word "parasite," as J. Hillis Miller explains in "The Critic as Host," in *Deconstruction and Criticism*, ed. Harold Bloom and others (New York: Seabury Press, 1979), 218–19, "is one of those words which calls up its apparent opposite. It has no meaning without that counterpart." The ambivalence of "recall" has been discussed recently by Polan, "Ruin," 38; Sperry, *Shelley's Major Verse*, 80; and Rieder, "The 'One,' " 781.

to the ego's formation. The mirroring of act 1 thereby creates "an irreducible dislocation of the subject in which the other inhabits the self as the condition of its possibility."[63]

Similar problems warp the unitive thematics of Asia and Panthea's dream-reading. Panthea's mediating efforts seemingly establish a circuitry through which metaphor can restructure a system of reciprocal exchanges as a drive toward unity. What we really observe in the dream-reading scenes are paradoxes substantiating Hogle's claim that "the movement of a text towards a reading is thus an attraction of both sides towards each other in which two palimpsests that have no clear foundations look to potential counterparts to give them their significance."[64] The interaction of Asia and Panthea dramatizes a cyclical oscillation between centering forces that acquire their power from the subjects they (futilely) seek to center. Shelley foregrounds this circular logic at the end of the Oceanides' exchange of dreams. Recounting her dream, Asia says "And then I said: 'Panthea, look on me' " (2.1.160) and gazes deeply into her sister's eyes. She plumbs the deep bottom of dream, retrieving a crucial, last-reached recollection. This climactic discovery reveals that the sisters have sought their lost dreams through a specular scene that was part of, in a sense the telos of, the very dream they seek to remember. When they stare into each other's eyes in act 2, the Oceanides unwittingly reenact the dream, so that their specular encounter, while seeming to occupy an extrinsic, privileged position from which it can fathom the mind's depths, is already present in the darkness it claims to illumine, a center simultaneously within and without the dreamwork it purports to center. When the final element of a dream remembered through an exchange of glances turns out to *be* that exchange of glances, both the dream scene and Shelley's metaphorical idealism turn themselves inside out.[65]

In all such scenes, metaphor operates as a mode of power in the service of power's eradication. In *Prometheus Unbound* this power is principally figured in Demogorgon as "the Primal Power of the world," in Mary Shelley's phrase ("Note on Prometheus Unbound. By Mrs. Shelley," *CW* 2:269). Rhetorically, he initially suggests allegorized specularity, mirroring-with-a-difference, but erupts into action as metaphor assimilating all it meets to its own nature. By this transition, from allegory to metaphor, Shelley figures a shift to power for

[63] Samuel Weber, *The Legend of Freud* (Minneapolis: University of Minnesota Press, 1982), 33.

[64] Hogle, "Shelley's Poetics," 191.

[65] For a deconstructive reading of Asia and Demogorgon's colloquy, see Rajan, "Deconstruction," 327–32.

the violent transformation of indeterminacy into "mighty law." For
Ross Woodman the resulting aggressions serve as the climactic con-
tradiction of Shelley's poem:

> Shelley condemns Milton's idealization of Christian distortions in his
> presentation of God as an angry and vengeful Jehovah who destroys Sa-
> tan. But, having rehabilitated Milton's Satan in Prometheus, Shelley then
> turns around and metes out the same vengeful treatment on Satan's ad-
> versary. . . . The central incongruity in the drama lies in Shelley's vision
> of love, on the one hand, and the awful judgment upon Jupiter, on the
> other.[66]

The point can be overstated—Shelley accepted the necessity of revo-
lutionary violence under certain circumstances—but is quite well
taken here. Demogorgon's repression of Jupiter acts as the organiz-
ing matrix of the poem's political ironies. What becomes most inter-
esting, however, is that this "central incongruity" arises at the nexus
of Shelley's debt to *Paradise Lost*. As a perspective on the linguistic-
political ironies of *Prometheus Unbound*, this nexus correlates incon-
gruity and tradition, offering the latter as an explanation of the for-
mer.

The allegorical subplots of acts 1 and 2 obligate Shelleyan value to
traditions that shape it as much as it shapes them. Shelley can recon-
figure Oedipal violence only by struggling with his own ghostly fa-
ther-figures: "the raising of the ghosts of Aeschylus and Milton in the
form of the play is analogous to the raising of the ghost of Jupiter
who repeats Prometheus's curse in its action."[67] *Prometheus Unbound*
validates the conservative conventions it criticizes, similarly, in the
very act of choosing them for criticism. Shelley's demythologization
of myth, in the instant of its accomplishment, becomes another myth
whose relation to the past is potentially as continuous as it is discon-
tinuous. Obviously, no text can command the traditions that con-
verge in it. No text can command its own meaning at every moment,
especially when it attempts to illegitimize the notion of command.
Shelley's poem remains sufficiently self-conscious about these prob-
lems to justify Carl Woodring's description of it as "a tempered, skep-
tical, scarcely illusioned romance."[68] The visionary pyrotechnics of its
finale can make *Prometheus Unbound* appear the *Paradiso* of English
Romanticism. Its beatitudes expand Shelley's prophetic optimism be-
yond its limit, however. By exposing the embattled urgency and inner

---

[66] Woodman, *Apocalyptic Vision*, 154, 165.

[67] Cronin, *Shelley's Poetic Thoughts*, 135.

[68] Carl Woodring, *Politics in English Romantic Poetry* (Cambridge: Harvard University
Press, 1970), 278.

flaws of a metaphorical idealism, the *Prometheus Unbound* project taught Shelley lessons that left him incapable of writing so whole-heartedly celebratory a poem again.

PROMETHEAN EROS

The political and linguistic ambivalence of *Prometheus Unbound* recurs in its vision of love. Curran has written that Shelley's "reliance on the sufficiency of Eros is the most radical assertion of *Prometheus Unbound*."[69] The assertion is so radical, ultimately, because awareness of unquelled ruin persistently shadows Shelley's images of love. This shadow is Demogorgon, not Jupiter. "Why, then, does Demogorgon, whose task is beneficent," Yeats justly asked, "bear so terrible a shape?"—and not merely in Jupiter's eyes, for the Oceanides also regard him as a "terrible shadow" (2.4.150).[70] Demogorgon is a figure of death, a shapeless blackness like Milton's Death, and the object of a descent beyond the border "Of Death and of Life" (2.3.58) based on the underworld quest of Aeneas. As the unknown, the other, he incarnates the sources of primeval fear, his amorphousness connoting the adaptability of menace to the mind's myriad vulnerabilities. Even his "coursers fly / Terrified" by his proximity (2.4.153–54). Yeats claimed that Demogorgon's terrifying power "was thrust there by that something which again and again forced [Shelley] to balance the object of desire conceived as miraculous and superhuman, with nightmare."[71] As Shelley's Echoes avow, only Asia can unleash Demogorgon:

> In the world unknown
>   Sleeps a voice unspoken
> By thy step alone
>   Can its rest be broken,
>   Child of Ocean!
>
>   (2.1.190–94)

The supreme imaginative audacity of Shelley's second act may rest on its dramatic vision of a world where Asia and Demogorgon—whatever words they happen to exchange—can actually meet. The scene of their encounter iconically brings together two opposite powers,

[69] Curran, *Shelley's Annus Mirabilis*, 117.

[70] W. B. Yeats, "*Prometheus Unbound*," in *Essays and Introductions* (New York: Macmillan, 1961), 420.

[71] Yeats, "*Prometheus Unbound*," 420. In "Shelley's 'Deep Truth' Reconsidered," *ELN* 13 (1975): 25–27, Roland Duerksen argues that the imageless Deep Truth is love; I would add that this perspective also associates the imageless Demogorgon with love.

Eros and Thanatos, and insists on their alliance. Demogorgon's volcanic eruption to the upper world represents Shelley's mythic prefiguration of Freud's account of how "a portion of the [death] instinct is diverted towards the external world and comes to light as an instinct of aggressiveness and destructiveness."[72]

The psychological drama of *Prometheus Unbound* renders this aggressiveness paternal. Shelley associates Demogorgon with Anchises and Prospero, and assumes Boccaccio's identification of Demogorgon as the father of the gods.[73] The poem then attempts to sever eros and violence by thematizing Oedipal catharsis. Love's apotheosis, like charity, begins at home. It arises with Prometheus' reorganization of the family: the Titan gathers Earth, Asia, Panthea, Ione, and the Spirit of the Hour, then retires to the Cavern of the Earth (3.3.124–75), a maternal womb that sanctions Prometheus' desire for Asia by involving it in repossession of the mother. The Titan's family can even accommodate the Spirit of the Earth, who calls Asia "Mother, dearest Mother" (3.4.24). Since the Spirit's attraction to Asia is clearly erotic—he is precociously "Wanton" (3.4.91)—his return evokes the possibility of resurgent Oedipal aggressions. Shelley circumvents this threat through the imminent sexual thawing of the Spirit's "chaste sister" (3.4.86), the Spirit of the Moon. The amorous gravitational dance of Shelley's two Spirits in act 4 diverts the incestuous impulse from parental to sibling outlets, divesting it of any threat to the father.[74] Supervising this familial reorganization is Demogorgon himself. In *Prometheus Unbound* Necessity is the father of the world. Shelley presents Demogorgon as a placated patriarch, a benevolent Ur-father who encourages and applauds the restoration of Asia to Prometheus.

The Titans' reunion accomplishes "a passing of the Oedipus complex,"[75] however, only so long as "passing" denotes the repression rather than the transcendence of patriarchal violence. *Prometheus Unbound* merely displaces libidinal aggressions to the latent phase of a

[72] Freud, *Civilization and Its Discontents*, SEF 21:119.

[73] Peacock, who mentions Demogorgon in *Rhododaphne*, acquainted Shelley with Boccaccio's identification (Wasserman, *Shelley*, 333). Demogorgon is likened to Prospero by many Shelleyans—Woodman, in "Androgyne," 225, for instance.

[74] Brown, *Sexuality and Feminism*, 214 and Kenneth Neill Cameron, *The Young Shelley: Genesis of a Radical* (New York: Macmillan, 1950), 298 n. 74, point out that Shelley believed that the perfect egalitarian state would eliminate incest interdictions. For the regressiveness of Prometheus' familial retreat, consider the comment that "Shelley's penchant for a household containing two or more women" may have had "some psychological basis in an unconscious attempt to reconstruct his childhood home" (Cameron, *Young Shelley*, 104).

[75] Waldoff, "Father-Son Conflict," 92.

cycle perfectly capable of restoring them. Shelleyan love remains embroiled in family romance through its investment in a familial ideal. Shelley's family accords Prometheus the role of father by ejecting all other males. It thereby reestablishes a patriarchal monopoly of libido and controls its female members, relegating Panthea and Ione to an asexual infantilism. Act 4 opens with the following stage directions: "*A Part of the Forest near the Cave of* Prometheus. Panthea *and* Ione *are sleeping.*" Not merely an inevitable decorum—Asia and Prometheus have retired to the cave to reconsummate their marriage—this is an exclusionary gesture that creates another primal scene, renewing the possibility of generational rivalry. Shelley may minimize this possibility when the earthly Spirit's desire for Asia is diverted to the Moon. But a diversion of libido first invested in the mother reconfirms the emergence of eros from the matrix (and mater) of the family. Similar ironies extend from act 3 to act 4.

By duplicating the Titans' lovemaking, the dance of Earth and Moon remains the sibling vehicle of a parental tenor. We witness a worshipful ritual in which the moon circles the Earth-as-center, "Gazing, an insatiate bride, / On [his] form from every side" (4.471–72). Shelley's portrait of the Moon as "a winged Infant, white / Its countenance, like the whiteness of bright snow" (4.219–20) casts cold, colorless lunar sexuality as mere potentiality until actualized by the male Earth, who thereby fathers the Moon as a responding lover. Female identity arises as a Cythna-like "second self," the derivative antitype of a privileged maleness. The Moon's lover can only approach her in a chariot inescapably reminiscent of Milton's "Chariot of Paternal Deity, / Flashing thick flames, Wheel within Wheel" (*Paradise Lost* 6.750–51). We can concede the point that this vehicle formalizes the partnership of father and son, and still find the image dismaying.[76] Transporting Earth to Moon from the scene of Satan-Jupiter's downfall, the car portrays the planetary masque of act 4 as a reflex of heavenly warfare and patriarchal self-aggrandizement. Shelley stresses the earthly child's bond to past values by the once buried, now exposed evidence of "cancelled cycles" and extinct life-forms (4.287–318). No celebration of progress, the cycles show Shelley's "horror of an earthly evolution that, operating through the principles of competition, rapine, and survival, had left a history that was the very an-

---

[76] Hogle remarks that when the chariot-driven Earth's eyes "become 'Heavens / Of liquid darkness . . . pouring' forth darkness visible (iv.225–30)," the result is "a burlesquing of Milton that pours Hell's tyranny out of what seems the throne of God's Anointed" (*Shelley's Process*, 199). Bloom studies the deific chariot as a trope of imaginative violence in *Poetry and Repression: Revisionism from Blake to Stevens* (New Haven: Yale University Press, 1976), 83–111.

tithesis of his ideal of love."[77] They thereby illumine the antitheses of ideal love. Since these subterranean depths are the site of Jupiter's imprisonment, they reemphasize the complicity of eros and power.

Such contradictions by no means overrule Shelley's feminism. They merely grant the inherent sexism of Western literary and philosophical traditions and the fragility of intentional meanings. The Oedipalism of tragic myth allowed Shelley to probe the connection of aggression and desire. But despite his aversion to "reconciling the Champion with the Oppressor of mankind" (Preface to *Prometheus Unbound*, 133), he inherited a myth of accommodations from Aeschylus, one that the related accommodations of Freudian theory clarify. The Oedipal complex explains the socialization of eros by affirming the sublimation of violence. Yet these saving sublimations remain phallocentric. As a result, Freud's Oedipal theory does violence in declaring violence banished by banishing the female from its explanations. It contributes to "a perversion—the repression of the mother—which lies at the root of Western civilization" by enacting a thoroughly patriarchal critique of patriarchy.[78] Just so, *Prometheus Unbound* covertly reinstates fatherly prerogatives in dramatizing the (ostensible) transcendence of fatherly tyranny. The Spirit of the apocalyptic hour may report the liberation of women (3.4.153–63), but she cannot liberate Shelley's text from vestigial paternalism. Prometheus rejoins Asia only through the dispensation of Demogorgon, whose final line tellingly pairs Life and Joy with Empire and Victory, and who dominates a world in which Prometheus is unchained not by Asia but by Hercules, the symbol of an indisputably male power.[79]

In *The Cenci* Shelley trades mythic archetypes for social realism. He also exchanges his Oedipal account of sexual violence for one more typical of his work. In *The Cenci* violence arises specularly, through an appropriative power the ego exercises toward its antitypical image. The tragedy implies retrospectively that the lyrical drama mystified

[77] Sperry, *Shelley's Major Verse*, 122. Woodring observes that the passages "suggest Georges Cuvier's theory of cataclysmic change rather than Erasmus Darwin's 'mighty monuments of past delight' " (*Politics*, 306).

[78] Jerre Collins and others, "Questioning the Unconscious: The Dora Archive," in *In Dora's Case: Freud—Hysteria—Feminism*, ed. Charles Bernheimer and Claire Kahane (New York: Columbia University Press, 1985), 251.

[79] I merely mention factors that qualify the poem's depiction of egalitarian sexuality. But for a useful corrective to my emphases, see Woodman's contention that "by releasing the 'one great mind' from the limited male image of it, Shelley through the androgyne felt he had released the 'great poem' from the burden of its essentially patriarchal past" ("Androgyne," 239); and the account of nonexclusive, nonhierarchical love in Alan Richardson, *A Mental Theater: Poetic Drama and Consciousness in the Romantic Age* (University Park: Pennsylvania State University Press, 1988), 135–37.

aggression by screening its involvement with mirroring and meta-phor—by using metaphor, in fact, to present the banishment of de-structive impulses. *The Cenci* dramatizes the death of the father in "the great war between the old and young" (2.2.38) and the symbiosis of wills linking oppressor and oppressed. In returning to *Prometheus Unbound*, however, it also exchanges the lyrical drama's peripheral violence for a contagious sadism. Contemplating retirement, Prome-theus imagines sitting with Asia to "talk of time and change / As the world ebbs and flows, ourselves unchanged" (3.3.23–24); the lines echo Lear's fantasy of exhausting "packs and sects of great ones / That ebb and flow by th' moon" through love and gossip shared with Cordelia (5.2.18–19). Prometheus' sanctuary, viewed in historical perspective and human terms, is a prison with tragedy at its center. *The Cenci* plumbs this tragic center by exploring the father-daughter implications of the *King Lear* allusion. Shelley's dark drama remakes Demogorgon's "inextricable" embrace of Jupiter and his plunge "into the bottomless void" (3.1.70–83) as Beatrice's fear that her father's spirit will "wind [her] in his hellish arms ... / ... and drag [her] down, down, down!" (5.4.66–67). *The Cenci* envisions the father's predatory sexuality as a universal principle, but makes his violence a violence done with mirrors.

Chapter 5

THE POLITICS OF RECEPTION

If thou deny, then force must work my way;
For in thy bed I purpose to destroy thee.
. . .
Thy kinsmen hang their heads at this disdain,
Thy issue blurred with nameless bastardy;
And thou, the author of their obloquy,
Shalt have thy trespass cited up in rhymes
And sung by children in succeeding times.
—Shakespeare, *The Rape of Lucrece*

SHELLEY projected *The Cenci* as the compensatory reflex of *Prometheus Unbound*, which his tragedy uncannily resembles. Stuart Curran has written that "on all levels of execution—the conflicts of character, thematic preoccupations, dramatic devices, even poetic imagery—*Prometheus Unbound* and *The Cenci* continually reflect one another."[1] This metaphor is an apt one, for *The Cenci* is the distorting mirror of *Prometheus Unbound*, a dark other in which banished aggressions return to plunder an entire world. The tragedy's "sad reality" (Dedication to *The Cenci*, 237) restores a necessary balance, satisfying the antithetical requirements of Shelley's moral imagination by reconsidering Promethean ideals from an opposite vantage point. Yet the two dramas are not simply "contrary means to the same moral end—the warning against the wrong and the advocacy of the right."[2] As specular doubles, *Prometheus Unbound* and *The Cenci* can effortlessly switch places, each acting the norm to the other's exception. Viewing them as "exactly opposite sides of the same moral coin"[3] elides the violence of *The Cenci* by automatically referring it to the moral criterion of *Prometheus Unbound*, making Beatrice the negative confirmation of an optimism left essentially untouched by the spectacle of her anguish. With *The Cenci* as with *Alastor*, critics evade the text's pessimism by

[1] Stuart Curran, *Shelley's Annus Mirabilis: The Maturing of an Epic Vision* (San Marino: Huntington Library, 1975), 121.

[2] Earl R. Wasserman, *Shelley: A Critical Reading* (Baltimore: Johns Hopkins University Press, 1971), 101.

[3] Wasserman, *Shelley*, 101.

referring the protagonist's destruction to an unfortunate and unnec-
essary mistake. From this perspective the play illustrates an ethical
exemplum—"no person can be truly dishonoured by the act of an-
other" (Preface to *The Cenci*, 240)—and its heroine, the woeful con-
sequences of discarding moral altruism as the ground of conduct.

The one critic who has powerfully resisted this interpretation is
Curran, who gamely admits that his alternative reading "has not
drawn many adherents in print."[4] For Curran, *The Cenci* confronts
Beatrice with a choice between nightmares rather than a choice be-
tween good and evil; she can be condemned only if we "impose upon
her world an ethic foreign to its exigencies"—with it making no dif-
ference whether that ethic comes from the *Defence of Poetry, A Philo-
sophical View of Reform, Prometheus Unbound*, or the Preface to *The
Cenci* itself.[5] Curran's darker view of the play strikes me as entirely
just. It has the supreme virtue of recognizing that Beatrice and her
world must be assessed together. The reciprocal interdependence of
self and world in *The Cenci* focuses Shelley's tragic vision, generating
a pessimism that ramifies from Beatrice to her society to the poet. In
this work writers are thoroughly implicated in the solicitations and
complicities of violence. Shelley's depiction of resistance as merely
consolidating power renders the poet's freedom illusory and *The
Cenci* his most despairing vocational myth.

DISTORTING MIRRORS

Shelley considered drama the literary form most intimately rooted in
the social fabric. He meant *The Cenci* to take its place in society, to
achieve the public dissemination of a London production, and he was
absorbed by questions of its stageworthiness and prospective impact
on an audience.[6] His July 1819 letter to Peacock calls *The Cenci* "emi-
nently dramatic," "fit for representation," devoted to a realism aimed
at "the greatest degree of popular effect," and no less stageworthy
for its concern with incest—for "such a thing as incest . . . wd. be ad-
mitted on the stage," surely, if handled with the "peculiar delicacy"
that *The Cenci* bestows on it (*Letters* 2:102). "Incest is like many other

---

[4] Stuart Curran, "Percy Bysshe Shelley," in *The English Romantic Poets: A Review of
Research and Criticism*, 4th ed., ed. Frank Jordan (New York: MLA, 1985), 646.

[5] Stuart Curran, *Shelley's "Cenci": Scorpions Ringed with Fire* (Princeton: Princeton Uni-
versity Press, 1970), 140. For a critique of Curran's position, and by implication mine
too, see Donald H. Reiman's review of *Shelley's "Cenci": Scorpions Ringed with Fire* in
JEGP 70 (1971): 682–84.

[6] For the circumstances of the play's composition, submission, and reception, see
Curran, *Shelley's "Cenci,"* 3–20, and Kenneth Neill Cameron, *Shelley: The Golden Years*
(Cambridge: Harvard University Press, 1974), 395, 636–37 n. 15.

incorrect things a very poetical circumstance," Shelley told Maria Gisborne in November 1819; "it may be that defiance of every thing for the sake of another," he added, "or it may be that cynical rage which confounding the good & bad in existing opinions breaks through them for the purpose of rioting in selfishness & antipathy" (*Letters* 2:154). Incest, by itself, may be either good or evil. As an artistic subject, it proves morally objectionable only if indelicately handled.

The appropriateness of sexual violence for dramatic representation rests, for Shelley as for Aristotle, on a certain notion of catharsis. The imitation of violence evokes but also distills or restructures the tragic emotions and, for Shelley, morally empowers the will. Of course, the greater the violence, the greater the necessity of artistic mediation, as Shelley allowed in the Preface to *The Cenci*:

> This story of the Cenci is indeed eminently fearful and monstrous: any thing like a dry exhibition of it on the stage would be insupportable. The person who would treat such a subject must increase the ideal, and diminish the actual horror of the events, so that the pleasure which arises from the poetry which exists in these tempestuous sufferings and crimes may mitigate the pain of the contemplation of the moral deformity from which they spring. There must also be nothing attempted to make the exhibition subservient to what is vulgarly termed a moral purpose. The highest moral purpose aimed at in the highest species of drama, is the teaching the human heart, through its sympathies and antipathies, the knowledge of itself. (239–40)

Tragedians avoid dogmatism. They show rather than tell, fulfilling a higher "moral purpose" by letting the freely responding heart discover its inherent benevolence by recognizing itself in the dramatized actions of others. Dedicated to a therapeutic mimesis, *The Cenci* aspires to the condition of classical tragedy as Shelley described it in the *Defence of Poetry*:

> The tragedies of the Athenian poets are as mirrors in which the spectator beholds himself, under a thin disguise of circumstance, stript of all but that ideal perfection and energy which every one feels to be the internal type of all that he loves, admires, and would become. The imagination is enlarged by a sympathy with pains and passions so mighty, that they distend in their conception the capacity of that by which they are conceived; the good affections are strengthened by pity, indignation, terror and sorrow; and an exalted calm is prolonged from the satiety of this high exercise of them into the tumult of familiar life. . . . In a drama of the highest order there is little food for censure or hatred; it teaches rather self-knowledge and self-respect. Neither the eye nor the mind can

see itself, unless reflected upon that which it resembles. The drama, so
long as it continues to express poetry, is as a prismatic and many-sided
mirror, which collects the brightest rays of human nature and . . . mul-
tiplies all that it reflects, and endows it with the power of propagating its
like wherever it may fall. (490–91)

Shelley wrote *The Cenci* as an idealizing, prismatic mirror designed to
promote the viewer's specular realization of his or her best self. The
play's "audience is to know itself by seeing itself reflected in Beatrice,"
to redeem itself through similarity.[7]

The redemption Shelley envisions once more reflects his moral ide-
alization of metaphor. Tragedy must mirror viewers—minds can rec-
ognize themselves only through resemblance—but must also leave
viewers morally "enlarged." With similarity as its affective premise,
Shelley's notion of educative catharsis presupposes the very thing
that constrains its power of promoting significant change. Shelley
uses the idea of latency to skirt this impasse: drama alters spectators
only through the liberation of native potentials, which negotiate sim-
ilarity and difference by prefiguring the self in its (potential) other-
ness. Much of this is wholly unobjectionable: our reactions to theater
certainly actualize potentiality or they would not be our reactions. In
both theory and practice, however, Shelley's need to reject dogma-
tism and retain poetry's moral affect tends to leave art alternately un-
necessary or ineffectual. The Shelleyan text either changes viewers
by imaging their beliefs, which easily dissipates change in reconfir-
mation, or fails to change them at all. Shelley often avoids these dif-
ficulties by writing poems addressed to the happy few who already
resemble him. Even with *The Cenci*, he must hypothesize essential
likeness by assuming the innate benevolence of human nature, uni-
versalizing his own "ideal [of] perfection and energy" as the object of
"every one" (*Defence of Poetry*, 490). Were Shelley to admit difference
into the interaction of play and viewer, granting a corrupt audience
the right to hoots and catcalls, he would risk disrupting the meta-
phorical symbiosis that mediates playwright and audience as a version
of self and antitype.

Yet *The Cenci* forced him to do just that. The play's prospective
relation to spectators, or readers, is proleptically figured in the play
itself, metadramatically incorporated in scenes of mirroring in which
one character will seek to reshape the values and actions of another.
We witness one such scene near the end of act 2, when Giacomo's
frustrated demands for justice lead him to the moral precipice em-
bodied in the word "parricide." There he temporarily halts:

[7] Wasserman, *Shelley*, 122.

> For he who is our murderous persecutor
> Is shielded by a father's holy name,
> Or I would—
>
>   (2.2.72–74),

and his speech stumbles into silence. Orsino quickly exploits the opening Giacomo has given him:

>   What? Fear not to speak your thought.
> Words are but holy as the deeds they cover:
> A priest who has forsworn the God he serves;
> A judge who makes truth weep at his decree;
> A friend who should weave counsel, as I now,
> But as the mantle of some selfish guile;
> A father who is all a tyrant seems,
> Were the prophaner for his sacred name.
>
>   (2.2.74–81)

"Words are but as holy as the deeds they cover": in *The Cenci* such dismissals of language as secondary to thought are mere stratagems for the verbal reconstitution of thought. Words enjoy a dangerous actualizing power in the world of Shelley's tragedy. If we trust "Imagination with such phantasies / As the tongue dares not fashion into words" (2.2.84–85), we do so because the fearful tongue has already pronounced those words to itself, silently, or there would be no fear. But this auditor within is not sufficient. So Shelley's characters turn outward, seeking the counterpart of desires that cannot be recognized until legitimated by their replication in another visage and voice.

This mediating other is the precondition of action. Thus Orsino's coaxing reassurances commit Giacomo to the murder plot and determine his death. Later Giacomo will understandably regret them, lamenting in Orsino's presence,

>   O, had I never
> Found in thy smooth and ready countenance
> The mirror of my darkest thoughts; hadst thou
> Never with hints and questions made me look
> Upon the monster of my thought, until
> It grew familiar to desire . . .
> . . . .
> . . . For what end
> Could you engage in such a perilous crime,
> Training me on with hints, and signs, and smiles,

> Even to this gulph? Thou art no liar? No,
> Thou art a lie!
>
>   (5.1.19–24, 49–53)

Orsino's response is one that, we will see, the reciprocal dynamic of their interaction always permits: "Men cast the blame of their un-prosperous acts / Upon the abettors of their own resolve" (5.1.25–26).

Orsino excessively minimizes his manipulative role, but his disclaimers raise pertinent questions. If he only showed Giacomo what he already desired, why was that specular revelation so irrevocably determining, so decisive for Giacomo's actions? What do mirroring images provide prospective agents that allow them to act? I would argue that Orsino rhetorically draws Giacomo into crime by subtly offering him a place in a community of coconspirators. Fearing parricide, Giacomo in part fears the isolation of sin—the irreversible commitment to individual action, the loss of habitualness, of a shared and familiar world, that crime can necessitate. He is afraid to be alone. Tempted to murder, he describes his state as Dantean moral solitude amid a "selva oscura":

> I am as one lost in a midnight wood,
> Who dares not ask some harmless passenger
> The path across the wilderness, lest he,
> As my thoughts are, should be—a murderer.
> I know you are my friend, and all I dare
> Speak to my soul that will I trust with thee.
>
>   (2.2.93–98)

Although he claims to fear Orsino as a "passenger" in this "midnight wood," Giacomo fears the darkness more. Orsino's imagined presence there, his strategic intimation of the companionability of crime, actually bolsters Giacomo's resolve. It is no accident, then, that professions and questions of friendship recur through Orsino's tempting of Giacomo: "My friend," "A friend . . . as I now"; "a friend's bosom / Is as the inmost cave of our own mind"; "I know you are my friend"; "Are you not my friend?" (2.2.68, 78, 88–89, 97; 3.1.336).

In this way the specular encounters of *The Cenci* are socializing exercises. They permit inchoate promptings to crystallize as recognizable motives by positioning them socially, connecting them to variant forms of themselves. The conversational exchanges of *The Cenci* corroborate Jerrold E. Hogle's claim that "there is simply no construction of an identifiable self in Shelley without a specific counterpart . . . helping to form that self's structure and possibilities in a mirror, an apparent reversal of non-identity into an identity visible to the subject."[8] The subject defines himself by accepting a role in a play written by an offstage prompter, an alter ego whispering lines that the subject claims for himself in the act of repeating them. His reward is refuge from autonomy, or aloneness, but at the cost of integrity. *The Cenci* everywhere validates Lacan's insistence that the specular constitution of the subject alienates the subject, providing a selfhood that, mediated by the otherness of the transposed image, remains riven by otherness.[9] So it is with the characters of Shelley's play once they gaze into the "mirror of [their] darkest thoughts." They are secretly victimized by a psychological parasitism, inhabited by an alien presence, a voice whispering and goading, yet unable to dispel their fear or heal the inner divisions of consciousness. In *The Cenci* there are only looking-glass selves, but the mirror that bestows the power of acting also falsifies the self that acts.

This phenomenon is disturbing for two reasons. First, its reciprocal logic makes it reversible. Dialogue in *The Cenci* often reads like a dark parody of the uncentered dream-readings of *Prometheus Unbound*. Like Asia with Panthea, Orsino with both Giacomo and the disoriented Beatrice of act 3 must complete a broken narrative. Does he do so by inferring speakers' intentions, so that preexistent preferences revert on them from the site of the other, or by insinuating his own intentions, imposing more than he reflects? The answer is both. When self-realization arises specularly, the subject is constituted by an other that takes its constitutive function, reflexively, from the very subject it constitutes. Each character plays both roles, with Giacomo functioning as Orsino's specular other even as Orsino acts as Giacomo's specular other. The people of *The Cenci* defensively make their dialogic partners the initiators of the plans they jointly create. Self and other reciprocally divide the origin between them, tossing responsibility back and forth like a stolen object that burns the hand. They do so from duplicity and anxiety. They *can* do so, however, only because the mutually constitutive interplay of self and other allows cause and effect to trade places indiscriminately.

These metalepses are perhaps more disturbing because they leave no one exempt. Shelley offers specularity as the model of emotional and intellectual realization throughout *The Cenci*. One murderer, not-

---

[8] Jerrold E. Hogle, *Shelley's Process: Radical Transference and the Development of His Major Works* (New York: Oxford University Press, 1988), 98. Hogle's case for the Shelleyan self as socially constructed disallows readings that evaluate Shelley's characters by assuming that they possess socially inviolable resources of will or innocence.

[9] Jacques Lacan, "The Mirror Stage as Formative of the Function of the I as Revealed in Psychoanalytic Experience," in *Écrits: A Selection*, trans. Alan Sheridan (New York: Norton, 1977), 1–7.

ing the pale cheeks of his companion, and the fearfulness they imply, is told, "It is the white reflexion of your own, / Which you call pale" (4.2.21–22); Lucretia's fear that Savella suspects her of murder, Beatrice remarks, works to "Write on unsteady eyes and altered cheeks / All [she] wouldst hide" (4.4.39–40); interrogated together, those accused of Cenci's murder, Lucretia conjectures, will demand "Each from the other's countenance the thing / Which is in every heart" (4.4.174–75), compelled by torturers "Whose questions thence suggest their own reply" (5.2.43). Beatrice herself plays the game. Bernardo calls her "That perfect mirror of pure innocence / Wherein I gazed, and grew happy and good" (5.4.130–31), but she too acts as a corrupting mirror, her gaze violently remaking Marzio in the image of her own self-exoneration, and thereby consigning him to torture (5.2.157–63). Beatrice also corrupted Orsino by showing him his own reflection, as he readily confesses:

> It fortunately serves my close designs
> That 'tis a trick of this same family
> To analyse their own and other minds.
> Such self-anatomy shall teach the will
> Dangerous secrets: for it tempts our powers,
> Knowing what must be thought, and may be done,
> Into the depth of darkest purposes:
> So Cenci fell into the pit; even I,
> Since Beatrice unveiled me to myself,
> And made me shrink from what I cannot shun,
> Shew a poor figure to my own esteem,
> To which I grow half-reconciled.
>
> (2.2.107–18)

Orsino is society's creature, a mere assemblage of roles instantly adaptable to "a new life, fashioned on old desires" (5.1.90) because he easily finds disguises and adjusts to circumstances. Yet he too is only "half-reconciled" to his desires, ambivalently divided within by the otherness mediating even the revelation of his emptiness. Construed as the power to inhabit the social world, the power to act, identity arises as the reflex of the figural substitutions that specularity allows. Yet the mirroring of desire and violence morally corrupts the subject it constitutes.

What then of Shelley's affirmation of tragedy as a mirror in which spectators behold and actualize a psychologically latent nobility? Can we distinguish Orsino's degrading "self-anatomy" from the redemptive "self-knowledge and self-respect" drama ostensibly promotes in viewers (*Defence of Poetry*, 491)? Earl R. Wasserman says yes, arguing that Shelley's drama internalizes a functional and significant difference between casuistical modes:

> Pernicious casuistry, operating on self-anatomy, reconciles one to the commission of error by persuading that error is justified [because evil is inherent in human nature]; sublime casuistry, by displaying the feebleness of such sophistry and leaving error unrelated to innate purity, leads the observer to that self-knowledge which is the end of tragedy. Consequently, Shelley's tragic heroine must not only engage in *pernicious* casuistry but be painted by the artist with *sublime* casuistry.[10]

This argument strikes me as utterly unpersuasive. It relies on technical suppositions about the nature and responsibilities of the will that *The Cenci* at best leaves highly unstable, and verges on a notion of providential election in which human action has no bearing on the soul's moral status. In many deconstructive analyses, Barbara Johnson comments, "the differences *between* entities . . . are shown to be based on a repression of differences *within* entities, ways in which an entity differs from itself"[11]—and Wasserman's pernicious/sublime distinction lends itself to just such deconstruction. The radiant and dark mirrors of *The Cenci*'s affective theory and dramatic action cannot be absolutely dissociated. Radiance and darkness are divergent yet interrelated facets of the same specular model. This harmony of opposites is the organizing paradox of *The Cenci*. "The preface and logic of the play present self-consciousness itself as the one process which can resolve the contradictions experienced by the spectator," Michael Henry Scrivener summarily remarks, "but no act of self-consciousness depicted in the play is exemplary."[12] As an experiment in redemptive mirroring, *The Cenci* backfires. It stages specular scenes that reverse Shelley's conception of its social role and threaten to turn the play inside out.

This reversal is more than a hypothetical problem. It is a problem with tangible, historically specific illustrations. Consider this review from *The New Monthly Magazine and Universal Register*:

> There is nothing in the circumstance of a tale being true which renders it fit for the general ear. The exposure of a crime too often pollutes the very soul which shudders at its recital, and destroys that unconsciousness of ill which most safely preserves its sanctities. There can be little doubt

---

[10] Wasserman, *Shelley*, 119–20.

[11] Barbara Johnson, *The Critical Difference: Essays in the Contemporary Rhetoric of Reading* (Baltimore: Johns Hopkins University Press, 1980), x.

[12] Michael Henry Scrivener, *Radical Shelley: The Philosophical Anarchism and Utopian Thought of Percy Bysshe Shelley* (Princeton: Princeton University Press, 1982), 193.

that the horrible details of murder, which are too minutely given in our
public journals, lead men to dwell on horrors till they cease to petrify,
and gradually prepare them for that which once they trembled to think
on.[13]

These moralistic reservations echo Orsino's explanation of "self-anat-
omy" corrupting people by familiarizing them with "darkest pur-
poses" (2.2.110–11). Here Shelley's specular aesthetics succeed splen-
didly, as a portion of *The Cenci* reproduces itself in the social world.
Instead of improving society, however, the mirrored passage is ac-
commodated to society's provincialism, offered as reflexive evidence
of the moral deficiency of Shelley's tragedy. And it is extremely im-
pressive evidence, for the review becomes a self-fulfilling prophecy
enacting the possibility of misguided response that it worries over.
The crucial point about such miscarrying of meaning is not that it
occurred—it always occurs—but that *The Cenci* unwittingly encour-
aged it. The play thematizes its own errant reception in the errancies
of the mirrorings it depicts. For the moment, we need merely see that
this paradox becomes the tragedy's subject. Despite the ideal of spec-
ular catharsis it presupposes, *The Cenci* does not so much solve as pose
the problem of mirroring. Shelley's play is another poem about po-
etry, an investigation of the indeterminacies of public discourse.

METAPHOR AND VIOLENCE

As the negation of Shelley's Promethean myth, *The Cenci* both reflects
and disfigures the metaphorical idealism of *Prometheus Unbound*. If
the tragedy's distorting mirror makes metaphor the trope of power,
it makes power the motive of desire. Francesco Cenci's cruelty must
be attributed partly to "a perverted sexual drive," an investment of
libido in the luxurious refinements of pain and fear.[14] "I was happier
than I am," the aging Count admits,

> While lust was sweeter than revenge; and now
> Invention palls:—Aye, we must all grow old—
> And but that there remains a deed to act

[13] From a May 1820 review, reprinted in *The Unextinguished Hearth: Shelley and His
Contemporary Critics*, ed. Newman Ivey White (Durham: Duke University Press, 1938),
182. In a May 1820 review in *The Edinburgh Monthly Review*, another conservative critic
urged Shelley to consider "that the perpetration of actual guilt, may possibly be to
some natures a pastime of scarcely a different essence from that which is afforded to
himself . . . by the scrutinizing and anatomizing discovery of things so monstrous"
(*Unextinguished Hearth*, 186).

[14] Carlos Baker, *Shelley's Major Poetry: The Fabric of a Vision* (Princeton: Princeton Uni-
versity Press, 1948), 144.

Whose horror might make sharp an appetite
Duller than mine—I'd do,—I know not what.
When I was young I thought of nothing else
But pleasure; and I fed on honey sweets:
Men, by St. Thomas! cannot live like bees
And I grew tired:—yet, till I killed a foe,
And heard his groans, and heard his children's groans,
Knew I not what delight was else on earth,
Which now delights me little.

(1.1.96–109)

Agony replaces "honey sweets" because of the connection of eroticism and subjugation. Cenci can easily make sexuality a means of aggression—the murderer turning rapist—because his aggressions were always merely displaced sexuality. *The Cenci* envisions eros as a derivation of the will to power. Desire "authenticates" individuals, allowing them to forget their emptiness by making another person the reflection and instrument of their will. Such mimetic desire ends in addiction and futility, in the accelerating exchanges of mastery and abjection that Hogle anatomizes so brilliantly.[15] But until these specular appropriations exhaust themselves, they destroy voraciously.

The sexual violence they traffic in is a metaphorical violence. The dramatic image of metaphor dominating *The Cenci* is the Count's rape of Beatrice. Like the phantasm of Jupiter repeating the words of Prometheus, or the "*O, follow, follow*" dream shared by Asia and Panthea, the rape signifies metaphor-in-action, establishing a point of coincidence for disparate beings. As the rape's incestuous character shows, the basis of this convergence is similitude. Only because Beatrice is a "particle of [his] divided being" (4.1.117) linked to him by family resemblance can Cenci break the taboos that goad his appetites. His sexual possession will formalize that resemblance. Beatrice will eventually share his infamy and even his venereal infection, he boasts. "What she most abhors," moreover, "Shall have a fascination to entrap / Her loathing will" (4.1.85–87). The rape can thereby psychologically transform her in the image of her father's depravity, her moral will "by its own consent [stooping] as low / As that which drags it down" (4.1.11–12). If Beatrice "ever have a child," Cenci implores,

May it be
A hideous likeness of herself, that as
From a distorting mirror, she may see
Her image mixed with what she most abhors,

---

[15] In particular, see the discussion of mimetic desire, objectification, and abjection in Hogle, *Shelley's Process*, 155–59.

Smiling upon her from her nursing breast.
And that the child may from its infancy
Grow, day by day, more wicked and deformed,
Turning her mother's love to misery:
And that both she and it may live until
It shall repay her care and pain with hate,
Or what may else be more unnatural.

(4.1.145–55)

In *The Cenci*, regrettably, this genealogical fantasy is an exemplary act of imagination. Beatrice's imagined infant will image "what she most abhors," her father, by memorializing the violence that impregnated her. Through a metalepsis of cause and effect, rape and child, Cenci presents the imposed similitude of his rape as itself a "distorting mirror"—metaphor as a "distorting mirror." Metaphor becomes by association a form of rape.

The metaphorical transmission of evil enjoys a success Cenci never foresaw when, replicating in Beatrice his willingness to murder, the victimizer becomes a victim of his own methods. All the specular encounters of *The Cenci* leave violence uncontrollable. The dynamic of self and other produces power as a consequence of uncentered exchanges in which the interdependence of self and other renders the locus of power indeterminate. Still, we would be unwise to stress the elusiveness of force in Shelley's play. Whatever their ultimate import, the indeterminacies of specularity work mainly to enfranchise power, allowing it to systematize itself by appropriating values not securely anchored elsewhere. Shelley can consequently use the self/other paradigm as his model of history unfolding. We have only to recall Romanticism's greatest theorist of history, Hegel, to recognize the potential for historical explanation inherent in self/other constructs.[16] *The Cenci* can in fact appear a negative image, in miniature, of Hegelian dialectic. Shelley exchanges state for Hegelian Spirit, but still conceives of political history as the self-aggrandizing appropriation of otherness by power.

Although not directed to large-scale historical representations, *The Cenci* shows the initiatives of public power at one crucial point: the papal legate's arrival with an official warrant for Cenci's death. The irony of Savella's arrival, moments after Cenci's murder, is so heavy-handed as to suggest that Shelley "saw the effect as vital to the signif-

---

[16] Alan Richardson discusses Shelleyan mirroring from a Hegelian perspective in *A Mental Theater: Poetic Drama and Consciousness in the Romantic Age* (University Park: Pennsylvania State University Press, 1988), 100–123.

icance of his play."[17] What need does this ironic event fulfill? Stuart M. Sperry describes Cenci's death as "the very end that *society* itself has belatedly ordained."[18] Savella's entry shows that there have been *two* plots to kill Francesco Cenci: the private plot of self-defensive vengeance and the public plot of legally sanctioned execution. The second, papal plot accords dramatic action a metaphorical structure in *The Cenci* by making Cenci's death occur at the (near) juncture of two analogous sequences of events. We cannot reconstruct Vatican machinations in any detail; the motives behind Cenci's condemnation may include his public blasphemy at the banquet or the near-depletion of his wealth, a source of papal revenue. Savella's arrival nonetheless throws open a door on the plot of history, the strategies through which public power seeks its ends.

The pope serves then as a figure of the historical process.[19] It is a process that externalizes itself only in glimpses—the pope himself never appears in *The Cenci*—because it acts solely through surrogate forms of itself. History, or political power, kills Francesco Cenci through the intercession of Beatrice and her conspirators, puppets driven to action by the state's strategic refusal to act. The pope is by no means the deliberate or self-conscious motive force of the private plot. He figures history as a vast field of impersonal relations motivated by various pressures. He also figures the injustice of social mandates. Like all parallel lines, the two concurrent death plots never converge. Savella arrives too late; there is no coincidence of public and private violence. That disjunction allows the pope to shape the essential form of Beatrice's actions, as tenor shapes vehicle, and then deny his complicity by disavowing mutual similarity. The metaphorical relation of Shelley's two plots succumbs to another appropriation of otherness by self. When the pope rescinds his toleration of Cenci and pronounces his death sentence, history secretly refashions Beatrice in the image of its newfound imperatives as Orsino manipulated Giacomo. Social events transpire as externalizations of power into duplicative agencies that power, as another exploitative father, engendered but will not recognize. Beatrice and her coconspirators are the bastard offspring of History.

[17] Stuart M. Sperry, *Shelley's Major Verse: The Narrative and Dramatic Poetry* (Cambridge: Harvard University Press, 1988), 132.

[18] Sperry, *Shelley's Major Verse*, 132 (emphasis added).

[19] The pope ironically personifies the "larger socio-political movement" that might alone save Beatrice for Laurence S. Lockridge, in "Justice in *The Cenci*," *The Wordsworth Circle* 19 (1988): 98. For Shelley's representation of a historical process inimical to the individual will in *Prometheus Unbound*, see John Rieder's discussion of "the plot of necessity" in "The 'One' in *Prometheus Unbound*," *SEL* 25 (1985): 787–800.

Power's strategies for concealing its operation are what interest Shelley most in *The Cenci*. Lacking a means to reverse or redirect authority, the tragedy turns from revolutionary agendas to ideological representations. Shelley recognized the authoritarian values latent in language from at least 1817, when *The Revolt of Islam* declared words one of evil's habitations (ll. 388–89). In *The Cenci* he emphasizes the treachery of language when Savella's suspicions are substantiated by the discovery of Orsino's letter to Beatrice (4.4.90–95). With their conviction virtually assured by this note, the surviving Cencis find themselves betrayed by *writing*. Shelley hints at the role of language in their deaths with the double entendres of the pope's death sentence: "Here is their *sentence*; never see me more / Till, to the *letter*, it be all fulfilled" (5.4.26–27, emphases added). Metaphor in particular serves tyranny best. The drama's patriarchal hegemony presupposes metaphor: since the pope considers "paternal power, / . . . the shadow of his own" (2.2.55–56), and since God reigns as "the great father of all" (1.3.23), power establishes itself here by organizing the familial, social, and religious spheres as interconnected versions of the trope of paternity, which is therefore made to appear inevitable through its sheer ubiquity. Metaphor sets the terms for both conformity and rebellion. It provides docile citizens reifying representations "that forever recast the life of the mind into their own image."[20] Yet the nonconforming Beatrice merely conforms at an ulterior level: her "psychological enslavement to the father principle" allows her to combat one father only by appealing to another in her prayers, validating the patriarchal ideology that destroys her.[21]

Shelley's treatment of ideological appropriation reflects his psychological argument. As the self is socially constructed, so are meanings socially determined. As specular exchanges of self and other are co-opted by the more adroit manipulator, so is the determination of truth subject to power. The impotence of words to arrest truth in a determinate formulation helps explain Beatrice's refusal to declare what happened to her:

> If I could find a word that might make known
> The crime of my destroyer; and that done
> My tongue should like a knife tear out the secret
> Which cankers my heart's core; aye, lay all bare
> So that my unpolluted fame should be
> With vilest gossips a stale mouthed story;

[20] David Quint's phrase, in "Representation and Ideology in *The Triumph of Life*," *SEL* 18 (1978): 639.

[21] Scrivener, *Radical Shelley*, 195.

A mock, a bye-word, an astonishment:—
If this were done, which never shall be done,
Think of the offender's gold, his dreaded hate,
And the strange horror of the accuser's tale,
Baffling belief, and overpowering speech;
Scarce whispered, unimaginable, wrapt
In hideous hints . . . Oh, most assured redress!

(3.1.154–66)

To speak is to risk becoming "subdued even to the hue / Of that which thou permittest" (3.1.176–77)—to risk according rape a vicarious life of its own in the annals of public discourse. Beatrice will reiterate these fears even after Cenci's death. They reflect her sense of the malleability of a "truth" dependent on social reception. Her trial (along with much else) justifies such fear. What establishes Beatrice's guilt is a substitutive logic directed to predetermined ends. Paolo Santa Croce, a sibling like Beatrice, killed his mother, a parent-figure like the pope; Paolo escaped, but social order requires the state to defend its prerogatives by killing Beatrice as a surrogate Paolo (5.4.18–27). The findings at Beatrice's trial precede the hearings that produce them. Marzio's confession is made and believed, then retracted but believed anyway; Beatrice's resolute silence alters nothing: "She is convicted, but has not confessed" (5.3.90). Her conviction effects a closure of myriad possibilities into a narrative of truth institutionally recorded and fixed in judicial archives.

IMAGINATION ON TRIAL

The courtroom scenes that dominate act 5 of *The Cenci* force judgments from readers. But who or what do these scenes put on trial? Beatrice, certainly, and with her the world she inhabits. Yet Baker remarked wittily that "in reading criticisms of the trial scene one sometimes gains the impression that it is not so much Beatrice as the author himself who is up for judgment."[22] In truth, Shelley *is* on trial in *The Cenci*, and with him the poetic imagination as a means of moral renovation. The play's ending gathers up imaginative problems developed earlier in order to probe their implications for the politics of writing. The reversible mirrorings that leave meaning socially constructed and ultimately indeterminate, the opportunity for misreading presented by such indeterminacy, the metaphorical structure of ideology—all recur in Beatrice's public addresses in acts 4 and 5. Be-

[22] Baker, *Shelley's Major Verse*, 147.

atrice consequently emerges as the play's predominant poet-figure.[23] Like Shelley himself, Beatrice must communicate a vision of sexual violence so as to promulgate justice, but cannot articulate that violence explicitly. Her courtroom rhetoric is an exercise in reconciling these irreconcilable demands.

The contradictions embroiling Beatrice have precise correlatives in Shelley's own efforts to address a public sitting in judgment. As Beatrice must stress the brutalization she underwent, explaining her motives to exonerate herself, so must Shelley stress the brutality of rape. This necessity accounts for an otherwise unaccountable circumstance. Shelley's version of the Cenci legend emphasizes not only the terror but the very *fact* of Beatrice's rape. His main manuscript source, the *Relation of the Death of the Family of the Cenci*, merely stated that Cenci "often endeavoured, by force and threats, to debauch his daughter Beatrice."[24] Shelley dramatically realizes this force, transforming "an originally questionable incest into a central event."[25] Since the centrality finally forestalled production of *The Cenci*, Shelley's decision to heighten the rape should seem curious. Why did he dilate on a sexual violence his sources minimized? In part because such violence struck him as basic to the story's tragic potential. And in part because *The Cenci* had to establish Beatrice's victimization in order to wrest the appropriate moral and political exempla from her plight. Only the representation of rape could leave spectators suitably horrified by the injustices of entrenched patriarchal privilege. We can explain the centrality of rape in *The Cenci* only by assuming Shelley's belief in it as fundamental to the moral catharsis he sought.

[23] Jeffrey N. Cox, in *In the Shadows of Romance: Romantic Tragic Drama in Germany, England, and France* (Athens, Oh.: Ohio University Press, 1987), 163, comments, "Shelley sees the dramatic poet as facing a situation much like that which Beatrice confronts. Like her, the dramatist must struggle against the 'circumstance and opinion' of his place and time in history to discover a mode of language that will communicate with those around him without betraying his imaginative vision." For Beatrice's experience as "a parable of the poet" tragically wedded to a single meaning, see Ronald Tetreault, *The Poetry of Life: Shelley and Literary Form* (Toronto: University of Toronto Press, 1987), 131. Ronald L. Lemoncelli uses the *Defence of Poetry* to depict Francesco as a poet-figure in "Cenci as Corrupt Dramatic Poet," *ELN* 16 (1978): 103–17. Curran treats Cenci as a Renaissance Genet, an artist conceiving of crime as an immortalizing art form (*Shelley's "Cenci,"* 73–75).

[24] *Relation*, reprinted in *CW* 2:160. The versions of the Cenci legend examined by Truman Guy Steffan in "Seven Accounts of the Cenci and Shelley's Drama," *SEL* 9 (1969): 601–18, at most limit Francesco to attempted rape. There is no rape in Pieracci's tragedy on Beatrice, which may have influenced Shelley, according to George Yost, *Pieracci and Shelley: An Italian Ur-Cenci* (Potomac, Md.: Scripta Humanistica, 1986).

[25] Curran, *Shelley's "Cenci,"* 43.

But what *The Cenci* offers with one hand it retracts with the other. The tragedy performs a dance of attraction and repulsion around the rape as an object of representation. We necessarily and easily infer rape in making emotional and dramatic sense of the drama, yet our need to infer is itself telling. The rape occurs offstage, as a lacuna between acts. It signifies a violence that spreads through Shelley's plot without directly entering it, never achieving representation except through the depiction of its consequences. Staging Beatrice's rape was unthinkable: that would have affronted theatrical censors, contemporary sensibilities, and even classical preferences for offstage cruelty. Shelley's play leans most heavily on Renaissance tragic conventions, however, and hardly exhausts the limited staging options available to it, granting Francesco a few leers and innuendos but forbidding him even a brief appearance in Beatrice's bedroom. There should be no doubt as to Shelley's deliberate elision of sexual violence, for it extends from action to dialogue. *The Cenci* refuses even to name the rape, as Shelley fully realized:

> In speaking of his mode of treating this main incident, Shelley said that it might be remarked that, in the course of the play, he had never mentioned expressly Cenci's worst crime. Every one knew what it must be, but it was never imaged in words. ("Note on The Cenci. By Mrs. Shelley," *CW* 2:158)

Beatrice's inability to report her father's crime reflects Shelley's aversion to verbalizing the facts of sexual assault. Rape thereby serves as a nexus of the play's ambivalence toward representation itself as a social act. Underlying the ambivalence is fear of the vicarious power of reimaged experiences, as Michael Worton suggests,[26] and a deep insecurity about audience. What we must recognize above all are the communicative costs exacted by this ambivalence.

In court Beatrice cuts an impressive figure, and not merely to Marzio. Conviction rings in her voice, compelling a sympathy born of accurate intuitions. Camillo describes himself defending Beatrice as someone "Pleading, as I could guess, the devilish wrong / Which prompted [her] unnatural parent's death" (5.4.16–17). To some auditors, at least, Beatrice's silence clearly speaks volumes. But it still leaves far too much unsaid in her encounters with authority. Beatrice fears playing into her enemies' hands through words. Like radical poets of Shelley's era, she clings to her "awareness of the conservative force of language and [engages] in a self-conscious struggle against

---

[26] Michael Worton, "Speech and Silence in *The Cenci*," in *Essays on Shelley*, ed. Miriam Allott (Totowa, N.J.: Barnes and Noble, 1982), 108–9.

it."[27] She tries to circumvent the inherited conservatism of language by placing words in novel contexts that estrange inherited meanings and dislocate preconceptions—Shelley's own strategy with the monarchical diction of *Prometheus Unbound*. " 'Tis most false / That I am guilty of foul parricide," Beatrice tells Savella (4.4.145–46). She believes herself guiltless presumably because the parricide was not truly "foul." She remains "more innocent of parricide / Than is a child born fatherless" (4.4.112–13), similarly, because in no sense that truly counts was Francesco Cenci a "father." Unfortunately this privileging of context over diction is subject to the same reversals that undermined certainty in the play's mirroring scenes. Beatrice's words do not remake audience expectations; audience expectations subvert the efficacy of Beatrice's words. Statements such as "'Tis most false / That I am guilty of foul parricide" hardly redefine "guilt" effectively. Instead, they seem brazenly hypocritical—Orsino-like corroborations of others' assumptions when those assumptions are known to be misled. In Beatrice's rhetoric indirection becomes equivocation. By mixing her disingenuous evasions with outright lies (her denial of seeing Marzio before), Shelley portrays her language as "legal quibbling and logic chopping."[28]

Yet the Romantic ventriloquism of *The Cenci* makes Beatrice's failure Shelley's at one remove. With Shelley too, the problems of dramatic indirection refer back to the merely implied occurrence of the rape. If we infer rape as the offstage event that *The Cenci* cannot name, we also infer rape as the wellspring of Beatrice's character development from acts 3 to 5—a transition from saint to murderer that remains one of the most teasing and contested cruxes in Shelley studies.[29] The mysteries of her character arise as unresolved issues in the psychology of violence as *The Cenci* engages it, or fails to. Count Cenci pursues the destruction of his daughter's moral will through the fascination of the abhorrent. When Shelley internalizes the issue in this way, forcing us to ask what Beatrice undergoes spiritually, he foregrounds the inscrutability of her development. At some point we may

[27] Richard Cronin's phrase, from *Shelley's Poetic Thoughts* (New York: St. Martin's Press, 1981), 8. For Cronin, this is one of the two options confronting radical poets forced to employ a language saturated with conservative connotations, and the one Shelley ordinarily chose.

[28] Melvin R. Watson, "Shelley and Tragedy: The Case of Beatrice Cenci," *KSJ* 7 (1958): 19.

[29] A useful synopsis of debate on the moral enigma of Beatrice appears in Sperry, *Shelley's Major Verse*, 130–31. The first influential argument for Beatrice's moral corruption was Robert F. Whitman, "Beatrice's 'Pernicious Mistake' in *The Cenci*," *PMLA* 74 (1959): 249–53, which supplanted earlier interpretations stressing Beatrice's moral heroism, and which has been challenged by Curran's existentialist interpretation.

begin "to suspect that the rape did more to expose than to pollute."[30] What are the subjective correlatives of the coarsening that gradually recasts Beatrice in her father's role? Did she put on his knowledge with his power? Did she discover an affinity for the forbidden in the midst of revulsion, a revelation, beyond any later power to forget, of the ego's wanton complicity in its own dissolution? Did she kill to prevent further rapes or to avenge the one that occurred? From what precisely is Beatrice recoiling in horror as she speaks so wildly at the beginning of act 3? Posing these unanswerable questions, *The Cenci* revolves around an absent center.

This absence is obviously overdetermined. It derives partly from strategies Shelley embraced in adapting his play to prevailing criteria of stageworthiness: incest would "form no objection," would "be admitted on the stage," Peacock was reassured, due to "the peculiar delicacy" of Shelley's dramatization (*Letters* 2:102). Precisely this notion of the language of tragedy makes *The Cenci* a tragedy of language. As the reflex of an evasive "delicacy," Beatrice's inability to say "my father raped me" shows the play internalizing the moralistic strictures of bourgeois propriety. Rape is eradicated from Shelley's writing, and from Beatrice's speech, by an imposition of power disturbingly rape-like itself. Violence becomes the violence of society, rape-as-blankness an aporia inscribed in Shelley's text by the unenlightened conservatism he detested. The unvisualized summit of Mont Blanc, the unsayable language of the dead in *Prometheus Unbound*—these vacancies promote revolutionary change by exposing the baseless fabric of power. The unimaged deep truth of *The Cenci* creates indeterminacies that allow authority to co-opt Beatrice through a misappropriation that validates privilege by confirming power. We witness a final metalepsis, the play's corruption by the debased world over which it aspired to wield reformative influence. Instead of compelling spectators to see themselves reflected in Beatrice, the distorting mirror of *The Cenci* compelled Shelley to see himself reflected in the forces that deny rape access to stage, courtroom, and even consciousness.

This complicity provides Shelley's investigation of writing its final tragic irony. *The Cenci* makes the poet a cooperative participant in the reconsolidation of oppression—a possibility Shelley may deny elsewhere but finally cannot deny here. The errancies of public reception shadowed Shelley's entire career. But *The Cenci* self-consciously thematizes those errancies. The play argues that, if reception determines meaning as a public construct, and if readers' responses can be nei-

---

[30] Terry Otten, *The Deserted Stage: The Search for Dramatic Form in Nineteenth-Century England* (Athens, Oh.: Ohio University Press, 1972), 30.

ther anticipated nor controlled absolutely, then texts are merely the
histories of their own (mis)interpretation. If circumstances reduced
"Beatrice Cenci" to the "deep and breathless interest" (Preface to *The
Cenci*, 239) gossip takes in scandal, Beatrice herself prophesies that
fate:

> Are centuries of high splendour laid in dust?
> And that eternal honour which should live
> Sunlike, above the reek of mortal fame,
> Changed to a mockery and a bye-word? What!
> Will you give up these bodies to be dragged
> At horse's heels, so that our hair should sweep
> The footsteps of the vain and senseless crowd,
> Who, that they may make our calamity
> Their worship and their spectacle, will leave
> The churches and the theatres as void
> As their own hearts? Shall the light multitude
> Fling, at their choice, curses or faded pity,
> Sad funeral flowers to deck a living corpse,
> Upon us as we pass to pass away,
> And leave . . . what memory of our having been?
> Infamy, blood, terror, despair?
>
> (5.3.30–45)

Although they project empty theaters, these extraordinary lines were
written to be declaimed in a crowded theater. They publicize Shelley's
awareness of the people's ability to trivialize the most morally harrow-
ing "spectacle," including *The Cenci*. By associating "the churches and
the theatres," Shelley blames religion for the degeneration of "Bea-
trice Cenci" into an idle amusement, a cautionary tale reminding the
multitude of the cost of ignoring papal law. Yet his words indict the
poet too. Delivering Beatrice into the hands of the public, Shelley
potentially makes the Cenci name "a mark stamped on [an] innocent
brow / For men to point at as they pass" (5.4.151–52), and enlists him-
self with the man Beatrice imagines saying, "I with my words killed
her and all her kin" (5.2.143).

We should understand why even Beatrice's fear of death signifies
fear of reading. Envisioning a death-world of repetitions that will re-
stage her rape endlessly (5.4.60–67), she fears a figure for the vicari-
ous afterlife granted fictions by empathizing readers. Shelley critics
often represent the aporias of his texts as strategic irresolution that
"rouzes the faculties to act" (as Blake might say) with inevitably ben-
eficial consequences. The simultaneous nobility and depravity of Be-
atrice "may, by engendering our internal debate, cause us to know

ourselves"—as if self-knowledge always proved therapeutic, so that the play's moral conflicts miraculously heal themselves merely in entering the affective register.[31] If there are unfailing reasons to celebrate the activation of the human will, they appear in the newspapers of neither Shelley's day nor ours. Yet Shelley criticism abounds in idealizations of the reader as the poem's actualization and resolution. These viewpoints forget would-be Werthers driven to suicide; they forget other possible reader-responses neither enlightened nor ethical. They use the "reader" to personalize and depoliticize the institutional forces that control the place Shelley has been granted in contemporary culture, a place of reading suspect in many ways. We cannot simply invoke the reader to save *The Cenci* for a provisional optimism. We read the play poorly in seeking to do so, for through its specular figures, *The Cenci* deconstructs its own theory of morally educative catharsis.

The pessimism of *The Cenci* follows from its prosecution of language as an instrument of oppression. By putting Shelley's own imagination on trial, his tragedy shows how the reversible potential of a metaphorical idealism can promote moral despondency. This pessimism about poetry is belied by a great deal in Shelley—including his completion of, and hopes for, *The Cenci* itself—but we should pause before discounting it as atypical. I argued earlier that the specular reciprocity of *The Cenci* and *Prometheus Unbound* allows each text to appear alternately as the norm that its counterpart violates. *The Cenci* will never seem one of its author's more normative productions. Yet G. M. Matthews rightly stressed the exceptional aspects of *Prometheus Unbound*, which

is unique among the major prophetic poems in having a "happy ending." Shelley's fullest picture of the immediate future is in *The Revolt of Islam* (1818), where massacre, famine, and disease reach their climax in the burning alive of the popular leaders. *The Mask of Anarchy* (written 1819)

[31] Wasserman, *Shelley*, 121. Despite both the careful *may* in this statement and the acknowledgment that Shelley did not believe self-consciousness to be always cathartic (111–12), Wasserman views skeptical irresolution in *The Cenci* (and in *Alastor* and *Julian and Maddalo* as well) as a deliberate strategy for forcing readers to resolve the text's dilemmas for themselves. Sperry has recently offered a version of the same reader-response argument. His analysis of the emotional dynamics of catharsis in *The Cenci* recuperates thematic disunity as a unifying lesson in love. Sperry's "spectator is propelled violently back and forth between two poles of supposition" until those poles become the limits of a more inclusive understanding of love as "an act incorporating but transcending mere forgiveness" (134, 140). To develop this viewpoint, Sperry must assume, or mandate, a particular response—here a sympathetic love for Beatrice that many readers and viewers no longer feel by act 5.

anticipated a far greater slaughter of unarmed civilians than at Peterloo. *Hellas* (1821) ended in the betrayal and massacre of the resurgent Greeks.[32]

To this brief overview we might add *Alastor*, which dramatizes the fatalism of supernal quests, *Adonais*, with its suicidal climax and "triumph of human despair,"[33] and *The Triumph of Life*, with its vision of the teeming throngs undone by death. One element of Shelley's career is a highly complex disillusionment with the world as "the place where in the end / We find our happiness, or not at all" (*The Prelude* 11.143–44). In *The Cenci* "world" denotes the public sector against which Beatrice and her creator struggled. After 1820 Shelley's major imaginative efforts took on an increasingly introspective and private quality, arousing even Mary's impatience with "visionary rhyme" (Dedication to *The Witch of Atlas*, l. 8). That marginalization of social realism is one legacy of Beatrice Cenci's "sad reality."

[32] G. M. Matthews, "On Shelley's 'The Triumph of Life,' " *Studia Neophilologica* 34 (1962): 104.

[33] Harold Bloom's phrase, from *The Visionary Company: A Reading of English Poetry* (Ithaca: Cornell University Press, 1961), 349.

Chapter 6

ITALIAN PLATONICS

Ye who intelligent the Third Heaven move,
Hear the discourse which is within my heart,
Which cannot be declared, it seems so new.
—Dante, *Convito* (Shelley trans.)

SHELLEY's completion of *Prometheus Unbound* and *The Cenci* left his major artistic concerns provisionally realized. Although he wrote continually in 1820, his poetic efforts were devoted principally to lyrics, satirical pieces, and jeux d'esprit like the "Letter to Maria Gisborne" and *The Witch of Atlas*. These texts form the alienating arc Shelley's imagination traversed before reverting to its abiding interests when he met Teresa Viviani, a young Italian woman imprisoned in an Italian convent until her marriage contract could be negotiated.[1] Teresa's plight catalyzed Shelley's deepest imaginative preoccupations. As an object of intense idealization and a "Poor captive bird" (*Epipsychidion*, l. 5), Teresa raised the problems of freedom and limitation that, in one form or another, had preoccupied Shelley for most of his career. While drawn to the moral and emotional drama of her captivity, he also grasped its poetic implications—its ability to serve as a parable of the poet's aspirations and challenges. Shelley explores these issues in *Epipsychidion*, which he completed in early 1821. The poem develops its erotic theme as an aspect of style, pursuing love through a rhetorical self-reflexivity unprecedented in his career. In *Epipsychidion* the interdependence of language and desire in the Shelleyan imagination achieves definitive illustration.

The desire Shelley dramatizes is ardently idealizing. Yet *Epipsychidion* remains a resolutely earthly poem, ending on an Aegean island that offers the ruins of history and the rhythms of nature as love's rightful sanctuary. These simultaneous drives toward spirit and body generate the poem out of their powerful antagonism. Criticism of *Epipsychidion* ordinarily resolves this antagonism by placing transcendence and earthliness at the initial and terminal points of a progres-

---

[1] For the Shelley circle's relations with Teresa, see Kenneth Neill Cameron, *Shelley: The Golden Years* (Cambridge: Harvard University Press, 1974), 275–77.

sion. Such readings stress the poem's progressive relocation of theo-
centric values on secular grounds. Unfortunately, this approach
overlooks the ultimate complicity of nature and supernature in *Epi-
psychidion*. The poet's desire for Emily modulates from the Seraphic (l.
21) to the bodily, from the supernal to the worldly, only because Shel-
leyan contraries imply one another from the start, so that the human-
ization of eros ironically leaves love more idealizing than ever. This
irony dissolves desire in isolation. If the reflexive formalism of *Epi-
psychidion* at first liberates figural errancies for a celebration of erotic
potentiality, it ends as the mirror of the poet's visionary narcissism,
the only basis for his projections of love and community. Despite its
invocations of the cosmos, *Epipsychidion* testifies to Shelley's circum-
scribed sense of emotional and artistic possibilities in 1821.

FIGURING THE INEFFABLE

As a muse, Teresa had the virtue of providing Shelley a creative out-
let for his reading. Mary Shelley admired Teresa as someone "of
great genius—who writes Italian with an elegance and delicacy to
equal the best authors of the best Italian age" (*LMWS* 1:165). To all
appearances, Shelley too associated Teresa with Italian literature, and
thereby found the occasion for an "Italian platonics" (*LMWS* 1:223)
that adds to its erotic glorification of Teresa a persistent evocation of
Italian love poetry. In 1821–1822, Timothy Webb observes, "the
combined influences of Dante, Petrarch, Boccaccio, Cavalcanti, and
Latini, the process of writing and translating in Italian, and the phys-
ical experience of the Italian landscape and climate all fused together
with Shelley's natural propensity for idealized infatuation to produce
a literary world of extraordinary potency."[2] Inspired by this world,
the "allegory" of *Epipsychidion* exemplifies the poet's "awareness of
the imaginative roots of poetic traditions, and . . . ability to transform
those traditions into self-critical vehicles of the autonomous Romantic

---

[2] Timothy Webb, *The Violet in the Crucible: Shelley and Translation* (Oxford: Clarendon
Press, 1976), 309. For Dante's influence on *Epipsychidion*, see Carlos Baker, *Shelley's Ma-
jor Poetry: The Fabric of a Vision* (Princeton: Princeton University Press, 1948), 221–24;
Earl Schulze, "The Dantean Quest of *Epipsychidion*," *SIR* 21 (1982): 191–216; and Rich-
ard E. Brown, "The Role of Dante in *Epipsychidion*," *Comparative Literature* 30 (1978):
223–35. Teresa herself wrote. Shelley's epigraph cites her "Il Vero Amore," available
as translated by Thomas Medwin, in his *The Life of Percy Bysshe Shelley* (London:
Thomas Cautley Newby, 1847), 2:70. In tone and style, Teresa's essay resembles *Epi-
psychidion*, lines 1–189, as do her occasionally florid letters to Shelley and Mary, re-
printed in Newman Ivey White, *Shelley* (New York: Knopf, 1940), 2:467–85.

imagination."[3] Shelley's interest in imaginative autonomy and its for-malist correlative—a self-referring, nonreferential poetics—explains his reliance on Dantean tradition above all in *Epipsychidion*.

With Dante's poetry, Shelley declared, love "became a religion, the idols of whose worship were ever present" (*Defence of Poetry*, 497):

> His *Vita Nuova* is an inexhaustible fountain of purity of sentiment and language: it is the idealized history of that period, and those intervals of his life which were dedicated to love. His apotheosis of Beatrice in Par-adise and the gradations of his own love and her loveliness, by which as by steps he feigns himself to have ascended to the throne of the Supreme Cause, is the most glorious imagination of modern poetry. (*Defence of Poetry*, 497)

Dante's idealization of desire especially impressed Shelley for its at-tention to problems of representation. Dante was the poet of the in-effable sublime. The *Vita Nuova* and *Paradiso* combine celebrations of love with awareness of the inadequacy of "*veste di figura, o di colore rettorico*" (Advertisement to *Epipsychidion*, 373). Shelley had decried the incapacities of words well before 1821, but *Epipsychidion* makes a passing lament into a central preoccupation. The poem's Dantean legacy stressed the inability of language to represent or actualize ref-erents. As a result of this preoccupation with its own expressive lim-its, Shelley's hymn to Emily (the renamed Teresa) repeatedly turns away from the world to seek meaning among its own formal rela-tions. *Epipsychidion* is therefore not only "a poem about poetry," a "poem about the difficulties involved in its own composition," but one in which the "language appropriate for Emily's 'created' world cannot be referential, tied to the prison world, but must be a language that is self-generating, spinning out of itself."[4]

This heightened reflexivity reveals the influence of various intellec-tual and literary traditions. The linguistic self-consciousness of Dante's work fascinated Shelley in part because it raised issues inde-

[3] Frank D. McConnell, "Shelleyan 'Allegory': *Epipsychidion*," *KSJ* 20 (1971): 103. My concept of allegory again comes from Paul de Man's "The Rhetoric of Temporality," in *Blindness and Insight: Essays in the Rhetoric of Contemporary Criticism*, 2d ed., rev. (1971; reprint, Minneapolis: University of Minnesota Press, 1983), 187–228.

[4] The quotations are from Harold Bloom, *The Visionary Company: A Reading of English Poetry* (Ithaca: Cornell University Press, 1961), 336; Timothy Webb, *Shelley: A Voice Not Understood* (Atlantic Highlands, N.J.: Humanities Press, 1977), 41; and Michael Henry Scrivener, *Radical Shelley: The Philosophical Anarchism and Utopian Thought of Percy Bysshe Shelley* (Princeton: Princeton University Press, 1982), 269. I am also indebted to Robert N. Essick's " 'A shadow of some golden dream': Shelley's Language in *Epipsychidion*," *Papers on Language and Literature* 22 (1986): 165–75, which stresses both the poem's self-reflexivity and its connection of language and love.

pendently formulated in nineteenth-century formalist traditions—in symbolist and art-for-art's-sake denigrations of realism, but in Romanticism too. Blake's claim that "Natural Objects always did & now do weaken deaden & obliterate Imagination in Me" strikes a note that recurs in some form throughout Romantic visionary poetry.[5] Romantic interest in both revolution and the sublime encouraged poets to minimize the representational bonds of language and nature, word and world. "If writing and speech have the same sort of 'sisterhood' as painting and poetry," and "if writing transforms invisible sounds into a visible language, then it is bound to be a problem for writers who want to be imaginative iconoclasts, who want images that are not pictorial"—images, for instance, appropriate to imageless deep truths or perfectible energies.[6] In a similar vein, Burke had expanded on eighteenth-century universalism to argue that sublime poetry should ignore the tulip's streaks. The prospect of poetry freed from referential ties occasioned celebration and anxiety in the English Romantics, but remained central to their sense of the psychology of visionary experience. It should hardly surprise us that these psychological prospects acquired formal analogues, literary modes designed to reinstate what Coleridge termed "the old antithesis of *Words* & *Things*."[7] In Romantic literature an Orphic poetry "whose sphere of activity is governed by a mythical or ideal unity of word and being" finds its inevitable counterpart in a hermetic poetry oriented toward the poem "as a self-contained linguistic structure."[8]

Hermetic formalism in the Romantic period reflected new ideas about signification, for it arose in part from empirical language theory, especially Locke's insistence on the referential arbitrariness of the sign, a doctrine that foreshadowed the structuralist idea of diacritical signification. Hans Aarsleff claims that the most widespread consequences of Locke's argument—"today we find them in Saus-

---

[5] Blake's marginalia to the *Lyrical Ballads*, in *Blake's Poetry and Designs*, ed. Mary Lynn Johnson and John E. Grant (New York: Norton, 1979), 446.

[6] W.J.T. Mitchell, "Visible Language: Blake's Wond'rous Art of Writing," in *Romanticism and Contemporary Criticism*, ed. Morris Eaves and Michael Fischer (Ithaca: Cornell University Press, 1986), 50–51. This essay is particularly useful for the politics of representation and writing in the Romantic period. Robert F. Gleckner surveys the paradoxes created by the Romantics' recourse to a language they considered inherently inadequate in "Romanticism and the Self-Annihilation of Language," *Criticism* 18 (1976): 173–89.

[7] A phrase from Coleridge's 22 September 1800 letter to Godwin, in *Collected Letters of Samuel Taylor Coleridge*, ed. Earl Leslie Griggs (Oxford: Clarendon Press, 1956–1959), 1:626.

[8] Gerald L. Bruns's terms, from *Modern Poetry and the Idea of Language* (New Haven: Yale University Press, 1974), 1.

sure's *Cours*, but they have played a prominent role ever since Condillac"—include above all the position that, "since words are arbitrary signs for our private ideas, they do not constitute an inventory of the world, a nomenclature, as they did in the Adamic language doctrine against which Locke was arguing."[9] The transition from signs to propositions in linguistic theory suggests that "words achieve meaning not through the correspondence of each of them with a particular idea, but through their relations one with another within the sentence."[10] Language does not mean by incarnating referents but by modifying structural relations among words.

When employed as the vehicle of an "Italian platonics," such self-reflexivity embroils Shelley in difficulties. While both Dantean idealism and empirical linguistics challenged the correspondence of language to "extrinsic" reality, their assumptions about representation differed radically. In the *Paradiso*—Dante's "perpetual hymn of everlasting love" (*Defence of Poetry*, 497)—the poet's exhaustion of language produces "a gradual attenuation of the bond between poetry and representation," resulting in an aesthetic construct where an event "has no existence, even fictional, beyond the metaphoric."[11] As its criterion of truth, the *Paradiso* replaces referential conventions with interrelated symbolic elements independent of the world. But Dante's nonreferential poetics ends by marrying metaphor to mimesis. His organization of the *Paradiso* around an attenuated "bond between poetry and representation" enhanced the poem's figural mimesis of cosmic structure. For Dante, the divine order of the universe is inscribed in the metaphorical structures of his poetic theory. He could allegorize "the gradations of his own love and [Beatrice's] loveliness, by which as by steps" he presents an overview of the universe (*Defence of Poetry*, 497) because his Christianity bequeathed him a metaphysics of hierarchical resemblance, a cosmos conceived as a chain of interlocking analogies. This structure grounds the resemblances of

[9] Hans Aarsleff, "Wordsworth, Language, and Romanticism," in *From Locke to Saussure: Essays on the Study of Language and Intellectual History* (Minneapolis: University of Minnesota Press, 1982), 375. For Shelley's ideas on language, I again rely on the first chapters of Richard Cronin, *Shelley's Poetic Thoughts* (New York: St. Martin's Press, 1981), and William Keach, *Shelley's Style* (New York: Methuen, 1984).

[10] Cronin, *Shelley's Poetic Thoughts*, 14.

[11] John Freccero, intro. to *The Paradiso*, trans. John Ciardi (New York: New American Library, 1961), x, xii. For a corrective to my oversimplification of Dante's problems and resources in approximating the ineffable, see Peter S. Hawkins, "Dante's *Paradiso* and the Dialectic of Ineffability," in *Ineffability: Naming the Unnamable from Dante to Beckett*, ed. Peter S. Hawkins and Anne Howland Schotter (New York: AMS Press, 1984), 5–21.

words, so that language operates as the reflex of ontological sanctions.

Shelley's rejection of Dantean theocentrism restricted the power of metaphor, cutting the referential moorings of language almost entirely. The "Italian platonics" of *Epipsychidion* encouraged Shelley's idealism and then frustrated its realization by invoking skeptical accounts of linguistic self-reference inimical to originary or integral values. Shelley's response, as Keach writes, was to set "about transmuting an apparent limitation into a strength. . . . by diverting attention from the actual to the potential," and converting "his sense of the inadequacy of language into an ideal of inexhaustible poetic meaning."[12] He pursues this conversion through an allegorizing of metaphor far more self-conscious than the rhetorical anarchism of *Prometheus Unbound*. The problem of ineffability shapes his Promethean myth without achieving emphatic articulation in it. Shelley's "beautiful idealisms" typically celebrate language as "a perpetual Orphic song, / Which rules . . . / . . . thoughts and forms" by imposing shape on their potentiality (*Prometheus Unbound* 4.415–17). More intensely concentrated on language, *Epipsychidion* remains more aware of linguistic limits. Like Shelley's Urania, the language of *Epipsychidion* is "chained to Time" (*Adonais*, l. 234). Here the flowers of rhetoric are "votive wreaths of withered memory," "winged words" ultimately just "chains of lead" which impede love's effort to represent its unrealizable object and conduct the fancy that would "measure" Emily to its "own infirmity" (ll. 4, 588, 590, 69–71).

The Romantic reflexivity of *Epipsychidion* acts as a rhetoric of temporality because it makes each "sign refer to another sign that precedes it" and assume its meaning by "repeating" another, "previous sign with which it can never coincide."[13] In the figural structures of *Epipsychidion*, language aspires to the condition of music. "We—are we not formed, as notes of music are," the speaker asks, "For one another, though dissimilar; / Such difference without discord" (ll. 142–44). The lines seemingly recall Prometheus' idealization of metaphor as "difference sweet where discord cannot be" (*Prometheus Unbound* 3.3.39), but in fact describe a mode of diacritical interplay. The comparison makes language a system of harmonic ratios in which elements "mean" through adjustments in their mutual relations rather than through any referential extension beyond the system encompassing them. Shelley's densely tropical successions continually dramatize such relational complexities:

[12] Keach, *Shelley's Style*, 28.
[13] De Man, "Rhetoric," 207.

> Seraph of Heaven! too gentle to be human,
> Veiling beneath that radiant form of Woman
> All that is insupportable in thee
> Of light, and love, and immortality!
> Sweet Benediction in the eternal Curse!
> Veiled Glory of this lampless Universe!
> Thou Moon beyond the clouds! Thou living Form
> Among the Dead! Thou Star above the Storm!

(ll. 21–28)

The rapid, destabilizing passage from image to image displaces its appositions through a progressively disfiguring sequence. This series dissolves presence amid geometrically compounded difference. Emily is the tenor of a cloud-hidden moon, of a storm-transcending star, of the likeness of moon to star, of a "Glory," both independently and in *its* relation to the moon, to the cloud, to the relation of moon to cloud, and so on through the proliferating relations-within-relations distributed among seraphs, women, and benedictions. The attempt to represent Emily's beauty must continue infinitely; she must be all things because no one figure can convey her. Emily is a "living Form / Among the Dead," a radiance in an otherwise "lampless Universe"— in short, a "differential nexus"[14] that exists as the reflex of variants in their own complex interrelation.

Such allegorization of metaphor transfers value through a differential circuitry that fragments the origin and the one among receding vistas. Shelleyan desire seeks "one life, one death, / One Heaven, one Hell, one immortality," as a consequence of the lovers' fusion as one "Spirit within two frames, oh! wherefore two? / One passion in twin-hearts" (ll. 585–86, 573-75), yet can conceive union only contrarily. *Epipsychidion* retains the one as an unrealizable paradox.[15] The poem also retains the origin as its revisionary link to Dante, but insists on

[14] Essick, "Shadow," 172. Emily's "divinity" subjects her to the law that "the universal Being can only be described or defined by negatives," as Shelley wrote in his "Essay on Christianity" (*CW* 6:232).

[15] In *Shelley's Process: Radical Transference and the Development of His Major Works* (New York: Oxford University Press, 1988), 263–66, Jerrold E. Hogle discounts this unitive reorientation on the ground that Shelley's representations of oneness assimilate its traditional identity to a transferential model so completely as to obviate any conflict between enduring traditional associations and newly introduced radical values, thus leaving the One merely another image of transference. This view effectively erases traditional ideas of the One as intellectually or emotionally functional elements of Shelley's poem. My own view follows Essick, who argues that the self-deconstruction of Shelley's metaphors "provides a rhetorical equivalent to the polymorphism of his desires," but who also describes the "ideal of erotic desire in *Epipsychidion* as . . . will to union" ("Shadow," 166, 168).

its fundamental belatedness. Shelley reassesses Dante's erotic sublimation as a psychological drama, transforming "Dante's transcendental allegorizing" into "an allegory of imagination itself."[16] *Epipsychidion* internalizes the Dantean "Supreme Cause" as an originating moment of consciousness, so that Dante's fiery words—"each is as a spark, a burning atom of inextinguishable thought; and many yet lie covered in the ashes of their birth"—are recast as "a fading coal" that language must retrospectively fan to brightness (*Defence of Poetry*, 497, 500, 504). What we discover as *Epipsychidion* proceeds, however, is that such integral moments are never present to consciousness. They are irrecoverably dispersed into synecdochic traces even when first recognized. Like all origins, they can be construed out of their diaspora only by retrospective projections of similitude—by metaphor. Yet *Epipsychidion* recognizes and accepts the failure of metaphor. Shelley rejects erotic and representational closure, willing the divorce of desire and its object, of word and world.

Enacting this rejection, *Epipsychidion* subjects desire to an open-ended process that gives value no place to rest. The poem temporalizes love through a version of the rhetorical metamorphoses that shaped *Prometheus Unbound*. Shelley's metaphors once more seek to incarnate unrealized desires, and are consequently proleptic. The inadequacy of their initial vehicle calls forth first one and then another substitute, engendering a metonymic series of figures mutually associated as surrogates of Emily. When this metonymic series reaches the point of chiasmal antithesis, it reverses itself and returns metaleptically to the potentiality that engendered it.[17] Antitheses recur throughout the poem—blitheness and dissonance, an unmoving star amid "the moving Heavens," "A smile amid dark frowns," or gentleness opposing rudeness (ll. 59–63)—as the poles of love's energies. The cycles through which metaphor migrates show the recuperative logic of coherence and collapse in *Epipsychidion*. They temporalize passion by leading it back to potentiality:

> Then, from the caverns of my dreamy youth
> I sprang, as one sandalled with plumes of fire,

[16] Schulze, "Dantean Quest," 203.

[17] See Daniel J. Hughes's seminal "Coherence and Collapse in Shelley, with Particular Reference to *Epipsychidion*," *ELH* 28 (1961): 260–83; and Essick's reference to "Shelley's recognition that the desire for union is one with the creation of differences through a reciprocal dynamic in which each gives rise to the other" ("Shadow," 168). I am also indebted to P.M.S. Dawson's brief notice of the connection of potentiality and perfectibility in *The Unacknowledged Legislator: Shelley and Politics* (Oxford: Clarendon Press, 1980), 96–97.

And towards the loadstar of my one desire,
I flitted, like a dizzy moth, whose flight
Is as a dead leaf's in the owlet light,
When it would seek in Hesper's setting sphere
A radiant death, a fiery sepulchre,
As if it were a lamp of earthly flame.

(ll. 217–24)

These "plumes of fire" are Apollo's contribution to an inherently vi-
sionary love. Since they allow the poet his flight toward the stars, but
cannot grant him his "one desire," he soon becomes a "dizzy moth,"
his language temporalizing the lodestar of desire as "Hesper's setting
sphere," love's star in its subjection to earthly cycles of day and night.
Springing actively toward the lodestar, the poet then finds himself
flying weakly like a moth, whose flight in turn "Is as a dead leaf's in
the owlet light" when it (the moth) flies toward Venus. The leaf simile
connotes an uncertain fluttering motion, yet inescapably suggests de-
scent as well, the dead leaf's autumn fall to the earth. If Shelley's
metaphor of ascent contains a downward spiral, if it turns on antith-
esis, unable to go up without going down, that is because the object it
seeks is a coincidence of difference. Yet "fiery martyrdom" would re-
plenish the fires of desire's "flight," ending one phase of the quest by
recycling eros to its matrices.

This Romantic allegory forces desire to go on until it is stopped,
and it is never stopped. In reverting from the world, Shelley's lan-
guage internalizes becoming as a facet of indeterminacy. The self-
referring imperative of *Epipsychidion* gives time the rhetorical form of
a broken dialectic. The poet is lured "towards sweet Death," for in-
stance, by antitheses grounded in diurnal and seasonal rhythms—"as
Night by Day, / Winter by Spring, or Sorrow by swift Hope" (ll. 73–
74). Similarly, when Emily becomes a

Reflection of the eternal Moon of Love
Under whose motions life's dull billows move;
A Metaphor of Spring and Youth and Morning;
A Vision like incarnate April, warning,
With smiles and tears, Frost the Anatomy
Into his summer grave

(ll. 118–23),

her figural status creates a beauty that exists amid opposition ("With
smiles and tears") and time, waxings and wanings that Shelley likens

to the cycles of the tides and seasons. As the pattern assumed by de-
sire, this rhythm aptly recurs as the lovers journey to their island

> while Night
> And Day, and Storm, and Calm, pursue their flight,
>
> . . . .
>
> Treading each other's heels, unheededly.

(ll. 418–21)

Presenting these circlings as desire's self-perpetuating vitality, *Epi-
psychidion* offers its inability to stabilize a referent as testimony to love's
unending process. By disclaiming representation, Shelley's poem par-
ticipates in the historical process by which, in Lovejoy's phrase, an
"originally complete and immutable Chain of Being [was] converted
into a Becoming."[18] Upward transcendence defers to ongoing lateral
movements on a temporal plane. The appeal of *Epipsychidion*, from
this perspective, lies in its ability to approximate the erotic optimism
of *Prometheus Unbound* from a conception of language stressing not
the Daedal power of the Orphic voice but the limitations of meta-
phor.

UNACKNOWLEDGED LEGISLATION

One legacy of Shelley's allegorized eroticism is a meditation on the
politics of love in the contemporary world. If the formal organization
of *Epipsychidion* enacts a temporal progression—since the three main
sections of *Epipsychidion* are devoted respectively to present, past, and
future—the progression ends by locating love among the ruins of his-
tory. For any poet with Shelley's revolutionary commitments, re-
demptive love must involve a political program, and the reputed es-
capism of *Epipsychidion* gives its displaced political theme special
interest.[19] The poem articulates a prophetic politics as a dimension of
its figural organization. Shelley's rejection of representation pro-
motes an ideologically motivated detachment. This willed isolation
decrees poets the legislators of the world, at least initially, but argues

[18] Arthur O. Lovejoy, *The Great Chain of Being: A Study of the History of an Idea* (Cam-
bridge: Harvard University Press, 1936), 325–26. Jerome J. McGann argues for the
newfound humanism of Shelley's later poetry in "The Secrets of an Elder Day: Shelley
after *Hellas*," *KSJ* 15 (1966): 25–41.

[19] For Scrivener, *Epipsychidion* celebrates "unity in a realm just beyond the reaches of
civilization. . . . [an] island which has avoided the corruption of history" (*Radical Shelley*,
270); for Dawson the poem shows the poet "consciously in retreat from the public
world" (*Unacknowledged Legislator*, 102). Carl Woodring scarcely mentions *Epipsychidion*
in *Politics in English Romantic Poetry* (Cambridge: Harvard University Press, 1970).

that their legislation can prevail only when they preserve an unacknowledged distance.

The aversive stance of *Epipsychidion* reflects a historically specific mood of liberal alienation. In the aftermath of the French Revolution the first Romantic generation had turned principally toward a conservative natural supernaturalism in which divisions succumbed to spousal reunion and threatened traditions were reconstituted in the name of Tory quietism. But after Waterloo and the formation of the Holy Alliance, the reactionary climate of European politics forced republican writers to admit their distance from the sources of political authority, even to cultivate such distance as a standard of political enlightenment. It is unquestionably due in part to a common liberal disenfranchisement that the work of the second Romantic generation cultivates ironic tensions and distances, scorn of conceptual closure, and immersion "in uncertainties, Mysteries, doubts, without any irritable reaching after fact & reason."[20] Shelley never courted his isolation or surrendered completely his passion for reforming the world. Still, the traditions of prophetic poetry and his own failure to secure an audience encouraged the consoling reflection that true power dwells apart. By breaking the congruence of word and referent, the allegory of *Epipsychidion* informs Shelley's rhetoric with a distance intended as an adversarial stance.

The disjunction of word and world also prompts a successiveness that enjoyed particular radical sanction. When *Epipsychidion* refuses closure in the interest of its own self-perpetuating energies, it enacts a linguistic version of Godwinian perfectibility. "By perfectible," Godwin wrote in *Political Justice,*

> it is not meant that [man] is capable of being brought to perfection. But the word seems sufficiently adapted to express the faculty of being continually made better and receiving perpetual improvement. ... The term perfectible, thus explained, not only does not imply the capacity of being brought to perfection, but stands in express opposition to it. If we could arrive at perfection, there would be an end to our improvement.[21]

[20] A phrase from Keats's "Negative Capability" letter, in *The Letters of John Keats*, ed. Hyder Edward Rollins (Cambridge: Harvard University Press, 1958), 1:193. For the antagonism of irony and closure in Romantic poetics, see David Simpson, *Irony and Authority in Romantic Poetry* (Totowa, N.J.: Rowman and Littlefield, 1979), 162, 190; the first chapter of Anne K. Mellor's *English Romantic Irony* (Cambridge: Harvard University Press, 1980); and Stuart M. Sperry's *Keats the Poet* (Princeton: Princeton University Press, 1973), 244–49.

[21] William Godwin, *Enquiry Concerning Political Justice and Its Influence on Morals and Happiness*, ed. F.E.L. Priestley (1793; reprint, Toronto: University of Toronto Press, 1946), 1:93.

In accepting Godwin's position on this issue, Shelley pointedly de-
clined the millenarian optimism of Thomas Paine. For Paine, a per-
fect form of government could be achieved: "at that point," Dawson
notes, "further progress would become unnecessary, and the ideal
government could be embodied in a definitive constitution. . . .
[whereas,] Godwin noted with disapproval, any settled constitution
acts as a check on progress."[22] Godwin's swerve from "perfection" to
"perfectibility" reflects a powerful intuitive sense that ideological cor-
ruption lurks in all codification, or by extension in any use of lan-
guage to fix determinate meanings. Shelley would soon decry linguis-
tic ossification in the *Defence of Poetry* (482); at the time *Epipsychidion*
was composed, he had already criticized the 1688 Parliamentary Act
as language designed to "arrest the perfectibility of human nature"
(*Letters* 1:264). His wariness of the power of legislative formulas to
foreclose change had motivated his praise of the amendable Ameri-
can Constitution in *A Philosophical View of Reform* (*CW* 7:11–12). The
open-ended dynamic of *Epipsychidion* pries similarly at the verbally
forged manacles of final truth.

Yet the self-recycling antitheses of Shelleyan allegory celebrate rev-
olutionary change in more specific ways as well. Historical cycles ap-
pear in Shelley's poetry as early as *Queen Mab*; they return in Pan-
thea's vision "Of cancelled cycles" in *Prometheus Unbound* (4.289) and
in the famous concluding question of "Ode to the West Wind"; and
they reemerge definitively when *Hellas* envisions "Cycles of genera-
tion and of ruin" (l. 154) as the dialectic of history. Stressing the al-
ternation of "Ruin and Renovation" (l. 718), the cycles of *Hellas* stress
"the dynamics of antithesis in the context of an unfinished struggle,"
and declare "such opposition . . . the very essence of history and mu-
tability."[23] The political themes of *Hellas* foreground the permanent
elements of Shelley's concept of history. His historical vision consis-
tently centered on the motifs of cycles, antitheses, and progressi-
vism[24]—in other words, on political analogues of the allegorical
structures of *Epipsychidion*. Supposedly the vehicles of an idealized,
ahistorical rapture, the visionary tropes of Shelley's poem have been
inscribed by the rhythms of historical change from the begin-
ning.

It is wholly appropriate that these rhythms should move *Epipsychi-*
dion toward its Aegean paradise. The island idyll concluding Shelley's

[22] Dawson, *Unacknowledged Legislator*, 59.

[23] Constance Walker, "The Urn of Bitter Prophecy: Antithetical Patterns in *Hellas*,"
KSMB 33 (1982): 36, 38.

[24] William Royce Campbell, "Shelley's Philosophy of History: A Reconsideration,"
KSJ 21 (1972): 43–63.

poem resituates its figural politics in polemical contexts that clarify
their republican import. Since this politics develops from the earlier
visionary passages, Shelley's main political images—the ruined tower
and the "age of gold" (l. 428)—are subject to the familiar rhetorical
transformations. Shelley's tower is Titanic in origin. Evoking "the
world's young prime" (l. 489), it becomes a funerary monument to
mythic unities that supposedly antedate history, unities symbolized by
the innocent incest of the gods ("his sister and his spouse," l. 492), a
perfected closure of like with like. In truth, the towering palace is a
human, cultural artifact. Its ruination measures the passage of histor-
ical time: Shelley's wistful "It scarce seems now a wreck of human art"
(l. 493) means that it is one, and expresses a distinctly historical nos-
talgia. Still, the legendary Titanism of the palace permits Shelley to
emphasize its natural, chthonian gestation:

> It scarce seems now a wreck of human art,
> But, as it were Titanic; in the heart
> Of Earth having assumed its form, then grown
> Out of the mountains, from the living stone,
> Lifting itself in caverns light and high:
> For all the antique and learned imagery
> Has been erased, and in the place of it
> The ivy and the wild-vine interknit
> The volumes of their many twining stems;
> Parasite flowers illume with dewy gems
> The lampless halls, and when they fade, the sky
> Peeps through their winter-woof of tracery
> With Moon-light patches, or star atoms keen,
> Or fragments of the day's intense serene;—
> Working mosaic on their Parian floors.

(ll. 493–507)

Fantasizing a natural origin for the building because it has been re-
claimed by the processes of nature, like Wordsworth's ruined cottage,
Shelley indulges the fiction of the palace coming full circle, reverting
back to its own matrices.

This reversal is figural, an effect of the parasitic flowers as tropes
of language.[25] In *The Revolt of Islam* Shelley had presented ruins as
"scrolls of mortal mystery" (l. 765), figures for history and language
as inherently belated and vestigial. *Epipsychidion* characterizes the

---

[25] My interpretation of the tower and its parasite vines is indebted to J. Hillis Miller's
"The Critic as Host," in *Deconstruction and Criticism*, ed. Harold Bloom and others (New
York: Seabury Press, 1979), 238–47.

tower as a linguistic palimpsest by draping it with flowers of rhetoric. Shelley's "parasite flowers" at once substitute for vanished lamps and suggest that figuration itself is the work of substitution as it hovers between the assertion of difference as loss (flowers in place of lamps) and the assertion of likeness as recovery (flowers illuminate the halls). In the same way, overgrown vines and ivy stand "in the place of" an erased imagery—but do the "*volumes* of their many twining stems" reinscribe this antique imagery or complete its obliteration? The passage repeatedly stages the failure of representation as an inevitable erasure of language by language: thus the seasonal withering of vines and flowers to a "winter-woof of tracery" reenacts this erasure and leads to another substitution, as their "volumes" give way to the alternating mosaic-work of sun or moon and stars (ll. 505–6). Moreover, the passage itself is already caught up in a larger chain of just such displacements: its fading flowers and the endlessly postponed return of their lost meaning recalls (in displaced form) the revolutionaries "to whom this world of life / Is as a garden ravaged," and whose suffering "Tills for the promise of a later birth / The wilderness of this Elysian earth" (ll. 186–89).

As in *The Revolt of Islam*, this "birth" is made all the more political by its Ionian locale (ll. 422, 542). Among the associations of Greece and its ruins in early nineteenth-century political argument (as Shelley well knew) the promise of historical rebirth loomed large. Both liberals and conservatives exploited the Ottoman subjugation of Greece in polemical broadsides. In a volume dedicated to George III, the Tory historian Gillies would compare ancient Athens and contemporary France in praising Britain's monarchical constitution, while the radical newspaper *Black Dwarf* even described Peterloo "in terms of the struggle between Turks and Greeks: the crowds now become 'each helpless Greek' while the yeomanry are transformed into 'ye English Janizaries of the *north*.' "[26] Greece's architectural ruins lent themselves readily to political symbolism, for they signified the degeneration of the Greek spirit under the Ottoman tyranny. Frederick S. N. Douglas commented, almost as if thinking of Shelley's chthonian tower, "it is scarcely credible how ill the glory of their ancestors is appreciated by the generality of the Greeks, who, dwelling amidst the ruins of former ages, are content to attribute them to an ideal Constantine, or in some districts to the agency of a supernatural

---

[26] Cited by Timothy Webb in his introduction to *English Romantic Hellenism, 1700–1824* (New York: Barnes and Noble, 1982), 29–30. Webb supplies several other examples of this kind of political symbolism.

power."[27] In *Childe Harold's Pilgrimage*, shattered Greek columns and temples "Commingling slowly with heroic earth" struck Byron as causes to mourn "Fair Greece! sad relic of departed worth!" (2.806, 693). In its contemporary contexts, the ruined tower of *Epipsychidion* would inevitably suggest a lost democratic past that revolutionary struggle might reclaim.

Similar republican associations surround Shelley's "age of gold" (l. 428). *Epipsychidion*, like Keats's *Hyperion*, depends on the fact "that the whole myth of the Fall from 'Saturnian rule' to 'a Tartarian darkness' had already been invested with strong contemporary overtones of a historical, political, and social kind."[28] The golden age had served as a commonplace for the millennial glories republicans expected from the French Revolution: in Wordsworth's *The Excursion*, for example, the Solitary's republican enthusiasm had inspired him to sing "Saturnian rule / Returned,—a progeny of golden years / Permitted to descend, and bless mankind" (3.756–58). With Wordsworth, the overthrow of those hopes encouraged a conservative retrenchment Hazlitt criticized as a betrayal of the "new and golden era" that followed the fall of the Bastille.[29] Like Hazlitt, Shelley sensed that Wordsworth's discovery of "sufficient hope" in the life of natural communion meant "Dismissing therefore all Arcadian dreams, / All golden fancies of the golden Age."[30]

The allegorical force of *Epipsychidion* draws Shelley's golden age back to its prototypes. His vision of future fulfillment with Emily turns to the past, presenting itself as a cyclical recurrence. Transvaluing its original, this return also rejects perfect closure with its source. Shelley's revisionist attitude toward the Saturnian tradition rests on two issues: the historicity of the "golden years" and, crucially, the need for sexual equality. In Greek myth, precultural unity with nature characterized golden age contentment. In *Prometheus Unbound*, conversely, Asia denigrates Saturn for denying people "The birthright of their being, knowledge, power, / The skill which wields the

[27] Frederick S. N. Douglas, *An Essay on Certain Points of Resemblance Between the Ancient and Modern Greeks*, 3d ed., corrected (London: John Murray, 1813), 80–81.

[28] Sperry, *Keats the Poet*, 176.

[29] William Hazlitt, "Observations on Mr. Wordsworth's Poem The Excursion," in *The Complete Works of William Hazlitt*, ed. P. P. Howe, centenary ed., 21 vols. (London: J. M. Dent & Sons, 1930–1934), 4:120. M. H. Abrams discusses the political symbolism of the golden age myth in the Romantic period in "English Romanticism: The Spirit of the Age," in *Romanticism and Consciousness*, ed. Harold Bloom (New York: Norton, 1970), 90–118.

[30] Shelley never read these particular lines, which come from *Home at Grasmere*, MS D, ed. Beth Darlington (Ithaca: Cornell University Press, 1977), ll. 633, 625–626, but similar imagery can be found, for example, in *The Excursion* 3.756–58.

elements" (2.4.39–40). Shelley's "Ode to Liberty" corroborates Asia's judgment by making Periclean democracy and culture the apex of human experience (ll. 60 ff.). That is why the neo-Virgilian chorus of *Hellas*—"The world's great age begins anew, / The golden years return" (ll. 1060–61)—rests its vision of renewal on the faith that "Another Athens shall arise" (l. 1084). This same historicizing emphasis recurs explicitly in Shelley's "Essay on Christianity":

> The wisest and most sublime of the ancient poets. . . . represented equality as the reign of Saturn, and taught that mankind had gradually degenerated from the virtue which enabled them to enjoy or maintain this happy state. Their doctrine was philosophically false. Later and more correct observations have instructed us that uncivilized man is the most pernicious and miserable of beings, and that the violence and injustice, which are the genuine indications of real inequality obtain in the society of these beings without mixture and without palliation. (*CW* 6:250)

By extolling a golden age, *Epipsychidion* glances back to classical pastoral. But the poem dislocates its classical models by supplementing nature with civilization. However paradisal Shelley's island, the love prevailing there is assuredly a love among the ruins of human history and the continuities of human culture—"books and music," "instruments with which high spirits" invoke "The future from its cradle, and the past / Out of its grave" (ll. 519–22).

With the issue of sexual equality, Shelley's historicism proves similarly revisionary. In *A Discourse on the Manners of the Antient Greeks Relative to the Subject of Love*, he had lamented the inferiority of women in Periclean Athens, observing that "women, thus degraded, became such as it was expected that they should become," beautiful neither intellectually, morally, nor physically: "their eyes could not have been deep and intricate from the workings of the mind," and in consequence "could have entangled no heart in soul-enwoven labyrinths."[31] In the mythic golden age, at least according to the *Theogony*, no women even exist: paradise was lost with the coming of Pandora. Avowing the revolutionary power of desire, *Epipsychidion* alters its classical precursors to foster egalitarian passion in the new golden age.[32] For Shelley the liberation of women was perhaps the most sublime achievement of Christian culture: "The abolition of personal and domestic slavery, and the emancipation of women from a great part

---

[31] Cited as published in James Notopoulos, *The Platonism of Shelley: A Study of Platonism and the Poetic Mind* (Durham: Duke University Press, 1949), 408.

[32] Harry Levin discusses the idea of an erotic golden age as a Renaissance contribution to the original Greek myth in *The Myth of the Golden Age in the Renaissance* (Bloomington: Indiana University Press, 1969), 24–43.

of the degrading restraints of antiquity. . . . [are the bases] of the highest political hope that it can enter into the mind of man to conceive" (*Defence of Poetry*, 496). Shelley's "Italian platonics" pursues a historical synthesis of the classical ideal with the achievements of Dante's era, during which "the freedom of women produced the poetry of sexual love. . . . and a paradise was created as out of the wrecks of Eden" (*Defence of Poetry*, 496–97).

Epipsychidion insists that these paradises are recoverable historical legacies, and urges their recovery by proclaiming their surpassing worth. Shelley's erotic politics adds history to the body as equally necessary for love's realization. He stresses the necessary role of women, partly as an index to the egalitarian inclusiveness of his communal ideal, but partly to charge sexual desire with causal force; if the enfranchisement of women produced the erotic idealism of Dante, then the recovery of Dante's inspiration might advance the cause of freedom in nineteenth-century Europe. Shelley's refiguring of Dantean idealism produces both transferential allegory and a social vision of egalitarian sexuality. Pursuing democratic ideals through a prophetic aloofness, *Epipsychidion* seeks its political ends indirectly. Nevertheless, the poem's historical sense refashions Shelley's erotic idealism as a revolutionary agenda aimed at extending human freedom.

ALLEGORY AND APOCALYPSE

Interpretations of Shelleyan allegory—with its chiasmal reversals from a value to its opposite—must themselves veer to an opposite position eventually. Having credited *Epipsychidion* for its achievements in temporalizing the ideal, we must turn back to examine the limitations of those achievements. Elements compromising the poem's humanism and historicism are not difficult to find. Shelley's glorification of the body accords poorly with the tendency of his rhetoric to exhaust and discard all mediating figures. How authentic is an affirmation of worldly possibilities, we must ask, that emerges from a figural practice consistently avoiding representational closure with the world? Is the amatory politics of *Epipsychidion* authentically revolutionary or feminist? Unlike *The Revolt of Islam*, Shelley's hymn to Emily denies its heroine even a ventriloquized voice. In some of the surviving fragments of *Epipsychidion*, Shelley toys with the idea of Emily as something other than a real woman (*CW* 2:378). And in another, more troubling sense, there really is no woman in Shelley's poem, where Emily mirrors the poet's narcissism and serves as the object of a rhapsodic lyricism leaving her the mere reflex of his rhetorical virtuosity. If the poem's attitudes to women and the body ap-

pear so ambivalent, how legitimate are its parallel claims to historicize
the supernal? Does *Epipsychidion* accommodate transcendent prerog-
atives to a rhetoric of temporality, or is its humanism covertly obli-
gated to idealist assumptions?

The ideological contradictions of *Epipsychidion* refer again to the
indeterminacy of causal priority in the relationship of imagination
and history. In 1821, as the *Defence of Poetry* shows, Shelley's sense of
the interaction of artists and the historical process stressed their mu-
tual influence, avoiding (as we would expect) a simplistic determinism
moving from either art to politics or politics to art. By refusing his-
torical determinism, however, Shelley created an Archimedean point
in which poetry, its limitations realistically acknowledged, could qui-
etly reassume its mediation of powers enthroned beyond history, in
the sanctum of the poet's soul. The aversive gestures of *Epipsychidion*
sanction political hope by appearing as signs of prophetic election,
traces of an exalted impartiality that grandly disdain the institutional
expediencies ordinarily conditioning and constraining authority. Al-
lied to this vocational myth is an optimism about causality. Because "a
Poet participates in the eternal, the infinite, and the one," "his
thoughts are the germs of the flower and the fruit of latest time" (*De-
fence of Poetry*, 483), the "source of whatever of beautiful, or gener-
ous, or true can have place in an evil time," which evil cannot ulti-
mately or essentially corrupt, since the imagination "is the faculty
which contains within itself the seeds at once of its own and of social
renovation" (*Defence of Poetry*, 493). Preserving its capacity for socially
unmediated origination, the prophetic imagination can direct histor-
ical progression while avoiding historical contingency. *Epipsychidion*
validates Hayden White's claim that "Romanticist historical thought
can be conceived as an attempt to rethink the problem of historical
knowledge in the mode of Metaphor and the problem of the histori-
cal process in terms of the will of the individual conceived as the sole
agent of causal efficacy in that process."[33]

Like *Prometheus Unbound*, *Epipsychidion* thematizes a merely condi-
tional assent to becoming. The poem foregrounds the allegorical
phases of its figures, emphasizing the differential temporality of lan-
guage, but still employs an idealist model. In the end, *Epipsychidion*
circumscribes its allegory within a metaphorical dualism, so that tem-
poralizing gestures translate events and values from a higher realm
to its lower duplication. If Shelley skeptically undermines the super-
nal origin, he reclaims it on another level by emphasizing paradigms

[33] Hayden White, *Metahistory: The Historical Imagination in Nineteenth-Century Europe*
(Baltimore: Johns Hopkins University Press, 1973), 80.

of derivation and consequence in his treatment of history. In these paradigms, history again functions merely as alienated spirit in the process of returning to itself, and allegory as alienated metaphor teleologically compelled to relapse on its own originating potentiality. In *Epipsychidion* allegory and metaphor enact a mutually constitutive oscillation in which neither can establish clear precedence. The rhetorical circlings of *Epipsychidion* neither historicize the ideal nor idealize the historical because the "beginning" can be continually reassigned. Appreciating the political resonance of Shelley's rhetorical structures, we could insist that they politicize desire. The claim can be effortlessly reversed, though, with the same evidence—the text's heterogeneity, its inclusion of both historical and visionary elements—used to support the opposite conclusion that *Epipsychidion* idealizes the historical.

With *Epipsychidion*, we could go on forever asking whether the historical historicizes the ideal or the ideal idealizes the historical. Eventually we might ask instead why each alternative can undermine and replace the other so easily. The reason, as in *Prometheus Unbound*, is their tautological relationship. Arguments for the transformation of spiritual prerogatives into materialist ones and arguments for exactly the opposite transformation are formally indistinguishable. They are obverse forms of the same argument, the concave and convex turnings of a single dialectical spiral. We have encountered symmetrical reversibility of this sort before, as the form contradiction assumes in a metaphorical idealism. In *Epipsychidion* the relationship of history and transcendence is metaphorically idealized: each is the negative form of the other, and each assumes the place the other vacates in the cyclical dynamic of the poem. They are made dialectical antagonists, specular avatars displaced into difference and antithesis, but only through incorporation into a system where each element inevitably recuperates its opposite because each covertly implied the other all along. Patterns characterized by the mutual displacement and recuperation of contraries are myths of loss and recovery as idealizing in their assumptions as any tale of Eden, and as open to deconstruction.

When difference works merely as an agency for the return of the Same, the differential process remains controlled by an overriding identity of origin and end (of Lucifer and Hesper). As a luminous figure initially present to the speaker, subsequently lost, but finally reattained, Emily herself symbolizes the longed-for juncture of origin and end in *Epipsychidion*. The poet undertakes a quest for similitude (for "one form resembling hers," l. 254) that proceeds through alienated forms of Emily to Emily herself. Yet this quest concludes happily only because the women encountered along the way—the lady of "electric poison," the fair, wise, and true, the Moon, Planet, and Tempest—are Emilys in disguise, links in a self-regulatory circuitry stubbornly oriented toward recovery.[34] When the departed *must* be restored, it never truly departed; Emily can be redeemed from her estrangement into surrogate figures only when those figures do not really estrange her at all. Similar tautologies emerge with the passage from love quest to island paradise. Pointing to Shelley's description of the misty island as a veiled bride, Hughes notes that "the island is actually to be linked with the hypostatized Emily-figure of the first two parts," so that the poem "serves to identify the ground of the [lovers'] encounter with the encounter itself."[35] The poet can reach the island because it represents a symbolic version of Emily, but can consummate his love for her there alone, so that the island reflexively grounds the love that creates it. As an idealized past, or historical figure, the island is guaranteed by Emily, but only after Emily, as a personification of certain traditions, assumes her meaning from the cultural ideal she then makes available.

Crediting the poem's secularizing power, humanistic readings of *Epipsychidion* seek to negotiate its paradoxes by arguing that Shelley's poem develops from an initial position to its contrary. These readings overlook claims that the "humanizing of metaphysics is still metaphysical."[36] They misapprehend the circular identity of opposites— origin and end, humanism and theocentrism. Views of *Epipsychidion* that regard its island idyll as the culmination of a naturalizing supernaturalism, for instance, fix the poem's dialectic at a point just before it reverts into the phase uncongenial to their reading. Shelley's address to Emily concludes with a mounting intensity—"Our breath shall intermix, our bosoms bound, / And our veins beat together" (ll. 565–66)—that is self-evidently sensual. Yet this apotheosis of the body quickly intensifies beyond bodily constraints. Shelley's lovers become figures of an energy that subsumes individual identity, making them

> Like flames too pure and light and unimbued
> To nourish their bright lives with baser prey,

[34] Hogle points out that this recovery-by-similitude is problematic: "To approach this newly unified, objectified, and uplifted absolute, the speaker must rush into a quest from one 'shadow'-woman to another (ll. 246–71), all of whom seem to harbor a few of the standard's qualities (making each attractive) yet each of whom soon reveals a lack or perversion of the rest, driving the speaker away and onward" (*Shelley's Process*, 281).

[35] Hughes, "Coherence and Collapse," 276.

[36] J. Hillis Miller, "Tradition and Difference," *Diacritics* 2 (1972): 9.

> Which point to Heaven and cannot pass away:
> One hope within two wills, one will beneath
> Two overshadowing minds, one life, one death,
> One Heaven, one Hell, one immortality,
> And one annihilation.

(ll. 581–87)

Here the attraction of Shelleyan eros to death could hardly be clearer. "This tug of death has been unrelenting throughout the poem," Earl R. Wasserman remarks, "and repeatedly pulls its frame of reference beyond the limits of a mortal existence."[37] The contraries of *Epipsychidion* spiral upward beyond mortality and mediation due to the logic of the economy circumscribing them. Allegory does not end in a humanistic pathos. The end of allegory is apocalypse, not as achieved transcendence but as a figure for the self-undermining accelerations of a metaphorical idealism.[38]

The envoy complicates but does not nullify this spiraling. Shelley turns from "the height of love's rare Universe" to "Marina, Vanna, Primus, and the rest" (ll. 589, 601), apparently spurning the visionary sublime for a human community. Still, the envoy fails to persuade as a conclusion.[39] It is urbanely conventional, a gracious concession to Shelley's audience, but nonetheless a tagged-on address to a text ("Weak Verses, go, kneel") that has addressed Emily from its first line. As such, the envoy is an addendum to the central situation and emotional drama of the poem. In a sense *Epipsychidion* doubles itself in ending, or falls in two in ending, with the speaker's address to Emily finishing at line 590, but with his language continuing until line 604. The two conclusions are linked by their concern with language, of course, and are by no means contradictory. They remain skewed, however, like the edges of a Cezanne table, and confess Shelley's inability to resolve the energies of his poem at a single point of coincidence.

Moreover, the envoy is itself ambiguous. It restates rather than resolves the poem's formative contradictions. *Epipsychidion* remains gracious about love to the end; in its choice of sheer intensity, the poem's

[37] Earl R. Wasserman, *Shelley: A Critical Reading* (Baltimore: Johns Hopkins University Press, 1971), 458.

[38] "Shelley was led by Eros to annihilate the world of his imaginative vision," Ross Woodman comments, "because the way of Eros is the way of transcendence," in *The Apocalyptic Vision in the Poetry of Shelley* (Toronto: University of Toronto Press, 1964), 197.

[39] See Jean Hall's discussion of the "sense of incompleteness" created by the envoy, in *The Transforming Image: A Study of Shelley's Major Poetry* (Urbana: University of Illinois Press, 1980), 122.

final crescendo suggests an abiding faith in desire. But when the Sun/ Moon/Comet cosmos of lines 345–83 narrows to a concluding portrait of just two lovers, the poet and Emily, Shelley's image of erotic community fails to survive even the text that formulated it.[40] Shelley reinstates in desire, as the basis of its redemptive power, a version of the same distance that marks his own estrangement from the sources of power. He takes a love supposedly capable of returning society to the golden age and, by cloistering that love's virtues, implicitly admits its susceptibility to corruption *by* society. The envoy reconfirms this dilemma. Shelley mentions a coterie: his three friends as distinguished from society at large ("the troop which errs, and which reproves," l. 603). Is the envoy, then, an affirmation of the necessarily social contexts of poetic meaning, or another confession of social isolation, and of preference for a transcendent world, "not here," but built "beyond the grave" (l. 598)? Does Shelley's concluding address prefer society or the ideal?

The answer, of course, is that he prefers both, envisioning a social microcosm based on refined appreciation of the ideal, a community of authorial likenesses. As even the envoy suggests, the idealism and historicism of *Epipsychidion* are not alternatives but partial formulations of a single encompassing faith. The inseparability of the ideal and historical appears climactically when Shelley's earthly idyll modulates into the rhapsodic "flight of fire" (l. 590) with which it began, returning the poem to idealizing beginnings it never truly abandoned.[41] When the genealogical quest of *Epipsychidion* continually dislocates the origin, it undermines notions of causation and beginning essential to any vision of ideal or historical order.[42] The ending of *Epipsychidion* shows history and the ideal collapsing together, as the poem's rhetorical energies accelerate beyond the economy that had organized them, leaving it shattered. Construed in its true breadth

[40] Newman Ivey White noted the inconsistency of the island idyll, dedicated to Emily alone, with the preceding description of love's cosmos, dedicated to Claire, Emily, and Mary (*Shelley* 2:268). In *Shelley's Major Verse: The Narrative and Dramatic Poetry* (Cambridge: Harvard University Press, 1988), 175, Stuart M. Sperry stresses the implicit sexism of Shelley's amatory cosmos: "With superb male egotism he surrenders himself up to the domination of [the women's] influence within a planetary system he himself has created, which is in fact a projection of 'this *me*,' the ideal and idealizing part of the self."

[41] In this connection, Neville Rogers shows in *Shelley at Work: A Critical Inquiry* (Oxford: Clarendon Press, 1967), 246, that in fact *Epipsychidion* "began with its ending": the island idyll was the first part composed.

[42] Paul de Man sets forth the problems of Romantic genealogy in *Allegories of Reading: Figural Language in Rousseau, Nietzsche, Rilke, and Proust* (New Haven: Yale University Press, 1979), 79–82.

and import, Shelley's idealism resides neither with history nor transcendence but with a recuperative dialectic that explains temporality as the substitutive alternation of the mundane and the ideal. By correlating figural self-reversal with the assent to silence, and by emphasizing linguistic inadequacies, the broken structures of *Epipsychidion* end in an allegorical impasse. The invocation of death and annihilation at the close of *Epipsychidion* signifies abandonment of the reciprocal exchanges allowing *any* value to appear as the complement of its antithesis. The poem finally refuses the very idea of a cyclical complicity of contraries—the total form of Shelley's metaphorical idealism.

The Lost Audience

The renunciation of idealism in *Epipsychidion* emerges with the poem's emergent death wish, its attraction to a closure inconsistent with its allegory. The inconsistency is dramatized and discovered in the course of the work. As a result, Shelley's rejection of a desire given to metaphorically controlled transferences can occur only as his poem concludes. Coming at the end of a lengthy metaphorical invocation, this rejection cannot entirely offset the ardor and delight that precede it. The result is a complex (and prophetic) ambivalence. Shelley's ambivalence betrays an increasing anxiety about audience. His defensiveness about his prospective readership follows inevitably from the political contradictions of *Epipsychidion*, for the poem's politics resides principally in its affective strategies, which try to coax a sympathetic response from readers. More directly than in his earlier erotic poems (except perhaps the reading scenes of *Prometheus Unbound*) Shelley internalizes in his poem its relationship to an audience, "the esoteric few" (*Letters* 2:263). He speaks to his poem and commands it to find the special readership its difficult sublimity demands. Through the fiction of Primus, Marina, and Vanna, *Epipsychidion* once again reverts to its beginning, for the envoy develops the self-consciousness about audience that motivated the elaborate machinery of Shelley's prefatory Advertisement.

That the Advertisement to *Epipsychidion* exists in several drafts shows how hard Shelley worked on it. In the Advertisement, unlike earlier Prefaces, Shelley does not restrict himself to political or editorial maneuvering. He wholly disowns his poem, attributing it to a deceased recluse who had purchased "one of the wildest of the Sporades" (373). He thereby seeks to disarm criticism in several ways. His fiction about "the Writer of the following Lines" tries to secure an unbiased reading for *Epipsychidion* by maintaining authorial anonymity, while his frank declaration that the writer's schemes were "hardly practicable" forestalls criticism on that point. By glancing at the *Vita Nuova*, Shelley borrows a kind of innocence-by-association for the sexual heterodoxies of his poem, and identifies an orthodox precedent for its complex visionary allegory. Last, he blandly offers his readers membership in a spiritual aristocracy if they will accept the poem as a test of their sensibilities and acknowledge its merits. All of this is quite cleverly managed; none of it worked. Reviewers ridiculed *Epipsychidion* for its figural experiments and lax morality, instantly identifying it with Shelley himself: "There is nobody capable of wasting such poetry on such a theme," one critic complained, "except only the unfortunate Mr. Shelley."[43]

Most instructive, however, is the fact that the narrative premise permitting Shelley to address his readers is the death of the fictive author of *Epipsychidion*. In the image of this harmless eccentric Shelley recasts his own identity, and then obliquely commits suicide by killing his alter ego, as if the death of the poet were a necessary precondition to reaching and influencing an audience. *Epipsychidion* found few readers in Shelley's lifetime. The poem was withdrawn shortly after its publication—appropriately, perhaps, for its retraction shows *Epipsychidion* reverting from the world one last time. Shelley's distrust of his audience underlies the vocational crisis of his final phase. The conviction of artistic solitude virtually tolls through his letters from this period: "I write nothing, and probably shall write no more. It offends me to see my name classed among those who have no name"; "I wish I had something better to do than furnish this jingling food for the hunger of oblivion, called *verse*"; "I write little now. It is impossible to compose except under the strong excitement of an assurance of finding sympathy in what you write" (*Letters* 2:331, 374, 436). Despite these feelings, and their exacerbation by Byron's presence,[44] Shelley continued to write. But he made little progress with *Charles the First*, the major project he had undertaken, and his 1821 depictions of poetic immortality and prophetic vision, in *Adonais* and *Hellas* respectively, are darkened in mood.

A similar disillusionment marks Shelley's depictions of history after *Epipsychidion*. In *Hellas* Shelley optimistically views history "as a pro-

---

[43] From a review in *Blackwood's Edinburgh Magazine* (Feb. 1822), reprinted in *The Unextinguished Hearth: Shelley and His Contemporary Critics*, ed. Newman Ivey White (Durham: Duke University Press, 1938), 282n.

[44] Charles E. Robinson discusses Byron's debilitating creative influence on Shelley in 1821–1822, and Shelley's compositional problems in general, in *Shelley and Byron: The Snake and Eagle Wreathed in Fight* (Baltimore: Johns Hopkins University Press, 1976), 203–21.

gressive evolution of Spirit that bends time's circle into a spiral reaching ever closer to absolute perfection."[45] But qualifying that optimism, as Wasserman admits, is the tendency of such idealist historicism to reject earthly meliorism for transcendence, and exchange history for apocalypse. Also qualifying it is the "bitter prophecy" of *Hellas* (l. 1099), the world-weariness that "overturns and denies the whole of *Hellas* in the last six lines."[46] The literary history of the *Defence of Poetry* attempts to counter Shelley's isolation by presenting cultural traditions, in their essential continuity, as a kind of timeless community. While admitting in the *Defence of Poetry* that social oppression can conceivably destroy poetry, Shelley argues for a contribution of individual texts "to that great poem, which all poets, like the co-operating thoughts of one great mind, have built up since the beginning of the world" (493). However assured or volatile this cooperative ideal appears in the *Defence of Poetry*, it continually fails in Shelley's late poetry. In *Adonais* the community of mourners similarly connotes an essential continuity supporting the participatory aspects of poetic composition. But *Adonais* also illustrates the way such continuities presuppose transcendent sanctions, skeptically calls those sanctions into question with greater force, and concludes with a speaker "borne darkly, fearfully afar" (l. 492) and utterly alone on his journey.

Darker still are the moral and imaginative perspectives of *The Triumph of Life*, the unfinished masterpiece of Shelley's final year. This poem envisions history as a procession of characters personifying the subjugations and illusions of "Life," including the errancies of language and delusions of passion. *The Triumph of Life* includes no scene of sexual consummation, although Rousseau's encounter with the "shape all light" clearly renders an erotic epiphany of sorts. Shelley's manuscript marginalia suggest that this encounter restages St. Preux's reaction to Julie's kiss.[47] What *The Triumph of Life* restages above all is *Alastor*, with its visionary drama and erotically enervating idealism. With *The Triumph of Life*, the antitype becomes temptress as metaphor becomes allegory. The allegory of *The Triumph of Life* redefines eros as the reflex of death, and places Shelley's career as a love poet in final, tragic perspective.

---

[45] Wasserman, *Shelley*, 413.

[46] McGann, "Secrets," 26.

[47] See Donald H. Reiman, "Shelley's 'The Triumph of Life': The Biographical Problem," *PMLA* 78 (1963): 539–40, 547.

Chapter 7

SHELLEY'S DEATH MASQUE

Hast thou, in some safe retreat,
Waked and watched, to hear the roar
Of breakers on the wind-swept shore?
Go forth at morn. The waves, that beat
Still rough and white when blasts are o'er,
May wash, all ghastly, to thy feet
Some victim of the midnight storm.
From that drenched garb and pallid form
Shrink not: but fix thy gaze, and see
Thy own congenial destiny.
——Peacock, *Rhododaphne*

IF NEITHER mad nor bad, Shelley by 1822 had become someone dangerous to know. Trelawny reports him frightening Jane Williams by speaking of solving "the great mystery" (committing suicide) when with her in a boat: "He is seeking after what we all avoid, death," Jane said; "I wish we were away, I shall always be in terror. . . . You won't catch me in a boat with Shelley alone."[1] While many of the events of Shelley's last year illustrate his increasing fascination with death, Jane's fears strike an eerie note. They prefigure the whelming tides of Shelley's drowning and his poetry—as when the "shape all light" of *The Triumph of Life* approaches hovering above water, and when Rousseau, despondent over her disappearance, plunges among "The thickest billows of the living storm" (l. 466), life's chaos envisioned as a wind-driven ocean. From the perspective of this storm, the defaced Rousseau—a "grim Feature," eyeless and discolored (ll. 185–90)—appears as a proleptic image of Shelley's corpse, with its fleshless face, so that the unfinished text and its deceased author can seem each other's inevitable counterpart.[2] Their similarity reveals the figural

[1] Trelawny's recollection of Jane's remark, reported in his *Life of Percy Bysshe Shelley . . . Amended and Extended by the Author*, as cited by Donald H. Reiman, "Shelley's 'The Triumph of Life': The Biographical Problem," *PMLA* 78 (1963): 544.

[2] Paul de Man takes the poem's unfinished state as evidence "of a fracture that lies hidden in all texts" due to the self-deconstructing force of language, which he terms "disfiguration" and links to the notion of "defacement" as the erasure of identity, in

logic of autobiographical forms, in de Man's view, and reflects on the internalized autobiography of *The Triumph of Life*, its refiguring of Shelley's life in 1822. It also reflects on poetic tradition, for "the image of the drowned man ... haunts English poetry whenever the poet envisages the possibilities of imaginative failure through the overreaching of his powers."[3] However sudden Shelley's death by water, his poetic development culminates in *The Triumph of Life* as appropriately as Shakespeare's development culminates in the rich and strange transformations of *The Tempest*.[4]

Shelley's career concludes aptly in *The Triumph of Life* because he returns to the same complex of desire, doubling, and death that his most ambitious love poetry engages from the time of *Alastor*. His return shows the mind's interminable self-reflections shattering all possibilities of relation.[5] "The triumph of life," declares John Hodgson, "is the failure of the imagination," and in a sense this is quite true.[6] Yet for Shelley in 1822, the failure of life is more accurately the triumph of imagination and the ubiquity of illusion. His great unfinished poem reveals "the common structure of desire which leads self-enchanter and ideologue alike into life-imprisonment by the representational image."[7] It is an imprisonment occurring at the juncture of repetition and death. This juncture is a moment demanded by logic but unavailable to consciousness—a fictive moment, hypothetically necessary but quite unreal, a moment of absence or nonbeing. As such it is a moment of death, not death as a power of randomness, as de Man suggests,[8] but death as a power systematically presupposed

---

"Shelley Disfigured," in *The Rhetoric of Romanticism* (New York: Columbia University Press, 1984), 120. De Man discusses the tendency of literary self-portraiture to promote tropological defacement in "Autobiography and De-Facement," where he connects autobiography and disfiguration by their common dependence on specular models incapable of maintaining their own closure (*Rhetoric of Romanticism*, 70–71). For the appearance of Shelley's corpse, see *Trelawny's Recollections of the Last Days of Shelley and Byron*, ed. Edward Dowden (London: Henry Frowde, 1906), 79–80.

[3] John Heath-Stubbs, *The Darkling Plain* (London: Eyre and Spottiswoode, 1950), 33.

[4] Ronald Tetreault argues, conversely, that *The Triumph of Life* disrupts the dominant tendency of Shelley's development in *The Poetry of Life: Shelley and Literary Form* (Toronto: University of Toronto Press, 1987), 248–57.

[5] Harold Bloom reads *The Triumph of Life* as a myth of the destruction of relational possibilities in *Shelley's Mythmaking* (1959; reprint, Ithaca: Cornell University Press, 1969), 220–75. Lloyd Abbey offers a similar argument in *Destroyer and Preserver: Shelley's Poetic Skepticism* (Lincoln: University of Nebraska Press, 1979).

[6] John Hodgson, "The World's Mysterious Doom: Shelley's *The Triumph of Life*," *ELH* 42 (1975): 619.

[7] David Quint, "Representation and Ideology in *The Triumph of Life*," *SEL* 18 (1978): 641.

[8] In "Shelley Disfigured," de Man writes that "*The Triumph of Life* warns us that noth-

by life, a force that constitutes life and consciousness, ordering them by serving as the secret they try hardest to conceal.

Organized around this secret, *The Triumph of Life* emphatically justifies M. H. Abrams's claim that "Shelley's view of human motives and possibilities became more and more tragic" in the course of his development—though it is somewhat tendentious to say so, since Abrams himself warns against the "tendency to dramatize Shelley's career by imposing on it the form of a tragic plot, moving inexorably to *The Triumph of Life*."[9] Yet Abrams's terminology—"tragic" as opposed, for example, to "nihilistic"—perfectly suits the gathering darkness of Shelley's poem. This darkness has proven difficult to ignore but easy to slight. Many readers still pass from the poem's pessimism to considerations that (the arguments contend) significantly counterbalance it. Motivating such readings is the uncritical assumption that the truth always lies midway between extremes and that the measure of scholarly acumen remains a judicious bowing to both left and right. Also motivating them is a specious humanism that, insisting on imagination as a source of enriching values, equates the text's power of moral illumination with its power to console. Shelley's poetry demands a critical humanism that will contemplate despair and violence in their irreducible reality, thereby granting human life the moral dignity of its pain. *The Triumph of Life* insists on that dignity, I believe, but does so *against* life by revealing the antithetical relation of imagination and world. Shelley's poem traces the power of isolation inhabiting every exercise of imagination to death as its origin and end. The poem's moral extremism makes it the most harrowing exploration of solitude in the English Romantic tradition, and the clearest expression of one aspect of the Romantic legacy.

REPETITION AND DEATH

The Triumph of Life, as its title reminds us, reworks Petrarch's *Trionfi*, especially the *Trionfo d'Amore* and the *Trionfo della Morte*.[10] Reviewing

---

ing, whether deed, word, thought, or text, ever happens in relation, positive or negative, to anything that precedes, follows, or exists elsewhere, but only as a random event whose power, like the power of death, is due to the randomness of its occurrence" (122).

[9] These quotations come respectively from M. H. Abrams, "English Romanticism: The Spirit of the Age," in *Romanticism and Consciousness*, ed. Harold Bloom (New York: Norton, 1970), 111; and the headnote to *The Triumph* in *The Norton Anthology of English Literature*, ed. M. H. Abrams et al., 5th ed. (New York: Norton, 1986), 2:760.

[10] Two particularly good accounts of Petrarch's influence on *The Triumph* are A. C. Bradley, "Notes on Shelley's 'Triumph of Life,' " *Modern Language Review* 9 (1914): 29–

the *Posthumous Poems of Percy Bysshe Shelley* in 1824, Hazlitt focused on Shelley's portrait of victorious *Morte* in trying to re-create the frenzied complexity of *The Triumph*:

> life, death, genius, beauty, victory, earth, air, ocean, the trophies of the past, the shadows of the world to come, are huddled together in a strange and hurried dance of words, and all that appears clear is the passion and paroxysm of thought of the poet's spirit. The poem entitled *The Triumph of Life*, is in fact a new and terrific *Dance of Death*.[11]

In an 1815 essay on masques, Hunt had attributed "the origin of the Trionfi or Triumphs of the Italian poets" to "the time of Lorenzo de Medici, when a party of persons, during a season of public festivity, made their appearance in the streets, riding along in procession and dressed up like reanimated dead bodies, who sung a tremendous chorus, reminding the appalled spectators of their mortality."[12] Certainly Shelley realized the eschatological possibilities of the triumphal masque. He recasts politics as cataclysmic myth in *The Mask of Anarchy* by making his reigning Anarch "pale even to the lips, / Like Death in the Apocalypse" (ll. 32–33). He takes those same possibilities as justification for combining his dependence on Petrarch with an equally obvious dependence on Dante's *Commedia*, particularly its fictions of pilgrim and guide and of a postmortal journey.[13]

Both the *Inferno* and the *Purgatorio* were crucial models for *The Triumph of Life* because Shelley shared Dante's interest in allegorizing the spiritual condition of death. Like Eliot's *Wasteland*, *The Triumph of Life* offers "death" as an ironic figure, a verdict on the moral debility of the living. At the same time, Shelley's poem takes the convention of

---

30, and Richard Cronin, *Shelley's Poetic Thoughts* (New York: St. Martin's Press, 1981), 202–7.

[11] William Hazlitt, "Shelley's Posthumous Poems," in *The Complete Works of William Hazlitt*, ed. P. P. Howe, centenary ed., 21 vols. (London: J. M. Dent & Sons, 1930–1934), 16:273.

[12] Leigh Hunt, "Some Account of the Origin and Nature of Masks," in *Leigh Hunt's Dramatic Criticism, 1808–1831*, ed. Lawrence Huston Houtchens and Carolyn Washburn Houtchens (New York: Columbia University Press, 1949), 117. "Lines written among the Euganean Hills" envisions a mariner hastily skirting the Venetian shore "Lest [its] dead should, from their sleep / Bursting o'er the starlight deep, / Lead a rapid masque of death" (ll. 138–40).

[13] Shelley's debts to Dante are summarized in Bradley, "Notes," 442–45. Numerous critics of *The Triumph of Life* have called it an *Inferno*. The most interesting discussion of Shelley's response to the *Purgatorio* appears in Timothy Webb, *The Violet in the Crucible: Shelley and Translation* (Oxford: Clarendon Press, 1976), 310–29, where Webb analyzes Shelley's translation of the Matilda scene from *Purgatorio* 28, the crux of his indebtedness to the *Purgatorio* in *The Triumph of Life*, where Matilda is one of the chief prototypes of Rousseau's "shape all light."

a postmortal existence seriously enough to appropriate it as a narrative context. Rousseau's "sleep and rising in the valley represent not birth but death," as Hodgson claims, "and the subsequent experiences he recounts represent his symbolic reenactment, after death, of his mortal life."[14] Hodgson's reading seizes on the inescapable implications of Shelley's re-creation of a Dantean otherworld and accounts for the centrality of *The Triumph of Life* in his poetic development. *Alastor* had shown its protagonist in quest of "Death on the drear ocean's waste" (l. 305) even as Laon and Cythna sought death on a funeral pyre; Prometheus and Asia had retreated to a postmortal cave beyond mutability; *Epipsychidion* had simultaneously invoked "one life, one death" (l. 585) as love's telos. The setting of *The Triumph of Life* encrypts the imagination by transferring its story into the regions of death.

This transference, as Hodgson notes, results in a drama of reenactments. A legacy of the *Commedia*, where the souls of Dante's Hell and Purgatory compulsively repeat their moral errors, these reenactments underlie the very structure of Shelley's death-world. His dark Shape "Crouching within the shadow of a tomb" recalls both Petrarch's and Milton's figures of Death,[15] as well as Demogorgon. A black and "Awful Shape," the chariot-driven Demogorgon also subjugates rulers of the world ("And Conquest is dragged Captive through the Deep") when he is not lingering in his cave of potentiality with "the inarticulate people of the dead" (*Prometheus Unbound* 3.1.51; 4.556; 1.183). Haunted by the "ghastly shadows" of the dead, Shelley's *Triumph of Life* is set in the same death-world mentioned by

[14] Hodgson, "World's Mysterious Doom," 598. In *The Unacknowledged Legislator: Shelley and Politics* (Oxford: Clarendon Press, 1980), 261 n. 1, P.M.S. Dawson challenges Hodgson's claim "that Rousseau's account concerns his post-mortal existence." But Hodgson clearly argues for a postmortal *setting* in which events and stories repeat earthly life, a position Dawson seems to accept, for he subsequently remarks that "as the post-mortal framework borrowed from Dante serves to show, Death cannot liberate Rousseau from Life" (281). Hodgson's argument has been accepted by Jerrold E. Hogle in *Shelley's Process: Radical Transference and the Development of His Major Works* (New York: Oxford University Press, 1988), 320, and by Charles E. Robinson, who suggests that Shelley wrote *The Triumph of Life* as a seventh *Trionfo* designed to follow the triumph of Eternity over Time with a triumph of Life over Eternity, so that "Life in Shelley's poem pursues man *even into the valley of Death* and should be termed the car of *Life-in-Death* which enthralls man beyond the grave," in *Shelley and Byron: The Snake and Eagle Wreathed in Fight* (Baltimore: Johns Hopkins University Press, 1976), 222–23.

[15] Petrarch's Death is "a woman shrouded in a dress of black," in *The Triumphs of Petrarch*, trans. Ernest Hatch Wilkins (Chicago: University of Chicago Press, 1962), 54. The resemblance of Shelley's Life and Milton's Death is noted by, among others, Donald H. Reiman in *Shelley's "The Triumph of Life": A Critical Study* (Urbana: University of Illinois Press, 1965), 29.

Prometheus' Mother Earth. She offered doppelgänger visitations as evidence of "two worlds of life and death," the second a mirrored dimension "underneath the grave, where do inhabit / The shadows of all forms that think and live" (*Prometheus Unbound* 1.195, 197–98). Shelley had returned to this phantom realm a few months previously, in *Hellas*, where the materialized image of Mahomet the Second tells Mahmud that

> The Anarchs of the world of darkness keep
> A throne for thee round which thine empire lies
> Boundless and mute, and for thy subjects thou,
> Like us, shalt rule the ghosts of murdered life,
> The phantoms of the powers who rule thee now.
>
> (ll. 879–83)

Recalling "the ghost of [his] forgotten dream," like Prometheus remembering his curse, Mahmud enters a dimension in which

> The Past
> Now stands before [him] like an Incarnation
> Of the To-come
>
> (ll. 852–54),

and in which the recovery of the dream replays an event from life. The death-world of *The Triumph of Life* is the mirrored inverse of the life-world, a repository of prophetic and retrospective shadows of earthly events, like Freud's atemporal unconscious. Borrowing the punitive scheme of the *Commedia*, *The Triumph of Life* portrays a people condemned to repeat the fatal errors of their earthly past, endlessly duplicating their obsessions.

Of course, this scheme also refashions the events of the first world, the life-world, as reenactments. Shelley's deathly pageant mirrors life, but in so doing it mirrors the doublings of experience. An aura of déjà vu haunts Shelley's speaker even before he encounters the spectral parade. Waking near a mountain on a summer morning, the speaker of *The Triumph of Life* knows

> That I had felt the freshness of that dawn,
> Bathed in the same cold dew my brow and hair
> And sate as thus upon that slope of lawn
>
> Under the self same bough, and heard as there
> The birds, the fountains and the Ocean hold
> Sweet talk in music through the enamored air.
> And then a Vision on my brain was rolled.
>
> (ll. 34–40)

The advent of trance, directing the mind to a newfound awareness, implies that in *The Triumph of Life* even beginnings restage prior occurrences. The production of "Vision" from this feeling of repetition implies in turn that imaginative acts are themselves repetitions, sequences of perceived resemblances between then and now. The poem later corroborates this suggestion. When Rousseau's story of imaginative awakening—the irradiated spring landscape, the oceanside cave, and so on (ll. 308–48)—reproduces the setting of the protagonist's vision, *The Triumph of Life* provides "two parallel accounts of the same experience."[16] The characters of Shelley's poem, like the characters of Joyce's *Ulysses*, inhabit a universe of recurring prototypes, passing through "sequences of situations and thoughts which are bound . . . by coincidence, with the situations and thoughts of other living and dead men and of fictional, mythical men."[17] Shelley's internalized focus foregrounds the repetitions of consciousness. Here thought and emotion retrace paths already taken, though only dimly remembered, as if all aspirations seek recoveries that might nullify an inherent belatedness.

With their air of uncertainty, the repetitions of *The Triumph of Life* belong to the second of two repetitive modes discussed by J. Hillis Miller. The first, Miller writes, "is grounded in a solid archetypal model which is untouched by the effects of repetition," and which "gives rise to the notion of a metaphoric expression based on genuine participative similarity or even on identity"—precisely the repetitive form implied by Shelley's metaphorical idealism.[18] The other, "Nietzschean mode of repetition," Miller adds, "posits a world based on difference":

> It is a world not of copies but of . . . "simulacra" or "phantasms." These are ungrounded doublings which arise from differential interrelations among elements which are all on the same plane. This lack of ground in some paradigm or archetype means that there is something ghostly about the effects of this second kind of repetition. It seems that X re-

[16] G. M. Matthews, "On Shelley's 'The Triumph of Life,' " *Studia Neophilologica* 34 (1962): 106. This parallelism has been widely noted. William Keach points to reflexive imagery as "one of the means by which Shelley suggests a complexly infolded and parallel relationship between Rousseau's experience and that of the narrator," in *Shelley's Style* (London: Methuen, 1984), 108.

[17] Richard Ellmann's useful phrase, from "The Limits of Joyce's Naturalism," *Sewanee Review* 63 (1955): 574.

[18] J. Hillis Miller, *Fiction and Repetition: Seven English Novels* (Cambridge: Harvard University Press, 1982), 6. Miller's summarizing treatment of this issue draws, as he indicates, on the thinking of Deleuze, Benjamin, and Nietzsche.

peats Y, but in fact it does not, or at least not in the firmly anchored way of the first sort of repetition.[19]

Shelley's poem re-creates precisely this uncanny ambience of repetitions unsure of themselves, evoking the opaque resemblances of dreamwork. Miller's allusion to Nietzsche is especially appropriate for *The Triumph of Life* because of the demystification of the phenomenology of causation in *The Will to Power*: "The fundamental fact of 'inner experience,'" Nietzsche argues, "is that the cause is imagined after the effect has taken place."[20] In *The Triumph of Life* repetition regressively seeks prior scenes left ghostly largely because they are created by the very gestures of "recurrence" they elicit. Shelley's poem may organize itself around inaugural moments, but they remain strangely fictive moments dispersed by every effort to stabilize them.

Dispersal becomes intrinsic to repetition in *The Triumph of Life* as Shelley links recurrence with its opposite: effacement. His poem stresses the "flight of time and with it the perpetual erosion of vision, together with the persistence of something deeply buried and enduring in imagination."[21] Like the word "recall" in *Prometheus Unbound*, repetition and erasure combine as elements of a single, self-contradictory structure that both reaffirms and cancels presence. The action of cancellation has been noticed by numerous readers fascinated by the flux of layered palimpsests the text cannot arrest. Here the mind's "realizations" dwindle into a state that, poised between oblivion and memories dimly sensed, tentatively redefines consciousness as a series of fadings within fadings—with awareness at best "held in suspension for a moment so that the mind can remember what it must forget," but only for a moment, so that each visionary episode "forgets the knowledge achieved by the forgetting that preceded it."[22] The complex backward-eddyings of forgetfulness, of ungrasped mysteries trailing away, underlie an insistence on mutability that counteracts Shelley's equivalent attention to doublings. Why this odd pairing of vanishings and recurrences?

The pairing makes repetition the reflex of evanescence, the mind's defensive reaction to temporality. Origins permit such compensatory gestures by giving human fears something to retrieve. That Shelleyan

---

[19] Miller, *Fiction and Repetition*, 6.

[20] Friedrich Nietzsche, *The Will to Power*, ed. Walter Kaufmann, trans. Walter Kaufmann and R. J. Hollingdale (New York: Random House, 1967), 265.

[21] Stuart M. Sperry's phrase, from *Shelley's Major Verse: The Narrative and Dramatic Poetry* (Cambridge: Harvard University Press, 1988), 187.

[22] Angela Leighton, *Shelley and the Sublime: An Interpretation of the Major Poems* (Cambridge: Cambridge University Press, 1984), 171; de Man, "Shelley Disfigured," 119.

origins are retrospectively projected merely emphasizes their structural necessity. This necessity illustrates Nietzsche's point that experience is always mediated by interpretation: "everything of which we become conscious is arranged, simplified, schematized, interpreted through and through."[23] Requiring the notion of source and derivation, these linear and cyclical paradigms require the origin. Consciousness as an organized state of intellection presupposes this nodal moment as a term structurally necessary but void of meaning and reality in itself. *The Triumph of Life* dramatizes originary absence most clearly in Rousseau's encounter with the "shape all light," who hears his questions and offers him her cup. Does he drink from it? Carlos Baker doubts that Rousseau drank, while Harold Bloom insists that he did.[24] We need not choose between these claims. The poem compares Rousseau to "a shut lily" vitalized by dew, allows that he "Touched with faint lips the cup she raised," and supplies his narrative of subsequent events, which reduce his mind to a sandy "shore" washed by tides (ll. 401, 404, 409). The actual moment of drinking *is* elided here, as no lips meet any liquid. Yet the framing of Rousseau's act powerfully implies his drinking: we have dewfall, lips touching a cup, and a wave bursting in foam on a beach. Two vehicles—"*as* a shut lily," a brain become "*as* sand"—enclose as prefiguration and aftermath a flowing implied by the logic of comparison but not literally registered in words.

These fascinating lines illustrate a displacement of origins that recurs throughout *The Triumph of Life*. Still, we cannot say that Shelley's poem reveals the absence of the origin, since the act of displacement presupposes the origin as a displaceable element. Just as words signify only through their places in a system, the Shelleyan origin is intrinsically vacuous but structurally functional. *The Triumph of Life* insists—the point remains no less crucial for its appearance of glib paradox—that the origin is not so much absent as present in its absence, present *as* absence. The Shelleyan origin is a negative epiphany, a moment of nothingness that is also a figure of death. *The Triumph of Life* becomes the mythic nightmare so many readers have felt it to be by unveiling the desirability of death. Shelley mingles desire and death in showing sensualists pursuing a fulfillment that is the dissolution ("the bright destruction," l. 154) of their being, and by characterizing life's worshippers, with telling indiscrimination, as "Some flying from the thing they feared and some / Seeking the ob-

[23] Nietzsche, *Will to Power*, 263–64.

[24] Carlos Baker, *Shelley's Major Poetry: The Fabric of a Vision* (Princeton: Princeton University Press, 1948), 267; Bloom, *Shelley's Mythmaking*, 269.

ject of another's fear" (ll. 54–55). The Chariot of "Life" clinches these
suggestions when, as Jerrold E. Hogle writes, the "traditionally invis-
ible or heavily veiled 'center' of the *Merkabah* . . . is turned by Shelley
into yet another reworking of Milton's amorphous Death."[25] Trium-
phally enthroned, death reigns as the secret obsession on which life's
longings converge.

Yet these images of death remain less important in themselves, fi-
nally, than in their reference to Shelley's absent origins. Constituted
by originary absence, human aspiration constitutes itself through its
structural dependence on death. In *The Triumph of Life* moments of
nullity are foretastes of death, moments of prophetic nothingness by
which consciousness, incorporating the knowledge of its eventual dis-
solution, incorporates its greatest terror as the secret motive of all
attachments to life. However complex and refined their sublimated
forms, desires emerge in our recoil from a knowledge of death car-
ried blindly within us, a knowledge implied by the images of death
scattered throughout a poem designed as an allegory of conscious-
ness. For Freud, of course, the repetitive character of the instincts
betrayed their deathward orientation, so that death and repetition
reconsolidate an alliance first apparent in the coincidence of death
and doubling in the doppelgänger.[26] If *The Triumph of Life* also carries
us beyond the pleasure principle, it does so by taking a distinctly Shel-
leyan direction. The poem disdains the Freudian sense of death's
somnolent seductiveness for an otherworld flushed by feverish and
chaotic motion. Shelley's meditation on doubling and desire nonethe-
less verges on Freud's tragic insight that "the aim of all life is death,"
and thereby achieves a Romantic uncanniness.

LOVE'S TRANSFIGURATIONS

The despondency occasioned by Shelley's exploration of repetition
and death ramifies through many issues. It takes the form of political
disillusionment, certainly, but centers on the dynamics of erotic ide-
alization as exemplified by Rousseau. Rousseau's interest in ideal love
largely explains Shelley's choice of him as a surrogate Virgil. Rous-

[25] Hogle, *Shelley's Process*, 332.

[26] Freud discusses repetition compulsion and the double in "The Uncanny," in *SEF*
17:234–36. My argument also relies on Freud's *Beyond the Pleasure Principle*, *SEF* 18:7–
64, which notes humankind's pleasure in repetition, views such pleasure as a regressive
attraction to sameness, and discovers in human instincts a longing for the undifferen-
tiated stasis of pre-existence, the origin-as-death. The phrase quoted in this paragraph
is from *Beyond the Pleasure Principle* (38). Leighton notes the quality of Freudian uncan-
niness of repetitions in *The Triumph of Life* (*Shelley and the Sublime*, 159).

seau's role here is understandably complex, involving his political iconoclasm and fame as a theorist of democracy. Still, the *Defence of Poetry* mentions Rousseau to enlist him among those writers who "have celebrated the dominion of love" (497). Shelley's presentation of him in *The Triumph of Life* accords with the treatment of passion in *La Nouvelle Héloïse* while also echoing Byron's famous description of him in *Childe Harold's Pilgrimage*:

> His love was passion's essence—as a tree
> On fire by lightning; with ethereal flame
> Kindled he was, and blasted; for to be
> Thus, and enamoured, were in him the same.
> But his was not the love of living dame,
> Nor of the dead who rise upon our dreams,
> But of ideal beauty, which became
> In him existence, and o'erflowing teems
> Along his burning page, distemper'd though it seems.
>
> (3.734–42)

Shelley's use of Rousseau as an exemplar of Romantic idealization naturally organizes the lines introducing the "shape all light," for the shape acts as Rousseau's erotic antitype. Shelley consequently associates her too with love. He compares her fading to the waning of Venus (ll. 412–13), and her "chrystal glass / Mantling with bright Nepenthe" (ll. 358–59) recalls the reference to "the sweet taste of the nepenthe, love" in *Prometheus Unbound* (3.4.163). She rightly approaches on feet "with palms so tender / Their tread broke not the mirror of [the river's] billow" (ll. 361–62) because in *The Symposium* Eros "never treads upon the ground . . . but lives and moves in the softest thing in the whole of nature."[27]

Through the mirror imagery surrounding the shape, *The Triumph of Life* can return to language, to Shelley's notion of love as a metaphorically conceived pursuit of integration. If Rousseau's visionary maiden recalls Emily, the veiled maid of *Alastor*, and other erotic antitypes in Shelley's poetry, she is also a muse figure from Hesiod, approaching to the accompaniment of a "ceaseless song" and "measure new," her poetic "feet" seeming to "blot" thoughts as ink is blotted (ll. 370–84). She enacts the unrelenting slippage of meaning that signifies "the mode of being of all figures."[28] As both an idealized object

[27] Plato, *The Symposium* 195e (trans. Michael Joyce). This passage incorporates Homer's description of Delusion in *Iliad* 19, as Quint notes ("Representation," 649 n. 11).

[28] De Man, "Shelley Disfigured," 109. For other associations of the "shape all light" with language, see, for example, de Man, "Shelley Disfigured," 113; Leighton, *Shelley and the Sublime*, 169–71; and Quint, "Representation," 649–50, the source of the com-

of desire and a figure with linguistic connotations, the luminous shape allows Shelley to reexplore the alliance of love and language. The poem's mental theater depicts desire crystallizing as an orchestration of substitutive crossings, as with the especially dense figural succession rendering Rousseau's projection of the luminous shape. As Shelley's recasting of Matilda singing and dancing near the river Lethe in *Purgatorio* 28, the "shape all light" lets Shelley experiment with that "imagery . . . drawn from the operations of the human mind" for which the Preface to *Prometheus Unbound* had praised Dante so highly (133).

Because it approaches desire and knowledge as philosophical problems of language, *The Triumph of Life* can appear remarkably contemporary in its interests—as if Shelley devoted his poem to pursuing the ultimate implications of the sign's arbitrary status in skeptical linguistics. In a sense, that is precisely what he did, reformulating as a problem of reading and representation the vocational crisis gripping him in 1822. Yet to all appearances, he took his inspiration less from the language theory of Locke or Monboddo than from Dante's poetry. Shelley simply accentuates his debt to the *Commedia* when Rousseau mentions Dante's story of "How all things are transfigured, except Love" (l. 476). The most complex figures of *The Triumph of Life* are Shelley's extrapolations from the rhetorical practice of the *Commedia*. In them he restructures the extended conceits by which Dante psychologized the traditional epic simile:

> Even as snow among the sap-filled trees
> along the spine of Italy will freeze
> when gripped by gusts of the Slavonian winds,
> then, as it melts, will trickle through itself—
> that is, if winds breathe north from shade-less lands—
> just as, beneath the flame, the candle melts;
> so I, before I'd heard the song of those

---

parison with Hesiod. Identifying the shape as "a figure of imagination itself," Earl Schulze sees her as an image of revisionary allegory opposed to the dogmatic ossifications of traditional allegory, in "Allegory against Allegory: 'The Triumph of Life,' " *SIR* 27 (1988): 31–62. My understanding of language in *The Triumph of Life* also depends on J. Hillis Miller's *The Linguistic Moment: From Wordsworth to Stevens* (Princeton: Princeton University Press, 1985). I am especially indebted to Miller's account of the logic compelling elements that are each other's contrary to switch positions in a "continual chain of melting antitheses" (*Linguistic Moment*, 122) that dissolves only to reform. For Miller, this nonprogressive pattern, which annihilates its constitutive antitheses without having the power of self-annihilation, is the "Life" Shelley's poem depicts; it is also an extremely accurate description of the "allegorizing of metaphor" pattern discussed in previous chapters.

whose notes always accompany the notes
of the eternal spheres, was without tears
   and sighs; but when I heard the sympathy
for me within their gentle harmonies,
as if they'd said, "Lady, why shame him so?"—
   then did the ice that had restrained my heart
become water and breath; and from my breast
and through my lips and eyes they issued—anguished.

(Purgatorio 30.85–99)

These lines probably account for Rousseau moving "as one between desire and shame / Suspended" (ll. 394–95). The pertinence of Dante's description rests not with specific echoes, though, but with its basic figural manner. The focus on consciousness, the patient, delicate tracing out of details and conditions ("when gripped . . . if winds"), the layering of comparisons within comparisons (as in the brief reference to the melting candle) can all be seen in Shelley's strategically involuted rhetoric. In a famous instance, Shelley describes the brain as a shoreline deer had run across, after which a wave crashed, half-erasing the deers' hoofprints, which a pursuing wolf then trod on, leaving its own prints intact until the crashing of a second wave, which falls even as it is mentioned—all of this (in its entirety) resembling the bursting of a previously unseen vision, which makes the luminous female shape fade like the morning star when its light recalls the odor of jonquils surrounding a Brescian shepherd as he readies himself for sleep (ll. 405–23). Celebrating the permanence of "the Love that moves the sun and the other stars" (*Paradiso* 33.145), Dante had extolled a love apotheosized in the revelation of divinity, a love that *is* transfigured, as Christ was before his disciples. Shelley's skeptical "transfigured" connotes "transferred by a figure." It refers to the action of figuration in its restless instability.

This notion of figuration organizes *The Triumph of Life* around an entirely demystified allegorizing of metaphor, as the "shape all light" shows. Shelley begins with metaphor when Rousseau first projects the shape. Her footsteps kiss the lake without breaking "the mirror of its billow" (l. 362), so that she dances toward Rousseau like likeness itself, accompanied by her own reflection as though she had wandered off the pages of "On Love." She seems "Partly to tread the waves" and "partly to glide along / The airs" (ll. 370–72) because in her liminality she apparently mediates earth and heaven, again like metaphor. Her ministering rainbow (l. 357), a symbol at least momentarily of covenant rather than mutability, implies as much. The shape resembles the Witch of Atlas as a child of sun and water, connoting "a union of the Absolute and the limited, the Eternal and the temporal" in symbolic language.[29]

Shelley broadens the range of the shape's reconciliatory power through references to time. His beautiful shape flings "Dew on the earth, as if she were the Dawn" (l. 353), yet wanes like a fading star "in the coming light / As veil by veil the silent splendour drops / From Lucifer" (ll. 412–14). Rousseau's idealizing response to her takes her temporal role-changing as an expansion rather than a metamorphosis or a loss of identity. The sun and the stars converge in the "shape all light," who unifies day and night as eros lends lovers an essential oneness. Here we begin and end with the same sunrise in process, as if everything—from the shape's appearance as Dawn, dispensing dew and music, to the "coming light" of sunrise in line 412—took place in a single, suspended moment.[30] Shelley's luminous lady wields the power of similitude to gather out of time's dispersal a moment of such plenitude that it seems like a glimpse of eternity. Yet this reading of the "shape all light" betrays the symmetrical reversibility to which all idealizations of metaphor are subject. If the shape can seem to assimilate contraries as unity, she can also seem to temporalize them as allegorical difference. The simultaneity of opposites (sun and moon) in Shelley's lady hardly decrees union or identity. Although beginning and ending with dawn, the moment of the shape's apparition occurs as a passing moment poised on the verge of its own disappearance. In changing from figure to figure, from sun to stars, the shape succumbs to the mutability that Shelley's passage everywhere acknowledges. She vanishes into a night generated by the passage in its inability to represent her, banished from perception by the self-disfiguring light she brings.

This temporalizing and disfiguring light is language as a power that continually disrupts the perceptual possibilities it creates. Correlating time and language, Shelley's transfigurative shape expresses the action of allegory as a temporalizing succession of differences. Rousseau's meeting with the shape introduces metaphor merely to dislocate it allegorically. In no other poem does Shelley break and scatter metaphor so dramatically into metonymic debris. Light, for example, is displaced among reflections, kindled treetops, rainbows, sun, moon, stars, the mind's "embers," the visionary chariot's unnatural glare, and so on in a compilation of vehicles that unrecognizably disfigure their initiating comparison. In *Epipsychidion*—where the

---

[29] Reiman, *Shelley's "Triumph of Life,"* 63.

[30] Jean Hall makes this point in *The Transforming Image: A Study of Shelley's Major Poetry* (Urbana: University of Illinois Press, 1980), 158.

speaker can exclaim, "See where she stands!" (l. 112)—Emily retains a dramatic *presence*, an apparent availability, that reincites the effort to represent her despite the continual failure of language. In *The Triumph of Life* the lapsing of metaphor into metonymy belongs to a complex process of loss. The wolf and deer tableau mentioned earlier illustrates the first stage of this process:

> "And as a shut lily, stricken by the wand
>   Of dewy morning's vital alchemy,
>
> "I rose; and, bending at her sweet command,
>   Touched with faint lips the cup she raised,
> And suddenly my brain became as sand
>
> "Where the first wave had more than half erased
> The track of deer on desert Labrador,
>   Whilst the fierce wolf from which they fled amazed
>
> "Leaves his stamp visibly upon the shore
>   Until the second bursts."
>
>   (ll. 401–10)

Here reading follows in the wake of meaning. We must infer the escape of the deer—they are never *there* in the simile, having "fled" by the time the wolf leaves its signature—only from the fading palimpsest of their tracks, imprinted in the sand. These inscriptions are writing. Words signify through the differences between successive markings in which the latter seek to retrace the former correlatively but also help to obscure them, just as the parasite flowers of *Epipsychidion* helped erode the imagery their "volumes" replace (l. 501). Shelley's scenario of flight and pursuit depicts language as a fading trace-structure of mutually unfitted elements, a differential network without positive terms.

This absence in language is what Rousseau drinks from the shape's cup: a realization of her fading that itself fades as he realizes it, so that his act of drinking becomes as dubious as the knowledge it dubiously confers. The narrative structure of *The Triumph of Life* depends similarly on a lacuna to connect the two chariot visions. Like the shared "*O follow, follow!*" dream of Asia and Panthea, the vision of life that the protagonist and Rousseau experience establishes a common ground where self and antitype touch almost as a hand can touch a mirrored surface reflecting it. This touching is interrupted, however, for Shelley interposes Rousseau's account of the luminous shape between the chariot visions. The shape therefore acts as a narrative bridge carrying readers from the chariot's initial appearance to its duplication in Rousseau's dream, mediating the two visions much as Panthea mediated Prometheus and Asia in the second act of *Prometheus Unbound*. Yet Shelley brilliantly denies the protagonist his own vision of the "shape all light."[31] The two versions of the chariot's passage are thus placed side by side like parallel lines, structurally adjacent but incapable of meeting. Due to the shape's simultaneous absence from the speaker's trance and intermediate position between the two trances, the poem's two visions are joined by the very event that disrupts their coincidence, allegorically linked by absence and difference.

The interposition of the "shape all light" between framing chariot visions of *The Triumph of Life* organizes the temporality of language as an oscillation between contraries, as the text moves from darkness to light to darkness. Drifting back to their matrices, Shelley's metonymic sequences succumb to the gravitational pull of chiasmus. The chiasmal reversals of *The Triumph of Life* often work as metalepses due to the poem's preoccupation with inaugural moments and transpositions of cause and effect. Rousseau's response to the shape's cup provides a case in point:

> "All that was seemed as if it had been not,
>   As if the gazer's mind was strewn beneath
> Her feet like embers, and she, thought by thought,
>
> "Trampled its fires into the dust of death,
> As Day upon the threshold of the east
>   Treads out the lamps of night, until the breath
>
> "Of darkness reillumines even the least
>   Of heaven's living eyes—like day she came,
> Making the night a dream."
>
> (ll. 385–93)

Rousseau extrapolates backward from the death of thought, reflexively discovering in such divestiture the vestiges of something previous. Shelley uses dawn imagery to suggest the metaleptic constitution of a supposedly prior state. Most remarkable, however, are the oppositional transfers complicating this false dawn as its description unfolds. The embers of consciousness are trampled into dust, and pre-

---

[31] As Miriam Allott emphasizes in "The Reworking of a Literary Genre: Shelley's 'The Triumph of Life,'" in *Essays on Shelley*, ed. Miriam Allott (Totowa, N.J.: Barnes and Noble, 1982), 262. The ability of Shelley's protagonist to "see" the radiant shape only insofar as she is part of Rousseau's vision—which his own concentrically encompasses—makes the antitype available only through an "other" version of himself (Rousseau as visionary counterpart).

sumably extinguished, but in a manner similar to the sun's appearance on the eastern horizon (so that light's diminishment is unexpectedly reversed into intensification), which, once introduced, is presented as the event that extinguished the stars (the reference to night harking back to darkness) in order to produce a day (back to light) that will endure until the night returns to reillumine the stars (and back to darkness). The passage returns to the nocturnal imagery that began it, but less by tracing a gradual circle than through continual veerings between antitheses.

Chiasmal reversal occurs throughout *The Triumph of Life*. Even Shelley's wolf enters the poem as the reversed afterimage of the deer's flight. A similar transposition informs Shelley's portrait of frenzied lovers crushed by the chariot, which leaves in its wake "Old men, and women foully disarrayed" (l. 165). As in the first act of *Prometheus Unbound*, where the consoling "Spirits do not merely replace the Furies—they *are* the Furies in another form,"[32] the elderly are the youthful sensualists of the previous lines (ll. 149–57) metamorphosed into their opposites by the passage of the chariot as a figure of temporal attrition. Of course, the most obvious of such metamorphoses relates Shelley's two major symbols, the erotic antitype and the triumphal chariot. *The Triumph of Life* associates the "shape all light" with Life by gender, by diction (both are "shapes"), by a common light imagery, as several critics have pointed out, and by their dreamlike quality—for "when Rousseau refers to Life as 'the new Vision,'" Dawson remarks, "his intention is to distinguish it from his former vision of the Shape, but his words reveal that both are 'visions.'"[33] This connection explains the aura of menace imbuing the radiant shape and her Circe-like offer of her cup, a fear that "bursts into actuality at the moment the cup is touched."[34] That bursting, the ap-

[32] Dawson, *Unacknowledged Legislator*, 115–16.

[33] Dawson, *Unacknowledged Legislator*, 273. To the claim that Shelley's "text even hints that the Shape should be identified with Life" (Dawson, 273) can be added Cronin's remark that "the appearance of the Shape all light parallels the appearance of the chariot" (*Shelley's Poetic Thoughts*, 215), and Tilottama Rajan's demonstration that "the language used to describe the Car is already present in the language used to describe the Shape all light," in *Dark Interpreter: The Discourse of Romanticism* (Ithaca: Cornell University Press, 1980), 68. The most interesting connection between these two shapes involves rhyme scheme: Reiman perceptively notes that the triple rhyme accompanying the arrival of the chariot—"form / storm / deform" (ll. 84, 86, 88)—recurs in Rousseau's response to the radiant shape's departure (ll. 464, 466, 468) (*Shelley's "Triumph of Life,"* 94).

[34] Balachandra Rajan writes that "the dew, the dawn, and alchemy are all signs pointing to creative transformation. Yet in the midst of all these associations, the word 'stricken' is also before us as the dark centre of the opening flower. The fear it congeals

pearance of the triumphal procession, does not substitute Eros for
Thanatos in the sense of replacing a value with a discrete opposite
value. Shelley's identification of the two visions implies that the "latter
shape is simply the . . . replica of the other."[35] When the "shape all
light" summons and then dissipates into the vision of Life, we witness
an inherently antithetical energy entering its contrary phase. The
amatory disillusionment of *The Triumph of Life* underscores the pow-
erlessness of any beneficent image, when allegorized, to forestall the
production of its opposite.

The chiasmal orientation of Shelleyan allegory portrays the mind's
temporalizing response to the ambivalence of experience. *The Tri-
umph of Life* recognizes the tendency of consciousness to organize it-
self dialectically, to see and name "according to antitheses."[36] But the
poem also stresses the involvement of antitheses. Shelley's opposites
are delusory moments in which the heterogeneity of consciousness
seems to vanish because a fixing of attention has briefly arrested the
mind's temporal flux. An entity's or value's self-differentiation, *The
Triumph of Life* insists, must not be misrepresented as a difference
between discrete essences.[37] By displaying the covert likeness of Life
and erotic antitype, Shelley's poem depicts the reversal of a value into
its opposite as an occluded tautology, a return of the Same in which
the cyclical recovery of value demonstrates that the form into which
it had been "alienated" was, in truth, always merely a surrogate ver-
sion of that value. As it demonstrates the logical reversibility of causal
sequences, *The Triumph of Life* deconstructs all cyclical retracings of
originary presence and myths of recovery. Shelley expends some of
his subtlest mockery on these myths. When the luminous shape leaves
Rousseau, who must cast about for consolation, he instinctively
reaches for imagery of diurnal cycles:

> "And as the presence of that fairest planet
> Although unseen is felt by one who hopes
>
> "That his day's path may end as he began it
> In that star's smile, whose light is like the scent
> Of a jonquil when evening breezes fan it,

---

bursts into actuality at the moment the cup is touched," in *The Form of the Unfinished:
English Poetics from Spenser to Pound* (Princeton: Princeton University Press, 1985), 191.

[35] Sperry, *Shelley's Major Verse*, 189.

[36] Miller, *Linguistic Moment*, 120.

[37] I refer to Barbara Johnson's "differences *between*"/"differences *within*" distinction,
from *The Critical Difference: Essays in the Contemporary Rhetoric of Reading* (Baltimore:
Johns Hopkins University Press, 1980), x.

"Or the soft notes in which his dear lament
The Brescian shepherd breathes, or the caress
That turned his weary slumber to content."

(ll. 416–23)

This subtly derisive evocation of pastoral associates cyclical recuperation ("That his day's path may end as he began it") with the childhood of the race and of poetry, dismissing it as Keats dismisses Madeline's self-sheltering immersion in dream: "As though a rose should shut, and be a bud again" (*The Eve of St. Agnes*, l. 243). The regressive character of such nostalgia explains its muted death wish—the Brescian shepherd's sense of night's beauty and sweetly wearied assent to darkness.

This darkness shadows eros especially. The alternating attractions and repulsions of passion, which Shelley compares to the collision of oppositely charged stormclouds (ll. 155–57), leave a residue of regenerative potentiality, an Aphrodite-like trace "of foam after the Ocean's wrath" (ll. 163). Yet that fertile trace, as Miller notes, can regenerate nothing more than the pattern of transposition itself, reversing the previous reversal to create a nonprogressive oscillation.[38] This pattern links love to powers ensuring its perpetual frustration. Like the Poet of *Alastor*, Rousseau projects his erotic antitype in an experience of visionary communion, and subsequently loses her. He reacts not by accepting existential contraries, or aspirations tempered "to the imperfection of the self,"[39] however, but by elegizing perfection as "forever sought, forever lost" (l. 431). Shelley conjectured in 1822 that "all discontent with the *less* . . . supposes the sense of a just claim to the *greater*" and, reavowing his idealism, took that supposition as "the right road to Paradise" (*Letters* 2:406). Rousseau also chooses Paradise: he loses rather than forsakes the radiant shape, and plunges recklessly into life's "living storm" (l. 466). Unlike the questing Poet of *Alastor*, Rousseau refuses to follow his visionary maiden or even to contemplate death as a pathway back to her. Until the end of *Epipsychidion*, Shelley's love poetry conceptualizes death as a fiery martyrdom capable of granting lovers perfected harmony. *The Triumph of Life*, as if to confirm Beatrice Cenci's worst fears, presents the afterlife as a perpetuation of life's repetitions at their most destructive.

[38] Miller, *Linguistic Moment*, 120–21, 124–25.

[39] T. Rajan, *Dark Interpreter*, 59. Rajan errs, in my judgment, in claiming that "*The Triumph of Life*, which seems at first to continue Shelley's sentimental commitment to a defeated idealism," rejects Schillerian sentimentality for a purgatorial humanism that "does not fall victim to the inevitable disillusion that follows the failure to attain the ideal" (59, 67). But she is certainly correct in claiming that the poem confronts readers with "a tragic knowledge into which every human being must be initiated" (61).

Critical options for minimizing this destructiveness are disallowed in advance by Shelley's demystified treatment of chiasmus. Idealizations of the poem's despair tend to fall into two categories. Taking the hint from Shelley himself, critics sometimes argue that the text's valorization of despair *as* despair presupposes joy (albeit a lost joy) as the standard of judgment.[40] As it moves from the negative to the positive pole negativity implies, this contention obviously effects a transposition of opposites. Responding to a pessimism created by the chiasmal reversals of the poem, these readings ironically depend on chiasmus themselves, but on recuperative reversals in no way sanctioned by the nonprogressive transpositions of Shelley's poem. Certainly despair and joy imply each other; the question rests with the particular way the poem conceives their mutual implication. The visionary disillusionment of *The Triumph of Life* evokes presence as the standard of meaning, but thereby raises a standard rendered unreachable by the same relational logic that erects it. As implied by the poem's omnipresent ambivalence—the beauty of the chariot, the threat posed by the "shape all light"—any reachieved fulfillment would, at the very moment of its recovery, merely carry to a subsequent level the same problem it purported to solve.

The second method attempts to circumscribe the text's darkness by confining it to one locus, to Rousseau ordinarily, attributing to him errors that the protagonist has not made and can avoid.[41] Yet Rousseau's "error" remains instructively nebulous. It is sometimes said to be excessive idealism, as with the Poet of *Alastor*, and sometimes ex-

[40] This point is usually made to qualify an acknowledged negativity, as in the remark that "the articulation of these forces [forgetting, obliteration, and erasure] depends upon the counterforces of remembering, literation, and repetition" (Keach, *Shelley's Style*, 192). But the point also occurs in arguments for humanistic balance in *The Triumph of Life*, as in Reiman's claim, "if life possesses grace that it is tragedy to lose, then *life* must have value and not be simply sound and fury signifying nothing. . . . Everywhere in 'The Triumph' the dark side of human experience is balanced by positive alternatives" (*Shelley's "Triumph of Life,"* 81, 84).

[41] For example, in order to argue that "there is an appropriate way to experience divinity, to 'love,' and it is possible to commune in however mediated a way with the Ideal," Michael Henry Scrivener must dissociate love from "loveless sexuality" in the depictions of both Rousseau and the frenzied lovers, and also Shelley's lines about Dante's vision of untransfigured Love from the poem's problematizing of Dantean theocentrism in its other debts to the *Commedia*, in *Radical Shelley: The Philosophical Anarchism and Utopian Thought of Percy Bysshe Shelley* (Princeton: Princeton University Press, 1982), 309, 313–14. For similar dissociative strategies in recent readings of the poem, see the distinction between Shelley, or his protagonist, and Rousseau (T. Rajan, *Dark Interpreter*, 69); the separation of Rousseau from both protagonist and reader (Schulze, "Allegory," 56); and Hogle's variation on this perspective: he regards the contrary oscillations of the text as part of a drama of choice that serves merely to "give [Shelley's] narrator and reader the option of choosing between repressed and accepted transference" (*Shelley's Process*, 334).

cessive rationalism, with Rousseau demanding too much certainty, we are told, in asking for the meaning of his life. But surely these are "the great but simple and inevitable questions, irresistible to human-kind,"[42] as Shelley implies by linking them to the request for happiness to last ("Pass not away upon the passing stream," l. 399). Rousseau hardly prompts the luminous shape's fading by asking the wrong questions—as if she would have lingered if only he had been silent—for she *is* fading, as a principle of language and desire. Readers should be wary of dissociating Rousseau and the speaker on any grounds when *The Triumph of Life* so determinedly stations them in parallel situations. We are occasionally reminded of the differences between Rousseau and Shelley's protagonist as if their failure to cohere absolutely should be found unusual. Yet the conspicuous resemblances linking these characters are the truly exceptional feature of *The Triumph of Life*, which need not have included such doublings and repetitions but which in fact foregrounds them. Dissociative readings do not restrict themselves to the relationship of these characters, of course, but metamorphose through separations of order from chaos, love from lust, and so on. Such readings slight the complicities of Shelleyan antitheses, misrepresenting differences within as differences between.

Attempts to redeem a value by severing its tie to its opposite are themselves the reversed forms of those arguments that discover affirmation in the relational logic by which despair implies hope. The latter argument insists on the connection between contrary terms; the former insists on the disconnection of mutually similar terms. These positions together comprise a single dialectical response to *The Triumph of Life*, one seizing on either the identity or utter alienation of Shelleyan contraries to still the text's indeterminate oscillations between them. We are sometimes told that *The Triumph of Life*, properly finished, might have moved in an opposite direction, from darkness to light. But readers who appreciate the allegorical force of Shelley's figural transpositions will find little comfort in the prospect of yet another reversal.

THE DELUSIONS OF IMAGINATION

The nightmare of *The Triumph of Life*, however unsettling its vision of love and language, is the nightmare of history. As "Shelley's encounter with his historical imagination,"[43] the poem is appropriately filled

---

[42] Sperry, *Shelley's Major Verse*, 192.

[43] Edward Duffy, *Rousseau in England: The Context for Shelley's Critique of the Enlightenment* (Berkeley: University of California Press, 1979), 126.

with actual historical characters and references to European politics. The triumphal procession of Shelley's poem, a pageant of imperial power, represents the historical process in its martial violence. Compared to the moon trembling on the verge of day, bearing with it "The ghost of [its] dead Mother" (l. 84), Shelley's chariot dramatizes the eruption of past into present. The car's driver is a blind charioteer who, as in *Hellas* (ll. 711–12), connotes the moral blindness of history. The illustrious great chained to the chariot reflect the zeitgeist's curtailment of mental freedom, for Shelley's "sustained metaphor of enlightenment as conquest has drafted the *philosophes* into the ranks of those motivated and traduced by power."[44]

It enlists poets in this same defeat. The triumphal parade's traditional associations allow it to signify the nexus of politics and prophecy, the politicization of poetry. "Shelley's chariot remains an emblem of the creative imagination," we are assured.[45] The suggestion has merit, and is obliquely substantiated whenever critics draw comparisons between the light imagery accompanying the chariot and the visionary "shape all light." Like all deific vehicles, the chariot is drawn by powers emanating from itself.[46] Like Shelleyan allegory, then, the triumphal car moves only in the wake of other versions of itself. Its vanguard lightnings, signs of poetic inspiration, herald the appearance of a vehicle occupied by masked and hooded figures, so that the chariot allegorizes the power of allegory, displacing inspiration into figural veilings. It will not do, in any event, to slight the chariot's dramatic context and construe its symbolism apart from the fact of its being *seen*, its appearance to a specific character as part of the accession of vision. Whatever its military associations, Shelley's chariot recalls the chariots of Ezekiel, Dante, and Milton; it recalls every "chariot of fire" conceived as a vehicle of the prophetic imagination.

By conflating historical and imaginative meanings in the car of Life, *The Triumph of Life* effects a coincidence of politics and poetry. They coincide in Rousseau too. Rousseau appears in *The Triumph of Life* not merely as the champion of idealizing desire in *La Nouvelle Héloïse*, but as the prophet of a revolutionary epoch. As in *The Revolt of Islam*, the political concerns of *The Triumph of Life* crystallize as "a

---

[44] Duffy, *Rousseau in England*, 111–12.

[45] Ross Woodman, *The Apocalyptic Vision in the Poetry of Shelley* (Toronto: University of Toronto Press, 1964), 186. Quint adds that Shelley's "allegorical figures do not point to some paraphrasable abstraction for which they have been substituted, but to their own function as imaginative representation" ("Representation," 640). For the specifically literary associations of Shelley's chariot, see Harold Bloom, *Poetry and Repression: Revisionism from Blake to Stevens* (New Haven: Yale University Press, 1976), 83–111.

[46] Bloom, *Shelley's Mythmaking*, 234.

thematic cluster around . . . the French Revolution."[47] This historical focus explains why Shelley's climactic moral pronouncement—the protagonist's reflections on the disjunction of "Good and the means of good" (l. 231)—follows his discovery of the "Fall'n" Napoleon. Again Shelley follows Byron's lead in canto 3 of *Childe Harold*, which also linked Rousseau and Napoleon. When Rousseau boasts, "If I have been extinguished, yet there rise / A thousand beacons from the spark I bore" (ll. 206–7), Shelley glances at the fire imagery with which Byron described Rousseau's political influence:

> For then he was inspired, and from him came,
> As from the Pythian's mystic cave of yore,
> Those oracles which set the world in flame,
> Nor ceased to burn till kingdoms were no more.
>
> (*Childe Harold's Pilgrimage* 3.761–64)

A version of the desire that teems "Along his burning page" (*Childe Harold* 3.742), Rousseau's oracular fire implies a politics of liberated love, an impassioned egalitarianism that "set the world in flame." We need merely remember Shelley's prayer to have his words scattered like "sparks . . . among mankind" ("Ode to the West Wind," l. 67), and his conviction of artistic isolation in 1822, to grasp the wishful pathos behind his choice of Rousseau for *The Triumph of Life*: even more so than the immensely popular Byron, Rousseau stood as an acknowledged legislator of supreme importance, a writer whose "words have acquired the power of actions."[48]

Shelley's poem reduces this renowned philosopher of social equality to "an old root," a paltry thing unkempt and blind (ll. 182–88). There is no greater measure of the bleakness of *The Triumph of Life* than its demotion of Rousseau to an impotent spectator of life's pageant. His "limp disengagement"[49] shows imaginative power shrunken to utter passivity. His solitude—Aristotle, for better or worse, is chained to Alexander—converges ironically with Shelley's own artistic position, as if all imaginative paths meet in common isolation. Why is Rousseau so ineffectual here? No doubt the reasons include a career molded by egotism and paranoia, but *The Triumph of Life* uses Rousseau less as historical personage than as artistic type. Rousseau's ruin follows from the differential "repetitions" of consciousness and language as contagious errors. His public failure reflects the unreliability of reading as a process for the transmission of ideas. The in-

---

[47] Scrivener, *Radical Shelley*, 310.
[48] De Man, "Shelley Disfigured," 103.
[49] Duffy, *Rousseau in England*, 115.

effectiveness of Rousseau as a teacher is precisely the point of Shelley's scenes of reading. His protagonist must interpret the triumph of life, interrogating the images that pass before him, even as readers must interpret *The Triumph of Life*. Rousseau's inability to supply certain answers, to guide and warn with the authority of Dante's Virgil, bespeaks an erosion of shared values between writer and audience. It exemplifies the Romantic radical's powerlessness to control adequately the response his writing will receive from society.

It is a commonplace that readings are repetitions with a difference, contributions to a hermeneutic succession that reconstructs the text by situating it socially. Given the exiled Shelley's political and artistic marginalization in 1822, such disfiguring reception posed a special danger. Shelley knew from painful experience that authorial intention can lose itself amid the receding horizons of its own indefinite history, or be temporarily frozen by consensus into a form congenial to power. The allegory of *The Triumph of Life*, a proliferation of inexact doublings in which each figure misappropriates its predecessor, underscores writing's openness to ideological misappropriation. Publish the *Discours sur l'origine de l'inégalité* and you create, by authoritarian reflex, the figure of Napoleon. The mind's creations acquire lives of their own, as Victor Frankenstein discovered, and can demolish what their creators cherish. Worse, the dependence of intention on reception politicizes the problem of metalepsis, which calls into question the causal linkages fundamental to traditional notions of historical meaning.[50] "History" becomes a narrative superstructure with a skewed and indeterminate relation to its social base. *The Triumph of Life* stresses that incongruity structurally. When Rousseau's earlier chariot-vision *follows* the protagonist's in the poem's narrative succession, the order of chronology (the processes of historical fact) and the formal sequences of poetry (the processes of vision) are misaligned: history's logic is not the logic of art. If the existential corollary of allegory is historical contingency, Rousseau's "living storm," the moral corollary of that contingency is simple irresolution. How can one choose when the grounds of choice remain so evanescent and uncertain, so thoroughly implicated in the flux they aspire to control? How can one act when the consequences of action may well turn motives and values inside out?

These are tragic questions, variants on the issues Hamlet brooded over. The tragic despondency of *The Triumph of Life* bespeaks Shel-

---

[50] Paul de Man discusses the collapse of genealogical and organic paradigms in Romantic representations of change in *Allegories of Reading: Figural Language in Rousseau, Nietzsche, Rilke, and Proust* (New Haven: Yale University Press, 1977), 79–82.

ley's sense of a life hedged round with mystery, of divergent moral choices meeting in common uncertainty and illusion. With this tragic mood Shelley's specifically historical pessimism relents to the "deeper fear that the poet is in danger of being overthrown by something in the nature of the poetic imagination itself."[51] "Born into romance," Geoffrey Hartman writes, "we replace one illusion with another, until the pain of being is the pain of imagination."[52] Romance celebrates the power to re-create and substitute fictions almost endlessly. Tragedy tends to view that power more as a Johnsonian "hunger of the imagination which preys incessantly upon life." In 1822 Shelley wrote respectfully of the predatory illusions of *Faust*, which he regarded as the tragedy of idealism, and which reminded him of "the reproaches of memory, & the delusions of an imagination not to be restrained" (*Letters* 2:406). The act of writing *The Triumph of Life* similarly confronted him with "the delusions of . . . imagination."

Strip the mind of its kingly robes, *The Triumph of Life* hints, send it naked into the storm, and it will instantly relapse into role-playing, trying enemies for ingratitude and exchanging old illusions for new ones equally necessary and fragile. Here, by the admission of its own title, is a representation of "Life," a political allegory immersed in the particular historical possibilities of Shelley's era. Yet it is a poem of ghosts and shadows, a "drifting phantasmagoria" in which "vision opens into vision, dream unfolds within dream, and the visionary perspectives . . . shift elusively and are lost."[53] The triumphal pageant depicts "the subjection of each man or woman to illusory figures projected by his or her desire"[54] on life's fragile, empty bubble (ll. 248–51). Shelley's most harrowing image of imprisonment in illusion is the Lucretian deluge of "Shadows of shadows" emitted by the crowd and sustained by the chariot. These simulacra signify social roles, the familiar postures of a performing self, the self-representations of deluded egotism. They imply that "the victims of Life are masked or veiled only as an onion is skinned,"[55] and define human identity as masks of vanity covering a vacuity. As egocentric projections, the masks of *The Triumph of Life* remain personalized despite their suggestion of social roles, so that Shelley's masked figures live alone in

[51] Dawson, *Unacknowledged Legislator*, 270.

[52] Geoffrey Hartman, *Beyond Formalism: Literary Essays, 1958–1970* (New Haven: Yale University Press, 1970), x.

[53] F. R. Leavis, *Revaluation: Tradition & Development in English Poetry* (London: Chatto and Windus, 1936), 231. These are terms of censure for Leavis.

[54] J. Hillis Miller's phrase, from "The Critic as Host," in *Deconstruction and Criticism*, ed. Harold Bloom and others (New York: Seabury Press, 1979), 233.

[55] Bloom, *Shelley's Mythmaking*, 251.

autonomous mental worlds. In *The Triumph of Life* the self-consciousness of the Romantic imagination enters a mode of tragic isolation.

Shelley experienced the subjugation of reality by illusion quite literally in the terrifying visions of his final months. These visions, especially the two famous doppelgänger episodes, exude a curiously fictive aura. In an August 1822 letter, Mary told Maria Gisborne how Edward and Jane Williams had appeared to Shelley in a dream, standing at his bedside "in the most horrible condition, their bodies lacerated—their bones starting through the skin," and warned him that "the sea is flooding the house & it is all coming down"; Shelley then "got up, he thought," when "suddenly his vision changed & he saw the figure of himself strangling me," reports Mary, who was lying in her bed (*LMWS* 1:245). The combination of libidinal and apocalyptic imagery makes this piece of dreamwork extraordinary, and it loses little interest from the perspective of Shelley's troubled relations with Mary—or from the perspective of his reading. Here his subconscious fills the lacuna in Victor's account of his monstrous double strangling Elizabeth in *Frankenstein*: "She was there, lifeless and inanimate, thrown across the bed. . . . The murderous mark of the fiend's grasp was on her neck."[56]

The second doppelgänger visitation again evokes a textual model. Mary's same letter mentions Shelley saying that he "had seen the figure of himself which met him as he walked on the terrace & said to him—'How long do you mean to be content' " (*LMWS* 1:245). Robinson astutely points out that this incident

> recalls Calderón's scene in which Enio confronts his skeletal second self in *El Purgatorio de San Patricio*, this scene having been provided by Shelley for Byron's use in *The Deformed Transformed*. In Byron's summary of this incident, the hero actually kills himself by killing his mantled doppelgänger "who in falling utters 'are you satisfied!' "[57]

Robinson interprets this incident as a veiled suicide threat, and in retrospect a prophecy of death. In any event, the episode affords another instance of life imitating art, or art explosively intruding into life, through Shelleyan doubling.

Such literary mediations of the return of the repressed dissolve the boundaries of illusion and fact. They also work, as I have suggested,

---

[56] Mary W. Shelley, *Frankenstein; or, The Modern Prometheus*, ed. James Rieger (1974; reprint, Chicago: University of Chicago Press, 1982), 193. Other readers have noticed this similarity—Sperry, *Shelley's Major Verse*, 223 n. 1, for instance. Doubles appear in some of the poems Shelley was reading in 1822: in Byron's *The Deformed Transformed* and Calderón's *El Purgatorio de San Patricio*.

[57] Robinson, *Shelley and Byron*, 220.

to render the circumstances of Shelley's death almost predictable, as if his dying repeated a literary model. For "when the mind figures his skiff wrapped from sight by the thunder storm," Mary Shelley asked, "who but will regard as a prophecy the last stanza of the *Adonais*" ("Note on the Poems of 1822. By Mrs. Shelley," *CW* 4:212–13). Shelley had been braving death with *The Triumph of Life* too, Mary reflected, so much of which "was written as he sailed or weltered on that sea which was soon to engulf him," and which itself trails "off into sketches of sailboats on its final [manuscript] leaf."[58] It is difficult to assess the transpositions of life and imagination or the deathly foreshadowings surrounding Shelley at this time. Clearly, he was brooding over his mortality, as Trelawny, Jane Williams, and his own writings testify. Just as clearly, his fascination with the grave was accompanied by hallucinatory delusions, among them doppelgängers as traditional harbingers of death. One need not take these doubles as restagings of literary scenes to sense a progressive interweaving of Shelley's art and life in 1822. For independent confirmation of that interweaving we can turn to *The Triumph of Life*, which makes the inseparability of dream and reality the nexus of its tragic vision. When Shelley abandoned *Charles the First* for *The Triumph of Life*, he discovered a form brilliantly suited to his preoccupation with the repetitions that haunt consciousness. Only Shelley's accidental drowning made this work his poetic testament. But only his portrait of a mind "dense with shadows . . . / . . . grey with phantoms" (ll. 481–82) produced a testament so fitting. *The Triumph of Life* is Shelley's death mask.

[58] "Note on the Poems of 1822. By Mrs. Shelley," *CW* 4:211; Sperry, *Shelley's Major Verse*, 199.

INDEX